Introduction

So what's the big idea?

While clearly there are more than 100 great ideas of all time, we're just getting started with this small, fascinating book. Consider this an introduction to some of the greatest achievements of human knowledge, the first volume in a profound survey of what every educated person should know. These great ideas have been articulated by some of the best teachers living today, excerpted from The Great Courses for your convenience.

Browse these pages for a peek into some timeless, influential insights. A small equation that changed how we understand the workings of the universe? Think Einstein. For the impact a young playwright had on his society, and ultimately ours? Read Shakespeare. To find a series of notes and chords or colorful brush strokes that will move you to tears? Discover the genius of Beethoven and Van Gogh. Examine why people pray, cultures develop and disappear, wars start and wars end, history reinvents, or simply why we are who we are. Learn about Jesus, Descartes, Newton, Melville, or Eisenhower, to name a few. There is so much here for you to explore.

Enjoy this diverse selection of lecture excerpts from courses by our gifted professors. Who are they? Why are they unique? Simple numbers tell the story: The Teaching Company chooses only the top 1 in 5,000 college professors to be on its faculty. That's part of the secret of our success and the reason that, on average, our customers rate our courses an 8.97 out of 10. This elite group will inspire you to visit a place where writers, artists, scientists, leaders—political and spiritual—took chances and changed the lives of those around them and those yet to come.

The good news? All of our courses are available for sale on DVD, audio CD, audiotape, transcript book, and downloads. And we guarantee your satisfaction for a lifetime because we want you to be our customer for a lifetime. **The best news? At least once a year, we reduce by up to 70 percent the price of each of our more than 200 courses.**

Read on. We are excited to share some of the greatest ideas of all time from the best and the brightest minds in our national academic community. We're on an adventure, an adventure carefully created for lifelong learners—without any homework, exams, or pressure. Join us on the journey. No packing required.

As always, we thank you for being our customer. Enjoy the read!

Tom Rollins
Founder
The Teaching Company

P.S. Tell us which great ideas you would like us to include in Vol. 2 at www.teach12.com/greatideas

The Great Courses®

presents

The 100 Greatest Ideas of All Time

Volume 1

The Teaching Company®

The Great Courses©
published by The Teaching Company

THE TEACHING COMPANY
4151 Lafayette Center Drive, Suite 100
Chantilly, VA 20151-1232

First published 2006
Copyright 2006 by The Teaching Company

Set in Adobe Caslon Pro 11 pt.
Printed in the United States of America.

ISBN 1-59803-273-9

Table of Contents

PHILOSOPHY

SCIENCE

Table of Contents

Table of Contents

ANCIENT HISTORY

Table of Contents

Table of Contents

The Adventure of Lifelong Learning

Most of us remember a time when discovery and the thrill of learning were forces in our lives. The adventure of learning often took place in a great classroom somewhere, in the hands of one great teacher. Is it possible to enjoy this experience again without going back to college? Absolutely. The Teaching Company's customers do so every day.

The Teaching Company brings engaging professors into your home or car through courses on DVD, audio CD, audiotape, transcript book, and download. Since 1990, great teachers from the Ivy League, Stanford, Georgetown, and other fine colleges and universities have crafted more than 200 courses for lifelong learners like you. It's the adventure of learning, without the homework or exams.

Students enjoy our courses in many ways:

• Some listen while commuting. One customer writes: "Since I've discovered The Teaching Company, I look forward to my driving time. Thank you for changing my commute from frustrating to fascinating."

• Some watch our courses instead of TV. We once asked a heart surgeon how he had found the time to watch hundreds of hours of our courses. He answered, "I skip the first half hour of junk TV each evening and watch a Teaching Company lecture instead."

• Some improve their minds and bodies at the same time by listening while exercising. "The Teaching Company has really great college lectures on tape. If I only let myself use them while I'm exercising, it's an extra motivation to stay in shape," Bill Joy, cofounder of Sun Microsystems, told MSNBC.

With more than 2,000 hours of material in literature, philosophy, history, fine arts, science, religion, and other subjects, our courses can become a treasured part of a life well lived.

When and why do courses go on sale?

Every course we make goes on sale at least once a year. This revolving sales approach allows us to provide you with great value and great service.

To find out which courses are on sale, please check our catalogs, newsletters, or website. The catalogs and newsletters clearly identify the courses currently on sale.

Praise for The Great Courses

"The Teaching Company ... has become a force in adult education by distributing lectures by professors from some of the nation's leading universities."

—*The New York Times*

"The professors can be outrageous, funny, controversial, and challenging. They make you think, and sometimes make you argue with them ... They might even convince you to learn more, study deeper, and buy more books. All that with no tests and no grades."

—*Austin American-Statesman*

"The Teaching Company ... does not believe in the dumb-and-dumber theory of American taste; [it is] a company that competes for people's leisure time by asking them to reach up, rather than stoop down."

—*Chicago Tribune*

"Whether they're commuting to work or hammering out miles on the treadmill, people have made [The Teaching Company's] digital professors part of the fabric of their lives"

—*The Christian Science Monitor*

"'I didn't want it to end!' 'It had me on the edge of my seat.' Those aren't blurbs from movie advertisements; they're comments about college lectures now available" on audio and video.

—*The Chronicle of Higher Education*

Customers' Praise for The Great Courses

"TTC courses have changed my life: I now enjoy insomnia, traffic jams, and being unable to find an appealing movie on Friday night."

—Lucille Day, Oakland, CA

"Whenever your tapes go on sale, I buy them for further learning. I feel it's like a savings account for the brain."

—Sally Strom, Newport, OR

"Outstanding courses. Well-prepared, superb professors. Makes me want to go back to college—but why settle for mediocre teaching?"

—David Powell, Raleigh, NC

One of the key thinkers in Western philosophic tradition, Plato's work centers on the life and thought of his controversial teacher, Socrates.

PHILOSOPHY

"To teach how to live with uncertainty, and yet without being paralyzed by hesitation, is perhaps the chief thing that philosophy in our age can still do for those who study it."

—Bertrand Russell

Taught by: Professor Daniel N. Robinson
Georgetown University and Oxford University

I Think, Therefore I Am

There is a joke going around—it has probably gone around too often now—about Descartes going into a bar and having a drink, and when the bartender asks if he'd like another one, Descartes says: "I think not," and disappears.

This is a joke that's designed to convey, if not philosophical subtlety, then the philosophical frivolity of Descartes doubting his own existence until he could come up with a good reason for it, namely, *Cogito, ergo sum*: "I think, therefore I am." Well, there isn't very much that's frivolous in Descartes, and his philosophical power is a matter of record. In fact, on some accounts, it is with Descartes, 1596–1650, that the modern period of philosophy is said to begin.

Well, what about this *Cogito, ergo sum*: "I think, therefore I am"? Here is a scholar desperate to avoid mere opinion, of all that is transitory or merely customary, of all that is but rank mysticism, superstition, prejudice. What he finds in the Scholastic lessons of his early Jesuit schooling is a logical rigor, but one that has no power of discovery. What he finds in Renaissance "science" is marred by magic, witchcraft, and hocus pocus—dogma posing as knowledge.

However, to avoid this, one may well find the scholar insensibly falling prey to skepticism; so, Descartes, like Francis Bacon, is looking for a method. How does one find the right method that spares one from self-deception and superstition, but also from the melancholy state of the total skeptic?

How Descartes sets about to accomplish this is summarized in two monumentally influential works published four years apart: his *Discourse on Method*, which appeared in 1637, and his *Meditations on First Philosophy*, published in 1641.

The *Discourse on Method* was written in French. He explains his rationale. By writing in French, "the language of my country," he says he is able to address an audience not already committed to the wisdom of the ancients, as are Descartes' teachers. In French, the *Discourse* was indeed accessible to a wide audience, and one that could only have been attracted immediately on reading these opening lines:

> Good sense is of all things in the world the most equally distributed, for everybody thinks himself so abundantly provided with it that even those most difficult to please do not commonly desire more than they already possess. The power of forming a good judgment, and of distinguishing the true from the false, is by nature equal in all men, but to be possessed of good mental powers is not sufficient; the principal matter is to apply them well.

The diversity of opinions and the constant tendency toward error arise not from unequal or insufficient rational power, but from faulty methods of inquiry and discovery. It is the purpose of the *Discourse on Method* to reveal how Descartes himself has fashioned a mode of inquiry designed to save himself from such errors. As he says, he is not proposing something that all must follow. Rather, as something of an intellectual autobiography, he will share with readers what has worked for one man, who just happens to be René Descartes. Well, this would be as if Einstein wrote a treatise

René Descartes was the first modern philosopher and the father of modern mathematics.

on how to think about problems in physics, noting that it is "just my way" of doing it.

There are, to be sure, any number of candidate methods available, and Descartes summarizes them. He is a student of the history of ideas, and he knows what has been tried before. His most illustrious contemporaries are products of intellectual history, and they are largely so faithful to the ancients as to be addicted to ancient conclusions. The problem with history as a guide is that a man who spends too much time in a distant land becomes a stranger in his own country, says Descartes. The problem with the study of history is that it simply removes one from the very context in which the insistent demands for knowledge are indeed most insistent. History is a guide, but it is not an answer. No two historical events are ever precisely the same anyway—such that all one could glean from that kind of inquiry would be generalities subject to interpretation, and indeed, endless disagreement.

For Descartes ... the right method begins with an utterly skeptical position ... with a profession of ignorance. "Not only don't I know anything, but I am positioned in such a way that what I think I know is probably laden with error, misapprehension, and confusion."

What about vaunted philosophy—could there be a better method than a philosophical one? Well, of course, philosophy doesn't have a single method, and in any case, if you consult the great philosophers of history, the salient fact that emerges is that they scarcely agree with each other on any major point. Thus, indeed, if philosophy were a reliable guide to truth, the "long debate" would have been concluded long ago.

What about mathematics, the queen of the sciences? Well, at least—and Descartes is a great mathematician—at least when a problem is solved mathematically, you know it. Unfortunately, those problems are at a level of abstraction so removed from the facts of the physical world and our place in it that it's not entirely clear you really can match them up with reality at all. There isn't anything wrong with mathematics, but in a certain sense, there also isn't anything really right about it as a method of inquiry. It is majestic as a method of analysis, an abstract method of representation, but, alas, not as a method of discovery.

For Descartes, these limitations led to a different approach. For him, the right method begins with an utterly skeptical position. The right method should begin with a profession of ignorance. "Not only don't I know anything, but I am positioned in such a way that what I think I know is probably laden with error, misapprehension, and confusion." It is with this orientation that one is committed to accepting nothing, unless it can prevail as an idea of such power and clarity and indubitability that I am simply powerless to doubt it. This is how Descartes wants to proceed. Descartes adopts the highest standard that must be met by anything presented as an object of knowledge. Anything that fails to satisfy that standard, he says, he is prepared to reject. ∎

Puis le diametre de ce verre n'a pas besoin d'estre si grand que pour la lunete precedente, ny ne doit pas aussy estre si petit que celuy du verre A de l'autre d'auparauant. mais il doit a peu prés estre tel que la ligne droite N P passe par le point bruslant interieur de l'hyperbole N R P : car estant moindre, il receuroit moins de rayons de l'obiet Z; & estant plus grand, il n'en receuroit que fort peu d'auantage; en sorte que son espaisseur deuant estre a proportion beaucoup plus augmentée qu'auparauant, elle leur osteroit bien autant de leur force que sa grandeur leur en donneroit, & outre cela l'obiet ne pourroit pas estre tant esclairé. Il sera bon aussy de

Voyés en la page 126.

A reproduction of a page from Descartes' *La Dioptrique*, written in 1637, in which he investigated the rules of the science of optics.

The preceding lecture was an excerpt drawn from The Great Course:

The Great Ideas of Philosophy, 2nd Edition
Course #4200

Humanity left childhood and entered the troubled but productive world when it started to criticize its own certainties and weigh the worthiness of its most secure beliefs. Thus philosophy began—that "Long Debate" on the nature of truth, the scale of real values, the life one should aspire to live, the character of justice, the sources of law, the terms of civic and political life—the good, the better, the best.

The debate continues, and one remains aloof to it at a very heavy price, for "the unexamined life is not worth living."

This course of 60 lectures gives the student a sure guide and interpreter as the major themes within Western philosophy are presented and considered.

Daniel N. Robinson

Daniel N. Robinson is a member of the Philosophy faculty at Oxford University, where he has lectured annually since 1991. He is also Distinguished Professor, Emeritus, at Georgetown University, on whose faculty he served for 30 years. He was formerly Adjunct Professor of Psychology at Columbia University.

Professor Robinson earned his Ph.D. in Neuropsychology from City University of New York. Prior to taking his position at Georgetown, he held positions at Amherst College, Princeton University, and Columbia University.

Professor Robinson is past president of two divisions of the American Psychological Association: The Division of History of Psychology and the Division of Theoretical and Philosophical Psychology. He is former editor of the *Journal of Theoretical and Philosophical Psychology*. Professor Robinson is author or editor of more than 40 books, including *Wild Beasts & Idle Humours: The Insanity Defense from Antiquity to the Present*, *An Intellectual History of Psychology*, *The Mind: An Oxford Reader*, and *Aristotle's Psychology*.

In 2001, Professor Robinson received the Lifetime Achievement Award from the Division of History of Psychology of the American Psychological Association, and the Distinguished Contribution Award from the Division of Theoretical and Philosophical Psychology of the American Psychological Association.

Lecture Titles

1. From the Upanishads to Homer
2. Philosophy—Did the Greeks Invent It?
3. Pythagoras and the Divinity of Number
4. What Is There?
5. The Greek Tragedians on Man's Fate
6. Herodotus and the Lamp of History
7. Socrates on the Examined Life
8. Plato's Search For Truth
9. Can Virtue Be Taught?
10. Plato's *Republic*—Man Writ Large
11. Hippocrates and the Science of Life
12. Aristotle on the Knowable
13. Aristotle on Friendship
14. Aristotle on the Perfect Life
15. Rome, the Stoics, and the Rule of Law
16. The Stoic Bridge to Christianity
17. Roman Law—Making a City of the Once-Wide World
18. The Light Within—Augustine on Human Nature
19. Islam
20. Secular Knowledge— The Idea of University
21. The Reappearance of Experimental Science
22. Scholasticism and the Theory of Natural Law
23. The Renaissance—Was There One?
24. Let Us Burn the Witches to Save Them
25. Francis Bacon and the Authority of Experience
26. **Descartes and the Authority of Reason**
27. Newton—The Saint of Science
28. Hobbes and the Social Machine
29. Locke's Newtonian Science of the Mind
30. No matter? The Challenge of Materialism
31. Hume and the Pursuit of Happiness
32. Thomas Reid and the Scottish School
33. France and the *Philosophes*
34. *The Federalist Papers* and the Great Experiment
35. What Is Enlightenment? Kant on Freedom
36. Moral Science and the Natural World
37. Phrenology—A Science of the Mind
38. The Idea of Freedom
39. The Hegelians and History
40. The Aesthetic Movement— Genius
41. Nietzsche at the Twilight
42. The Liberal Tradition—J. S. Mill
43. Darwin and Nature's "Purposes"
44. Marxism—Dead But Not Forgotten
45. The Freudian World
46. The Radical William James
47. William James' Pragmatism
48. Wittgenstein and the Discursive Turn
49. Alan Turing in the Forest of Wisdom
50. Four Theories of the Good Life
51. Ontology—What There "Really" Is
52. Philosophy of Science— The Last Word?
53. Philosophy of Psychology and Related Confusions
54. Philosophy of Mind, If There Is One
55. What makes a Problem "Moral"
56. Medicine and the Value of Life
57. On the Nature of Law
58. Justice and Just Wars
59. Aesthetics—Beauty Without Observers
60. God—Really?

If you would like to order this course, please contact us at:

Phone: 1-800-TEACH-12

Web: www.TEACH12.com

For more information on our pricing policy, see page 245.

Taught by: Professor Robert C. Solomon
The University of Texas at Austin

What Is Existentialism?

Existentialism might be conceived of as a movement rather than a series of doctrines. In the literature that has come out in the years when Existentialism first became popular just after the Second World War, and ever since, it often has the connotation of being a particularly "gloomy" philosophy—one that is obsessed with the notions of anxiety and dread.

Existentialism can actually be a very invigorating and positive-minded philosophy. The "no excuses" idea, in part, says we do have control over our own lives. It is often thought that Existentialism is an atheistic philosophy. It is true that some rather notorious atheists were Existentialists, most notably Jean-Paul Sartre, who gave the movement its name. Søren Kierkegaard was also an Existentialist—one might say the "first" Existentialist—and he was devoutly religious. In today's terms he would probably be counted as a Christian fundamentalist. He is not the only one—Martin Buber, the Jewish Existentialist; and some of the more recent Christian Existentialists, like Karl Barth. One finds the entire spectrum, and one can put the nature of God well within the Existential tradition.

One can trace the movement as far back to Socrates who said famously, "One should know thyself," and took great responsibility for his own behavior, defended the virtues, and was very much the individual. It has been traced back to Heraclitus, before Socrates, a philosopher who defended that impermeability of life and who often delighted in contradictions and dark sayings. St. Augustine was sort of a proto-Existentialist, because his *Confessions* are so inward looking, and he is so concerned with the questions of who he was and what he was going to do.

Existentialism as we know it today is best represented in five figures: Kierkegaard, Nietzsche, Heidegger, Camus, and Sartre. Albert Camus is possibly the easiest to understand, but he also captures the sensibility that represents Existentialist thinking. He explains why so many students over the last 50 years have become enamored with the movement. Søren Kierkegaard was a Danish philosopher who worked roughly in the middle of the 19th century. Friedrich Nietzsche has some differences with Kierkegaard and some of the later philosophers, but nevertheless fits in with this sequence. Martin Heidegger, a German philosopher at the beginning of the 20th century, was actually very influential in terms of setting up the kind of philosophy—both Existentialism and what is today called postmodernism—that still rules many universities today.

Before there was a term for it, Søren Kierkegaard espoused many of the fundamentals of the philosophy of Existentialism.

Finally, Jean-Paul Sartre gave the movement its name, and is probably the single most influential Existentialist. Typically when people talk about Existentialism, it is Sartre's ideas they have in mind.

Nevertheless, it is not a school. There are all sorts of differences. Just to start with the obvious, Kierkegaard was a devout Christian and Nietzsche was famously a rather vitriolic atheist. In the same way, if you consider politics, Existentialism is often considered a kind of left-wing conspiracy. But, the truth is that while Sartre was a Marxist; Nietzsche was, if anything, a kind of reactionary; Kierkegaard was completely apolitical; and Martin Heidegger by contrast was a fascist. When we talk about Existentialism, it is very important not to try to pin it down

Toward the end of his life, Nietzsche went insane. Is it possible to detect the approach of his madness in his writings?

too much to begin with; not to try to define it in terms of this or that doctrine—this or that set of beliefs.

The movement is defined best of all by Jean-Paul Sartre. He had a very long career in which he changed many of his ideas, but one of the things that he said in a very late interview captures Existentialism. He said, "I have never ceased to believe that one is and one makes oneself of whatever is made of one." The language is a bit convoluted; many of these figures tend to enjoy rather difficult language. The idea that—as he put it in his earlier writings, "we make ourselves"—that there is a sense of self-creation here, is going to be very important in understanding Existentialism.

There are three central themes in Existentialism. The first is the emphasis on the individual. Many Existentialists were truly eccentric. Kierkegaard defined himself against the reigning passions and doctrines of the age. In particular, when Kierkegaard was philosophizing, much of Danish society—and certainly the whole idea of Christianity—was wrapped in the idea of collective consciousness, sometimes summarized as the Holy Spirit, or in the secular realm summarized by the term "bourgeois." Kierkegaard, by contrast, defined himself as the individual. In fact, he said what he would like written on his tombstone was simply "The Individual."

Nietzsche was another great eccentric. Nietzsche wrote pretty much in isolation and lived in isolation for most of his mature life. He sometimes would reach out to an audience, but it is always interesting that it is a very select audience, and he dedicates his books to "the very few." One of the tricks that Nietzsche uses quite effectively is he writes as if he is writing for you, the singular reader alone. He really has a kind of mini-conspiratorial tone that makes us think it is just us; we are different and we are especially different from all of them.

This notion of individuality takes different forms. Camus, when he was in Algeria where he was born and spent most of his life, found himself very much at odds with both the French population, of which he was a member, and the Algerian population, who were fighting for independence. He gains his reputation as a courageous individual in part by taking a very independent stance, one he continued when he was in Southern France during the occupation by the Nazis.

Jean-Paul Sartre takes individuality in a different direction. Individuality basically comes down to the idea of individual *Nietzsche was another great eccentric. Nietzsche wrote pretty much in isolation and lived in isolation for most of his mature life. He sometimes would reach out to an audience ... but he dedicates his books to "the very few."* choice. It is the heart of Sartre's philosophy that we are always making choices—we make them as individuals. It doesn't matter if the whole society or the whole world makes them at the same time. The responsibility that he talks about is always the responsibility of the individual for making his or her choices and accepting the consequences that flow from it.

The second theme is the importance of the passions. If you look back through the history of philosophy, one thing that is striking is the fact that the passions are very often the whipping horse. Philosophy is defined as reason or the love of reason. Wisdom is often considered to be a version of reason—being reasonable. There has always been a kind of undercurrent of opposition here.

Again, Heraclitus was someone who fully recognized the power of the passions. Of course, the Greek playwrights before him—the great tragedians—they were very keen on the power of the passions, which they sometimes demonized, but

Considered the finest writer of Existentialist literature, Albert Camus was the author of *The Stranger* and *The Fall*.

nevertheless were very clear that these are very important elements in human life.

It is Kierkegaard who is going to define what it means to really exist—that special notion of existence that is going to give rise to the term "Existentialism." To really exist is to be passionate. In particular, it is to passionately commit oneself to a way of life; in Kierkegaard's case, to passionately commit oneself to Christianity. He talks about "passionate inwardness." So, we are not talking about passions here fully expressed and exploded on the stage so much as we are talking about passions that one might feel and not show. Kierkegaard makes a good deal out of talking about the truly passionate person not being the one who is dramatically visible for everyone else. The truly passionate person is the one who is quite inwardly contained and defined by his or her passions.

We often have the idea that the passions take us over, that the passions happen to us—the idea from the ancient world that the passions are often intermittent bouts of insanity. But for the existentialist, it is very clear that to live is to live passionately. Nietzsche is well known as a very passionate philosopher. When you read his work it is filled with all sorts of excitement and enthusiasm. To put it in a rather trivial way, he uses more exclamation points that probably any other philosopher in the history of the subject. He is always expounding and enthusing. He is always praising, condemning. But in his life itself it is very clear that while he was a very quiet and courteous man, his philosophy and his life were defined by some really exciting, dramatic, grand passions. He encourages us to live according to our passions.

The third and possibly the most famous theme in Existentialism—and certainly most central theme for many philosophers—is the concept of freedom. What freedom means is something which has been highly debated. It is one of the ironies of history that virtually every regime in every country, from the most authoritarian to the most anarchistic, has defended freedom. Freedom gets defended in many different ways. There is a distinction in philosophy between freedom in the political sphere and freedom in a more personal way, or sometimes freedom in a more metaphysical sense. There is a so-called "free will" problem that philosophers are well concerned with. There is a sense in which neither of these is the kind of freedom that the Existentialists are primarily concerned with. As for political freedom, Sartre, in particular, comes out as a vigorous defender of freedom. It is really parasitic on a much more basic note of freedom that lies at the heart of his philosophy.

As for metaphysical freedom, whether there really is freedom, free

Hold up a mirror to your life. Do you like what you see? Existentialism is a philosophy that challenges you to take control of your life. To accomplish this, you must be willing to be honest, to strive to succeed, and to take responsibility for your actions.

will, in the very nature of things—this is a question none of these philosophers address very directly, except in the negative. Nietzsche, for example, makes fun of it and says that the very idea of a free will, of a subject who is detached from the causal nature of the universe, is really just a kind of illusion.

The kind of freedom that they do talk about, and the kind of freedom which is absolutely essential for understanding what we are going to be doing, is that sense of personal freedom which is neither political nor metaphysical but has very much to do with how we think of ourselves, how we behave, how we think about our behavior. Kierkegaard has a nice little aphorism that sums up a good deal of this. He says, "People hardly ever make use of the freedom that they do have, like freedom of thought. Instead, they demand freedom of speech as compensation." The idea is that freedom has to do with making choices. It has to do with deciding how you are going to live your life.

Freedom also has to do with taking consequences. Once you have made your choice, you can't say, "I didn't anticipate that. I don't take responsibility for that." Having chosen, you are then responsible for what follows as well.

Freedom is often connected with reason. In much of the history of philosophy, to be free is to act rationally. What we find in the existentialists a very different kind of thesis. In the ancient Greeks, it was often said that acting in accordance with reason makes us free; acting according to the passions makes us a slave. The Enlightenment philosopher David Hume, in the 18th century, said that instead, reason is and ought to be the slave of the passions.

There are quite a few who did want to say something like, "The passions are not really the monsters that they have been portrayed to be." It is rather that passion motivates us. Without passion, there is no motivation. It is the passions that give meaning to life; without passions, life is meaningless.

Passions give life meaning, and it is through passionate commitment that we give our lives the particular meaning that they have.

What Existentialism is really all about is how we live our lives. It is complained that Existentialists don't really give us enough advice about what we should do—they really just say things like: "Take responsibility for your actions." One might conceive of that not so much as a weakness but as a great strength and very central to the idea of Existentialism itself.

You don't tell people what they should do. What is central to all these figures is what *you* should do—how you live is up to you. It is up to you to make the choice. One could argue that Existentialism really has had its greatest impact and power in America. We have always been a society which has prided itself on our sense of responsibility.

What Existentialism talks about and constantly hammers away at is the idea that we are responsible; we do have choices, no matter how complicated or fast-moving the world is, no matter how superficial those around us might be. We are in charge of our lives. We have to make the choices. We have to understand exactly how dark life can be and what to do with that, as well as figure out where joy lies and pursue that, as well. ∎

The preceding lecture was an excerpt drawn from The Great Course:

No Excuses: Existentialism and the Meaning of Life
Course #437

The message of Existentialism, unlike that of many more obscure and academic philosophical movements, is about as simple as can be. It is that every one of us, as an individual, is responsible—responsible for what we do, responsible for who we are, responsible for the way we face and deal with the world, responsible, ultimately, for the way the world is.

Lecture Titles

Robert C. Solomon

Robert C. Solomon is the Quincy Lee Centennial Professor of Business and Philosophy at The University of Texas at Austin, where he has taught for more than 30 years. He received his undergraduate degree in Molecular Biology from the University of Pennsylvania and his Master's and Doctoral degrees in Philosophy and Psychology from the University of Michigan.

Professor Solomon has won many teaching honors, including the Standard Oil Outstanding Teaching Award; the President's Associates Teaching Award (twice); and the Chad Oliver Plan II Teaching Award. In addition, he is a member of Academy of Distinguished Teachers at UT, which is devoted to providing leadership in improving the quality and depth of undergraduate instruction.

If you would like to order this course, please contact us at:

Phone: 1-800-TEACH-12
Web: www.TEACH12.com
For more information on our pricing policy, see page 245.

The Great Minds of the Western Intellectual Tradition, 3rd Edition

Course #470
Lecture 36

Taught by: Professor Alan Charles Kors
University of Pennsylvania

Newton and Enlightened Science

Isaac Newton entered Trinity College in Cambridge University in 1661. Every other college at Cambridge was dominated by the Aristotelian Scholastics, but Trinity College, Cambridge, was the one college in the university that was a Cartesian stronghold. That had a profound influence on the education of Isaac Newton because he was introduced to Descartes as an undergraduate.

Descartes had founded analytic geometry, which made extraordinarily easier the sorts of calculations in which Kepler had engaged. Newton, then, early on was a student both of Descartes' mechanical philosophy and of higher mathematics.

Shortly after receiving his bachelor's degree at Cambridge, Newton had to abandon the university because of the plague, which emptied the university as people went to their various homes. Newton spent 18 months in the countryside at Woolsthorpe, an unparalleled 18 months in the history of human thought, during which time he did nothing less than alter the history of the world.

What were the accomplishments of Newton's 18 months in Woolsthorpe following the receipt of his bachelor's degree? One, he was thinking about the problem of astronomy, the orbit of the Moon, what kept it in that orbit, when, in fact—I am pleased to report, for such stories rarely are true—an apple did fall as he was sitting thinking about astronomy in the field. Newton began to speculate on what

Trinity College, part of Cambridge University, is one of the oldest universities in the world. Newton became a Professor of Mathematics there at a young age.

would be the nature of a force that accounted at one and the same time for the Moon maintaining an orbit around the Earth without falling, coming closer; and the apple falling from the tree toward the center of the Earth. Assuming that it was the same force, what would that force be, and what could it account for?

He worked his way to the view that there was a force that varied directly according to two masses anywhere in the universe and that varied inversely according to the square of the distance between them. To work out his calculation in terms of the Earth and the Moon and the solar system, he needed a precise, accurate account of the circumference of the Earth, but he didn't have his books with him and he put down the wrong figure, and as he related it, he very nearly had solved the problem. In fact, he had arrived at the law of gravity but did not know himself to have done so, and, quite typical of Isaac Newton, when he returned to the university, he put those papers in a drawer and forgot about them for 20 years. He was someone who often forgot to take meals unless reminded.

In order to work out that theory of a force of gravity, Newton had to arrive at an understanding of the essential laws of mechanics that governed matter in motion, the nature of velocity and time and acceleration, the nature of inertia—which he now articulated as linear inertia,

Unable to attend classes at Oxford because of the plague, Newton, in 18 months of work at his family's farm in Woolsthorpe, England, altered the history of the world.

that matter unless acted upon by another force, if moving in a straight line continued in a straight line, if at rest remained at rest—and, his third law of motion, that for every action there is an equal and opposite reaction. So Newton had discovered the law of gravity and laid the foundation, with his three laws of motion, for the future of Western physics.

In order to deal with the multiple variables of time, motion, mass, and distance, the analytic geometry was insufficient, so Newton also created the infinitesimal calculus, and, interested in finding things to fill his mind during the 18 months, he began experimenting with a prism on the nature of light, and, with his experimental discovery of the composition of light, laid the foundation of modern optics, the science of light. He also did work that changed the nature of mathematical understanding of numerical series.

So, in 18 months in the countryside, in his early 20s, Isaac Newton had discovered the law of gravity, laid the foundation of modern physics with his three laws of mechanics, created the infinitesimal calculus, founded the science of modern optics, and advanced the frontiers of mathematical understanding. When he returned to Oxford, he spoke about this work to almost no one, and, in fact, it was al-

The work had mathematics of a difficulty that almost no one in England or on the continent could understand, and yet the work was an absolute watershed in the history of science and, indeed, in the history of our culture.

most by chance that he showed his work on the calculus to his professor, Isaac Barrow, who held the leading chair in mathematics in Great Britain. On seeing Newton's work, Barrow immediately resigned his chair in favor of his young student—probably the last time *that* ever will happen in the history of higher education.

Nearly 20 years later, in 1684, a group of scientific minds, Edmund Halley, Sir Christopher Wren, and Robert Hooke, were discussing the problem of gravity in a coffeehouse in London, and they were trying to come to terms with what Newton had been thinking about some 20 years before—the problem of falling objects, the orbits of the planets, and the problem bequeathed by Huygens's work on the pendulum, which is extremely interesting in light of Newton's formula of inertia as linear, that motion occurs in a straight line unless acted upon by another force. All Western science agreed, from the Greeks through the 17th century, that the circle was a natural inertial motion that seemed to make sense of the heavenly bodies and their motions and, indeed, of so much of the world.

Huygens's work on the pendulum is on centrifugal force, the swinging globe. If you swing a globe attached to a chain or string around your head and get it going in a perfect circle and then let go, it doesn't continue moving in a perfect circle; it flies off in linear motion. Newton, indeed, had been working on the problem of the orbit of the Moon and of the planets as looking for a force that acted as the chain did for the swinging ball. What would be the force that could alter, acting upon linear inertial motion, the movement of a planet into an orbit?

Well, Wren, Halley, and Hooke are thinking on this same problem but find the mathematics far too difficult for them, and they've heard that there is a great mathematician at Cambridge, Isaac Newton. They send Edmund Halley down, and Halley asks Newton, "What do you think would happen to the orbits of the planets and the Moon if there were a force that acted upon them according to the two masses and in inverse proportion to the square of the distances between them?" which is what the data suggested but what they could not prove, and Newton immediately said, "They would be elliptical orbits as described by Kepler," and Halley said, "How do you know that?" and Newton said, "Oh, I pretty nearly worked it out some 20 years ago," and Halley said, "Where are the papers?" and Newton began rummaging through drawers.

Newton convinced a culture that the world was ordered and lucid and knowable, that the human mind was capable of understanding the architecture and design of God in creation by means of a quantitative physical science.

When he found it, and Halley saw that Newton had plugged in a wrong figure for the circumference of the Earth, and that with the right figure everything in the cosmos fell into place, Halley was beside himself, and at his own expense and at his urging, he led Newton to develop his general system of the laws of motion and the law of universal gravitation, and these were published in 1687 as the *Philosophiae Naturalis Principia Mathematica*, the *Mathematical Principles of Natural Philosophy*, better known simply as the *Principia*. The work was published in Latin. The work had mathematics of a difficulty that almost no one in England or on the Continent could understand, and yet the work was an absolute watershed in the history of science and, indeed, in the history of our culture.

Newton's *Principia* was a mathematical demonstration of the Copernican hypothesis as proposed by Kepler. I had said that Galileo rejected Kepler's laws of planetary motion because they had not been demonstrated. One might say they don't get demonstrated until the space program, and, based on calculations from Keplerian models, things actually do land upon the Moon, but, in another sense, it is Newton's *Principia* that offers the scientific demonstration of Kepler's laws and the Copernican model. Assume the law of gravity, that there is a force that is equal to mass one times mass two, divided by the square of the distance between those masses, and assume linear inertia, and the Copernican solar system precisely as described by Kepler's laws of planetary motion follows. And that theory not only predicts the very universe that is open to our experimental gaze, but it predicts as well the behavior of tides, the reappearance of comets; in short, huge ranges of phenomena that had seemed inexplicable to the human mind.

Readers of the *Principia* who could not follow its demonstrations could read its predictions, could learn that those predictions held and were experimentally confirmed. Readers of the *Principia* could see Newton's demonstration of why all other physical systems that had been proposed, including Descartes', would lead one to a different universe than we observed, and they were convinced by popularizers, by the word of experts, and by the drama of predictions that came true about data. Newton accurately had described the world and the forces that governed that world, and for the first time, the human mind understood the system of the world in which it found itself. Newton convinced a culture that the world was ordered and lucid and knowable, that the human mind was capable of understanding the architecture and design of God in creation by means of a quantitative physical science.

The role of Newton's predictions in convincing even those who could not understand his work led to a moment of cultural scientific enthusiasm the likes of which we rarely see. Edmund Halley, a sober astronomer, penned an ode as a preface to Newton's *Principia* that concluded, "Nearer the Gods, no mortal may approach." Alexander Pope, the great British poet, penned Newton's epitaph, still visible in Westminster Abbey. It said, "Nature and nature's laws lay hid in night; God said, 'Let Newton be,' and all was light." A hundred years later, Napoleon asked his great court astronomer if there ever would be another Newton. He answered, "No, sire, for there was only one universe to be discovered."

But not all who read Newton were impressed. One of the most illuminating and most influential debates in the history of Western thought is that between the Newtonians and the Cartesians. The Cartesians had wanted to strip the Aristotelian universe of what they saw as its magic, its superstitious explanations, and substitute a mechanistic explanation in which we understood all problems of physics as problems of the communication of force by matter in motion to matter in motion.

For the Cartesians, the only way that force could be communicated from one part of matter to another part of matter was by direct contact. Think of a billiard table: You walk in, in the midst of a highly complicated shot on a pool table, and you infer, because there is no magic, what ball struck what balls, going from the original cue shot and the cue ball striking a ball—God's original cue shot being the one of interest there—that then produced the universe of matter in motion that we observed. For the Cartesians, the Newtonian explanation of gravity as action at a distance, two masses with nothing between them affecting each other with gravitational pull, sounded like the Aristotelians and their secret, or occult, forces in nature.

Science, Newton believed, should not make things up; it should admit ignorance when it does not have data ... that, absent experimental data, one admits ignorance.

When Cartesian-type mechanists made fun of the Aristotelians, they did so in the following manner. In Molière's *Le Médecin malgré lui*, there is a scene at the Aristotelian School of Medicine where the doctoral candidate in medicine is asked, "Why does opium put one to sleep?" and he answers, "Because of its dormitive power," and they all go, "Learned, learned, learned." That's what this sounded like to the Cartesians. Why do the planets hold their orbits? Because of their gravitational power. In the Cartesian universe, everything is a problem of fluid mechanics. They are certain that, between all the planets, the Earth, and the Moon, there is a fluid, and we are dealing with whirlpools of motion that can be understood in terms of the direct communication of force by matter to matter. Action at a distance seems to them a return to occult forces.

Originally Newton wanted an explanation of how gravity could operate, of how that force could be communicated. Was it magnetism, for example? But, unable to derive gravity from anything else, Newton made a virtue out of a necessity, explaining that natural philosophy science can only demonstrate that a certain force operates in the world, not why or how. For the Cartesians, an explanation of how the world operates should account for how the world got to be this way in the first place. For the Newtonians, this was the universe that God created, and these were the laws that governed it, and it could be demonstrated that these were the laws.

Science, Newton believed, should not make things up; it should admit ignorance when it does not have data—an argument that John Locke will build deeply into his own theory of knowledge—that, absent experimental data, one admits ignorance. But Newton also loved the fact of the universe that he had discovered, for he was a deeply religious man, and he was appalled by the Cartesian notion that God created a universe of fixed mechanical laws—that God had to proceed in this way, that God's will necessitated inertial motion in the world.

For Newton, the system of the world was a demonstration of God's omnipotence and freedom in contrast to the necessity under which Descartes' God labored, having to do things this way or that to be rational and perfect. For Newton, the universe was comprehensible. Why these laws were the laws that God had chosen—that was known to God alone, and science did not penetrate beyond experience and knowledge of how nature operated and what laws governed it to why that should be the case.

Newton, indeed, wrote more about scripture and religious chronology than he did about physics and astronomy. He was a deeply religious man—what we now would call a Unitarian—however, very unorthodox in his Christianity, but found a powerful side of his science to be its demonstration of God's omnipotence and freedom and wisdom.

For Newton, the design of the universe proved the existence of God. He reasoned: If matter had been placed in any other way in the world, at different velocities there would be a gravitational collapse of all matter. But he assumed a static universe such as we observed it and saw the placement and velocities chosen by God to have avoided a gravitational collapse, showing us a proof of God's design and existence.

But Newton's greatest legacy to his civilization is that which Alexander Pope understood, a sense that all could be order and clarity and light. Newton, by the success of his method, bequeathed a great confidence in the method by which he had reached his conclusions: observation, induction, the mathematization of motion, quantitative—not qualitative—knowledge, predictive value, and experiment. God did not intend us for ignorance. We now had a method by which to use our minds, and, for so many in Europe, this was a model that now could be extended to the whole of natural knowledge. ∎

The preceding lecture was an excerpt drawn from The Great Course:

The Great Minds of the Western Intellectual Tradition, 3rd Edition
Course #470

For 3,000 years, humanity has grappled with life's most fundamental questions. What is real? What should be the purpose of my life, and how should I lead it? Who or what is God? How can there be freedom in a world determined by causal laws? When is it legitimate for one person to have power over others? What is justice? Beauty? These are the crucial questions that thoughtful men and women have pondered since civilization began. The most brilliant minds in history focused on these questions—and their search for answers has left us an intellectual legacy of unsurpassed depth and richness.

Great Minds of the Western Intellectual Tradition, 3rd Edition is a comprehensive survey of the history of Western philosophy from its origins in classical Greece to the present. The course is an 84-lecture, 12-professor tour of Western philosophical tradition and covers more than 60 of history's greatest minds.

Alan Charles Kors

Alan Charles Kors is a Professor of History at the University of Pennsylvania, where he has been teaching since 1968. He received his Bachelor's degree from Princeton University and his Master's and Doctoral degrees from Harvard University.

Professor Kors is the author and editor of several books on European intellectual history, including *D'Holbach's Coterie: An Enlightenment in Paris; Atheism in France, 1660–1729: The Orthodox Sources of Disbelief;* and *Anticipations of the Enlightenment in England, France, and Germany.* He is editor-in-chief of the four-volume Oxford University Press *Encyclopedia of the Enlightenment.*

Professor Kors has served as a member of the Council of the National Endowment for the Humanities and on the editorial boards of several scholarly journals. He has received postdoctoral fellowships from the American Council of Learned Societies, the Davis Center for Historical Studies at Princeton University, and the Smith Richardson Foundation.

Professor Kors has won two awards for distinguished college teaching and the Engalitcheff Award for defense of academic freedom. With Harvey A. Silverglate, he is co-author of *The Shadow University: The Betrayal of Liberty on America's Campuses.* He is president of the Foundation for Individual Rights in Education.

ecture Titles

If you would like to order this course, please contact us at:

Phone: 1-800-TEACH-12

Web: www.TEACH12.com

For more information on our pricing policy, see page 245.

The Will to Power: The Philosophy of Friedrich Nietzsche
Course #415
Lecture 5

Taught by: Professor Robert C. Solomon
and Professor Kathleen M. Higgins
The University of Texas at Austin

Nietzsche and the Greeks

Nietzsche was obsessed with the Greeks. He discovered them as a schoolboy, and one can only imagine the fantasies he must have had as a very young man. They stayed with him throughout his life. In fact, his last crazed note, well into his period of insanity, was signed Dionysus.

There's a contrast that goes throughout his philosophy between the ancient Greeks and modern bourgeois Christianity, and there is a sense in which understanding what he liked or what he loved about the Greeks is essential to understanding what he disliked and sometimes despised about modern society. He was, of course, a classics professor. He knew his ancient texts very well. The Greece that he really admired, though, was not the Greece that you would expect him, as a philosopher, to have loved. He thought that the Greece of Socrates, Plato, and Aristotle was already in some sense decadent. The Greece that Nietzsche really praised and admired was the Greece of Homer, the Greece of the ancient tragedians. His first book, *The Birth of Tragedy*, talks at great length about the ways tragedy became possible for the Greeks and, consequently, the ways tragedy has become unthinkable for us now.

He felt Greece should be a kind of model, and he despised his fellow scholars. He called them "scholarly oxen" who worried about Greek grammar, who worried about Greek philology, who worried about when such and such was written or performed—but didn't spend even a minute fantasizing about what it would be like to live as a Greek and, in particular, what it would be like to live as a Greek today. The

Philosophy

Greece that he admired is very much the Greece depicted by Homer, the Greek attitude toward life was something that was enviable and was clearly something missing in the modern world.

If you think about the tragedies that were written by the great Greek playwrights (this is all before Socrates)—plays like *Oedipus, Antigone,* the plays about the Trojan women, Prometheus—what you realize is that it's a model of life that we have trouble understanding. It's so cruel. The idea of fate driving Oedipus to do these awful things, a curse that had been cast on his father, now extending to him, which would extend in turn to his daughter Antigone. The idea of realizing that one had done something awful, murdering your father, marrying your mother, and consequently putting your own eyes out because you had seen too much. That kind of vision to us is just plain awful, and one of the themes of *The Birth of Tragedy* is how it was different for the Greeks, and how, when they saw these tragedies performed, something different was going on.

In fact, the theme of *The Birth of Tragedy*, at its very core, is that tragedy is a real, honest recognition of what life is all about. To be sure, Oedipus, Antigone—these are people who faced dilemmas, situations that none of us really would like to face, but the truth of it is we all are going to face our own dilemmas. We all have to face up to death. We all have to face up to the bad things in life, and the question is: How do we do that? Do we accept it as the way things are, or do we rationalize it away? The idea in *The Birth of Tragedy* is that the Greek view of tragedy was possible because two different strains of thought or two different strains of feeling came together in a remarkable way.

The one, the Apollonian, the rationalistic, saw tragedy as something that happens to the individual. It's a real, personal loss. On the other hand is the Dionysian, and the Dionysian is connected up with what you might call the suprapersonal—it's the idea of ourselves as part of the flow of life. If you think about the Bacchanalian revels, one of the things that's most pronounced about them is a loss of the sense of self, a sense of going with the flow, a sense that one is part of life and that what happens to one as an individual really is of no great importance. That sense of overriding passion of identity with the whole as opposed to a kind of rational individualism is what Nietzsche thinks allows the Greeks to come up with this notion: on the one hand, something awful happening to an individual; at the same time, understanding this as something beautiful.

The Birth of Tragedy makes a distinction, however, between two different sets of Greek authors. Nietzsche sees the early great tragedians, namely Sophocles and Aeschylus, as very much in tune with this merging of the Apollonian and the Dionysian, getting the two in balance, whereas the third of the great three Greek tragedy writers, Euripides, Nietzsche condemns. He condemns him in particular because of his linkage—which is debatable in classical circles—with Socrates in particular. With Euripides and with Socrates, that's when Greek thought and Greek culture goes into decline. The difference was that Sophocles and Aeschylus saw tragedy as something that's inexplicable, something that could not be rationalized. You watch *Oedipus* or *Antigone*—both plays by Sophocles—and the overwhelming sense you come away with—apart from the beautiful poetry—is that life is really a mystery; the things that happen to people can't be explained.

With Euripides, however, Nietzsche says rationalization enters the picture—Euripides and Socrates tried to explain tragedy in such a way that human beings could ultimately think their way through it. That's precisely what Nietzsche wants to say one could *not* do. He also thinks that the ancient Greeks had, as one of their primary virtues, the fact that they believed that life itself was a struggle. The tragedies make this very clear.

Nietzsche thought this sense of agony, this sense of struggle, was what made the Greeks so beautiful, and the struggle itself became an artistic form. The idea of looking at life as a struggle even extends to such supposedly genteel professions as philosophy. One often talks about Socrates in terms of his love of the truth, his pursuit of wisdom, but you don't have to read much of Plato to see right through that.

What Socrates really loves is a good argument, to get down and dirty in the streets and show he is the smartest guy of all. The important thing is winning arguments. Socrates is often contrasted with the Sophists, a school of philosophers who were his contemporaries. I sometimes think of them as the ancient equivalent of law school because in democratic Greece their function was to teach people the art of rhetoric and how to win arguments. Socrates contrasts himself on the grounds that that's all they do. What he is about, on the other hand, is the truth. But the truth is that Socrates wasn't against the Sophists so much as he was one of the best of them.

The idea of Greece's agonistic also explains, in Nietzsche's terms, why Greece declined. In the early days of Greece there were constant wars between the city-states and invasions from the Persians, and so there was always a struggle. Nietzsche said, "As long as the Greeks had a struggle going on they knew what life was about and they were great. As soon as they found themselves in a period of relative peace that kind of inner instinct for struggle turned against themselves—and that's when they started to decay." ■

The preceding lecture was an excerpt drawn from The Great Course:

The Will to Power: The Philosophy of Friedrich Nietzsche
Course #415

Among shapers of contemporary thought—including Darwin, Marx, and Freud—Friedrich Nietzsche is perhaps the most mysterious and least understood. His aphorisms are widely quoted, but as both man and thinker he remains an enigmatic figure.

Lecture Titles

1. Why Read Nietzsche? His Life, Times, Works, and Themes
2. Quashing the Rumors About Nietzsche
3. The Fusion of Philosophy and Psychology
4. "God Is Dead"—Nietzsche and Christianity
5. **Nietzsche and the Greeks**
6. "Why the Greeks Were So Beautiful"—Nietzsche on Tragedy
7. Nietzsche and Schopenhauer on Pessimism
8. Nietzsche, Jesus, Zarathustra
9. Nietzsche on Reason, Instinct, and Passion
10. Nietzsche's Style and the Problem of Truth
11. Nietzsche on Truth and Interpretation
12. "Become Who You Are"— Freedom, Fate, and Free Will
13. Nietzsche as Moral Psychologist—Love, Resentment, and Pity
14. Nietzsche on Love
15. Nietzsche and Women
16. Nietzsche's "Top Ten"
17. Nietzsche on History and Evolution
18. What Is Nihilism? The Problem of Asceticism
19. The Ranking of Values—Morality and Modernity
20. Nietzsche "Immoralism"— Virtue, Self, and Selfishness
21. *On the Genealogy of Morals*— Master and Slave Morality
22. Resentment, Revenge, and Justice
23. The Will to Power and the *Übermensch*
24. Eternal Recurrence—Nietzsche Says "Yes!" to Life

Robert C. Solomon

Robert C. Solomon is the Quincy Lee Centennial Professor of Business and Philosophy at The University of Texas at Austin, where he has taught for more than 30 years. He received his undergraduate degree in Molecular Biology from the University of Pennsylvania and his Master's and Doctoral degrees in Philosophy and Psychology from the University of Michigan.

Kathleen M. Higgins

Kathleen M. Higgins is Professor of Philosophy at The University of Texas at Austin where she has been teaching for more than 20 years. She earned her B.A. in Music from the University of Missouri at Kansas City and completed her graduate work at Yale University, receiving her M.A., M.Phil, and Ph.D. in Philosophy.

If you would like to order this course, please contact us at:

Phone: 1-800-TEACH-12
Web: www.TEACH12.com

For more information on our pricing policy, see page 245.

The scientific method is a cyclic process of inquiry based on observation, synthesis, hypothesis, and prediction that leads to more observation.

SCIENCE

"Science is the attempt to make the chaotic diversity of our sense-experience correspond to a logically uniform system of thought."

—Albert Einstein

Comets!

Comets are diffuse, luminous patches that move across the sky from night to night and sometimes have a long tail. We see them every few years, and sometimes a bright one every few decades.

In March and April of 1997, when Comet Hale-Bopp graced our skies, it was the best comet in about two decades. It was easy to photograph, in fact, it was hard to get a bad photograph. Even in the middle of cities, people obtained reasonably good photographs of Hale-Bopp.

The word *cometa* in Greek means "hairy star;" people thought that these were stars that somehow developed hair, like a brush or a ponytail or something. In fact, a comet isn't a star at all. A comet is a dirty snowball that comes in from very far away, and as it approaches the Sun, the Sun's energy evaporates the snow. The Sun's radiation and its solar wind push the particles, the gas, and dust from which the comet is made away from the Sun.

That tail then reflects the sunlight, and it is that phenomenon that we see as a comet. Nothing is actually burning, there's no hair, and it's not a star. It's just a small snowball, in some cases a kilometer in diameter, in some cases up to 10, in other cases very small indeed. It just lights up because it's being evaporated.

A comet's tail always points away from the Sun. It doesn't always follow the head of the comet. It follows the head of the comet on the way in, but on the way out, the tail actually leads the head of the comet, because it's pointing away from the Sun. The tail curves a little bit behind the comet's head, and that's because of Kepler's third law. The particles come streaming out and then are farther from the Sun; according to Kepler's third law, they then have a longer orbital period about the Sun, so they drag behind a little bit. The head is on a faster orbit when that happens.

A comet has a nucleus, which is perhaps one to 10 kilometers in diameter, and then an evaporated region, a coma, which is considerably bigger. It is from this coma that the gases and the dust are pushed away. The ions (the ionized gases) are pushed

The most famous of all periodic comets, Comet Halley is visible from Earth every 75–76 years and was the first comet to be recognized as periodic in nature.

away very rapidly by the Sun's charged solar wind. The ions are very light and go streaming away from the comet very quickly, so they appear to go in a straight path. The dust gets pushed less.

It's pushed nearly as much, but the dust particles are more massive, so they're harder to accelerate. They don't move away from the comet's coma as easily, and you can actually see their orbit then deviate from the orbit of the comet more easily. There's a sort of a hydrogen envelope that surrounds the whole thing.

The most famous of all comets, Comet Halley, is what's called a periodic comet. It comes by every 76 years, so it has a closed orbit around the Sun, and we see it come near the Sun and light up roughly every 76 years.

In 1910, it was a fabulous sight. It had a very long tail because we were viewing it from a favorable geometry. In 1910 the Earth went through the tail of Comet Halley, the last bit of the tail. The tail is nearly a perfect vacuum. It's not quite as good a vacuum as interplanetary space, but it's a better vacuum than what's achievable here on Earth. Even though the tail has various noxious gases, such as cyanide and others, there's no real need to worry when you go through the tail of a comet, although some people made a lot of money in 1910 by selling various potions that would save them from this cyanide.

Most of the tail, by the way, is water-ice, or evaporated water, evaporated carbon dioxide, dry ice, methane, and things like that. In 1986,

A close-up view of Comet Halley taken by the ESA spacecraft Giotto in a carefully orchestrated flyby in 1986.

the geometry was much more unfavorable, so it wasn't such a spectacular sight.

Giotto was a spacecraft that approached Comet Halley in 1985 and 1986 and took some very detailed pictures of it. In them you can see that the comet is kind of shaped like a peanut. It's maybe 16 kilometers in length with the widest point something like 10 kilometers.

The emission of the gas and dust from the comet nucleus is quite irregular. The sunlit side is heavily lit up, so it evaporates quite readily, but the dark side, the side facing away from the Sun, is not heated very much. It is icy cold and the gases don't evaporate away. It's really the part of the comet that's facing the Sun that evaporates. Sometimes comets tumble. They rotate, so all parts of the comet might suffer some evaporation along the way, but other comets might preferentially face the Sun and the backside won't evaporate nearly as much as the side that's facing the Sun.

Giotta provided a beautiful close-up view of the comet, although it couldn't quite reach the surface and scoop up a chunk and bring it back to Earth. It wasn't going to come back, but it did get some good pictures.

If you look at the orbit of Halley's Comet, you can see that it's a beautiful illustration of Kepler's law. The comet zips past the Sun in a short amount of time, so that the area that a segment from the Sun to the comet sweeps out is equal to the area swept out when the comet is far from the Sun and moving slowly. That's Kepler's second law.

Edmund Halley has his name attached to Halley's Comet because he noticed that a number of comets in the history of human viewing of the heavens seemed to occur in periods of around 75 to 76 years—a great comet of about the same brightness showed up roughly every 76 years. He postulated that this was the same comet. He predicted the next appearance of this comet and, indeed, it did appear when predicted, so it was named after Edmund Halley.

When you look at Halley's Comet, you can see the fine structure in the tail. That structure can change daily as new bits of gas shoot out from the comet's nucleus. The corollary of this is that with every passage around the Sun, a periodic comet loses some of its material. It's flowing away from the comet nucleus never to return, so it's losing mass each time. That means that periodic comets slowly wither away and essentially burn out. Not that anything's burning, they just kind of evaporate away; they disintegrate.

When that happens, the remaining material of the comet can actually spread out in its former orbit. Suppose there's rocky, dusty material left that didn't evaporate away and maybe some ice chunks associated with that material. The comet breaks up and then it just kind of dissipates throughout the orbit. A little chunk breaks off here and there. Then again, by Kepler's third law, the different pieces will have slightly different orbital periods around the Sun. Hence, what is initially just a small separation between two chunks gradually grows after many orbits into a large separation between those chunks. A comet that's disintegrating gradually spreads out over the entire orbit of the comet and the orbit broadens a little bit.

Sometimes, if that orbit happens to be in the Earth's orbital plane, the Earth will pass through the swarm of comet debris. That means that there will be a larger than normal number of chunks moving through Earth's atmosphere at that time. That gives rise to a meteor shower. When you have a lot of little bits of gravel, pebbles, and ice zipping through the atmosphere, you get a meteor shower. You can see maybe one or two meteors per minute, much better than the usual average rate of the so-called sporadic meteors, which is maybe half a dozen to a dozen per hour at best.

A good time to look for meteor showers is when the Earth is passing through the orbit of an old disintegrated comet. In some instances, that can even happen twice per year for a given comet, giving rise to different meteor showers.

Occasionally, the material is highly clumped. If the comet has only begun to disintegrate recently, then much of the orbit is relatively free of debris and there is a lot of debris in the clump that's still breaking apart. In that case, you can get a meteor storm, because the Earth moves through a whole conglomeration of these particles and you can get up to a few per second in those cases.

If you look at a picture of a meteor shower—captured through a time exposure—you will see meteor streaks. If you extrapolate these streaks, you see that they appear to come from a common point, called the radiant of the comet. That occurs because the Earth is approaching the swarm of comets from a particular direction and they're all coming at us as in a tube. There's something like a tube of material approaching us.

That tube has a vanishing point. It's like railroad tracks that you see from far away. The railroad tracks vanish in the distance, at infinity, so to speak. The telephone poles seem to vanish at that same point as well. In a similar way, all these parallel tracks coming towards us, like railroad tracks, seem to emerge from a particular direction simply because that's the convergent point of all those parallel tracks.

There are well-publicized meteor showers throughout the year. One recent shower that was particularly impressive was the Leonids, which occurs every November 17.

Meteor showers have this radiant, and in newspapers you can sometimes see announcements of meteor showers that are named after the radiant point. The Geminids, which appear in December, seem to radiate from Gemini. The Perseids in August, another famous meteor shower, radiate from Perseus.

In general, the radiant is not necessarily the best place to look because right at the radiant, the meteors are by and large coming right at you, so they don't make very wide streaks across the sky. You want to look a number of degrees away from the radiant because they will be going through the atmosphere more broadside and the streaks will tend to be larger.

There are well-publicized meteor showers throughout the year. One recent shower that was particularly impressive was the Leonids, which occurs on November 17 every year. On November 17, 1999, Earth passed through the main clump of the comet that had disintegrated to form an orbit that normally produces the Leonids. Usually we pass through a part of the orbit that doesn't have very many particles in it, but every 33 years we pass through the main clump.

Apparently in 1833 the storm was a fantastic one, and a woodcut from 1833 shows that the sky was almost literally falling. Remember, this is back when people did not know what meteors were. You can imagine the reaction people may have had when it looked as though the whole sky was raining down on them—up to 100,000 meteors, according to some reports, in a single hour. Contrast that with the six or seven per hour you might see on a normal night. ∎

Engraving of a particularly heavy meteor shower in 1833

The preceding lecture was an excerpt drawn from The Great Course:

Understanding the Universe: An Introduction to Astronomy, 1st Edition
Course #180

Astronomy, the science of the universe, exists because Einstein's awe-inspiring insight is correct. Even more thrilling is this: What we comprehend about the universe has increased dramatically in recent years.

This course taught at this time, by this professor is a scientific adventure. We have the good luck to be alive during a golden age of astronomical research and discovery. Twenty years ago, the universe was thought to be a very different size and age than we think it is now. Fifteen years ago, black holes and planets around other stars had not yet been observed. Now, they are discovered every month. Fifteen years ago, scientists could not find the 90 percent of the universe that was "missing" if the Big Bang theory was true—and they still have many questions.

With this course, you can share in the almost daily excitement as we learn more about the universe.

Alex Filippenko

Alex Filippenko is Professor of Astronomy at the University of California at Berkeley. He received his Bachelor's degree in Physics from the University of California at Santa Barbara and earned his Ph.D. in Astronomy from the California Institute of Technology.

Dr. Filippenko's research accomplishments, documented in over 430 published papers, are among the most highly cited in the world. He has been recognized with several major awards, including the 1997 Robert M. Petrie Prize of the Canadian Astronomical Society. He was a Guggenheim Fellow in 2001 and a Phi Beta Kappa Visiting Scholar in 2002.

Science magazine credited Professor Filippenko and his international team of astronomers with the top "Science Breakthrough of 1998" for research on exploding stars (supernovae) which shows the universe is expanding at an accelerating rate, propelled by mysterious "dark energy." Moreover, he leads the world's most successful robotic search for exploding stars.

At UC Berkeley, Dr. Filippenko's teaching awards include the Donald S. Noyce Prize for Excellence in Undergraduate Teaching in the Physical Sciences, and the Distinguished Teaching Award. He was also voted the Best Professor on campus in student polls four times, in 1995, 2001, 2003, and 2004. He recently won the 2004 Carl Sagan Prize for Science Popularization from the Trustees of Wonderfest, the Bay Area Festival of Science.

Lecture Titles

If you would like to order this course, please contact us at:

Phone: 1-800-TEACH-12
Web: www.TEACH12.com
For more information on our pricing policy, see page 245.

The Joy of Science
Course #1100
Lecture 43

Taught by: Professor Robert M. Hazen
George Mason University and the Carnegie
Institution of Washington

What Is Life?

The most basic question in biology must be: What is life? It might surprise you to learn that in spite of thousands of years of study of living systems, there is no single definition that has been widely accepted. No one can give an exact definition of life.

Y
ou might say, "Oh, I know life when I see it," but it turns out that many of the traits we associate with living things are not observed in all life forms. Furthermore, many objects are clearly not alive, even though they have aspects of living things.

You know that birds are alive, you know that dogs are alive; but of course, not all living things move. By the same token, there are some things that aren't alive—like streams, rivers, and fire—that do move but aren't alive. So coming up with a precise definition of life is not such a simple matter. Many biologists would argue that it's impossible to define life in any simple way. Nevertheless, there are six traits that are shared by all living organisms.

First of all, all known organisms are highly complex chemical systems. They have thousands of interdependent molecular components. The simplest life form is far more complex than the most advanced products of any human technology, and will be for at least hundreds of years to come, most likely. In terms of the chemistry of life, we have a term

Coming up with a precise definition of life is not a simple matter. Many biologists would argue that it's impossible to define life in any simple way.

called metabolism; it's the collective chemical repertoire of a living organism. Even the simplest life forms are capable of hundreds of different chemical reactions, and these reactions wouldn't occur otherwise

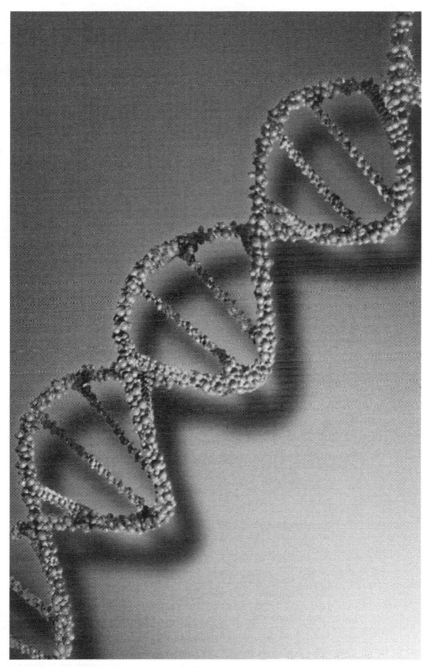

The DNA molecule contains four bases that, when ordered in a particular pattern, create a template for storing human genetic code.

in nature. They don't occur spontaneously; they occur only in living things. Most of life's chemical reactions require enzymes; they are molecular catalysts. They greatly increase the efficiency of reactions, and the catalyst, or the enzyme itself, is a molecule that does not change in the process of facilitating that chemical reaction.

The second characteristic of all life: All organisms are composed of cells, which is the unit in which metabolism occurs. Many organisms, including bacteria and yeast, are single-celled organisms. But most known species, including all the plants and all the animals, are multicellular, composed of many cells, sometimes tens or hundreds of trillions of cells collected together in a single organism. A human being, for example, contains about 100 trillion cells.

All organisms grow and develop. Most organisms change form and capabilities as they get larger. For example, a seed develops into a flower.

Third, all organisms obtain and use energy. Energy is the ability to do work, to exert a force over a distance. Every organism needs to feed, it needs to grow, it needs to reproduce—and so it has to have energy. Plants, and many single-celled organisms, obtain their energy directly from the Sun through a process called photosynthesis. Most animals, on the other hand, obtain energy, directly or indirectly, from plants. They eat plants, or they eat organisms that have eaten plants, and so forth. There are a few simple one-celled organisms that have been found to get their energy directly from Earth's inner heat. They get the energy from chemistry; in fact, they eat rocks, essentially.

The fourth characteristic of all life on Earth is that all organisms reproduce using the same genetic mechanism. A genetic mechanism is a way of processing information, passing that information from one generation to the next to the next. It turns out that this aspect of information passing from one generation to another is key to all organisms. There are three characteristics about this genetic code you should remember. The first is that each individual reproduces its own species; like begets like. The second is that offspring inherit genetic instructions from their parents through a molecule called DNA—it's actually a molecule, DNA—that carries information that passes from one generation to the next. Finally, the genetic information of offspring can differ from that of the parents. This gives you a way of reproduction with variation, and that variation is key to living things, the fact that one generation can differ slightly from the previous one.

The fifth characteristic of all life: All organisms grow and develop. Most organisms change form and capabilities as they get larger. For example, a seed develops into a flower. A fertilized human egg—a single cell—develops into the 100 trillion cells that are a human being. This implies that all organisms have to gather atoms, and they have to gather energy. There's no way you can go from a single cell to 100 trillion cells unless you use a lot of energy, and a lot of new atoms and molecules in the process.

The sixth characteristic of all life is: All organisms respond to changes in their external environment while they maintain a relatively constant internal environment. This point has a couple of subtexts. First of all, there has to be an inside and an outside to all living things. The inside is in some way controlled, chemically and physically.

Furthermore, organisms can respond in significant ways to the external influence. Some of these are obvious. Larger animals, for example, may cause smaller animals to scurry away; that's a kind of response to your environment. But plants also respond to environmental changes. For example, the direction of the flowers following the Sun; the fact that roots, as they penetrate deep into the ground, will change their direction, seeking water or going around obstacles ∎

The Joy of Science
Course #1100

English novelist and scientist C. P. Snow classed certain scientific ideas with the works of Shakespeare as something every educated person should know. One such idea, according to Snow, was the second law of thermodynamics, which deals with the diffusion of heat and has many profound consequences.

He might well have added Newton's laws, the periodic table of elements, the double-helix structure of DNA, and scores of other masterpieces of scientific discovery.

Now, Professor Robert M. Hazen introduces these and other great ideas in 60 lectures that explore the fundamental discoveries and principles of all of the physical and biological sciences—physics, genetics, biology, astronomy, chemistry, meteorology, thermodynamics, and more.

Robert M. Hazen

Robert M. Hazen is the Clarence Robinson Professor of Earth Science at George Mason University in Fairfax, VA, and a research scientist at the Geophysical Laboratory of the Carnegie Institution of Washington.

Dr. Hazen received his Bachelor's and Master's degrees in Geology from the Massachusetts Institute of Technology. He earned a Ph.D. in Earth Science from Harvard University and did post-doctoral work at Cambridge University in England before joining the Carnegie Institution. At Carnegie, Dr. Hazen's research focuses on high-pressure organic synthesis and the origin of life.

Professor Hazen has authored 15 books including the bestselling *Science Matters: Achieving Scientific Literacy* and *The Sciences: An Integrated Approach*. He has written more than 220 articles for both scholarly and popular publications such as *Newsweek, Scientific American, The New York Times Magazine, Technology Review,* and *Smithsonian Magazine.*

He has received the Mineralogical Society of America Award, the American Chemical Society Ipatieff Prize, the Educational Press Association Award, the American Crystallographic Association's Science Writing Award, and Fellowship in the American Association for the Advancement of Science.

Lecture Titles

If you would like to order this course, please contact us at:

Phone: 1-800-TEACH-12

Web: www.TEACH12.com

For more information on our pricing policy, see page 245.

The Mystery
of *The Federalist Papers*

Often, statistical reasoning can contribute to decisive arguments in matters that seem very difficult to resolve, and even to issues that don't appear to have any statistical component to them at all.

Consider the following example:

In 1787 and 1788, Alexander Hamilton, James Madison, and John Jay wrote a series essays about the Constitution, advocating that the Constitution be accepted by the people of New York. These were *The Federal-Papers*. The goal of these papers was convince people to vote for the Constitution, and the men wrote a total 85 essays. They didn't sign the papers with their names; they were all published under the pseudonym Publius.

Of these 85 essays, the authorship was clearly known in all cases except for about a dozen. Alexander Hamilton was known to have written 51 of these 85 essays; John Jay was known

THE
FEDERALIST:
A COLLECTION

C. M. Hare

ESSAYS,

WRITTEN IN FAVOUR OF THE

NEW CONSTITUTION,

AS AGREED UPON BY THE FEDERAL CONVENTION,
SEPTEMBER 17, 1787.

IN TWO VOLUMES.

VOL. I.

NEW-YORK:

PRINTED AND SOLD BY J. AND A. M'LEAN,
No. 41, HANOVER-SQUARE,
M,DCC,LXXXVIII.

In a series of anonymous newspaper essays during 1787 - 88, soon published in book form (1788) as The Federalist, Alexander Hamilton, James Madison, and John Jay strongly advocated ratification of the Constitution.

Frontispiece of *The Federalist Papers*, a propaganda piece that sought to convince New Yorkers to vote for the new U.S. Constitution.

to have written five; James Madison was known to have written 14; and Madison with Hamilton wrote three together. This left 12 disputed *Federalist Papers*. People had disputed the authorship of these essays for many, many years, and some contended that Hamilton was the sole author, and others asserted that Madison was the author. No one thought Jay was—so it was between Hamilton and Madison. Arguments were presented, based on all sorts of things, as you'd expect—namely, what positions were presented in the disputed articles, and issues about their style of writing, and so on. But none of these arguments was powerful enough to settle the dispute.

In 1964, statisticians Frederick Mosteller and David Wallace published a book called *Inference and Disputed Authorship: The Federalist*, in which they approached the question from a statistical point of view. They recognized that different individuals develop habits of word usage that are rather distinctive from person to person. In the case of Hamilton and Madison, there were many known examples of writing by each of the two. Because they had these sources, counting the frequency of the use of different words was a very possible thing to do.

In particular, Mosteller and Wallace viewed the use of unimportant words as particularly significant, with the idea that the unimportant words more or less just arose independently of the content being conveyed. This method of analysis is called discriminant analysis—trying to discriminate between, in this case, the word usage of Hamilton versus the word usage of Madison.

They used many words, but one specific word—to ground the discussion—was the word "upon." Hamilton was fonder of the word "upon" than was Madison. In Hamilton's extant writing, he used "upon" at the rate of about six words per 1,000; that is, six occurrences of the word "upon" per 1,000 words in his writing, on average—whereas, Madison only used the word "upon" less than 1 time per 1,000 words, overall.

By looking at the actual *Federalist Papers* in question—the ones of disputed authorship—several such words were analyzed, and the relative frequency of the use of those words by Hamilton versus Madison in the previous known writing versus the unknown writing, that kind of analysis was used to try to distinguish the authors.

The evidence and the reasoning from it are rather persuasive, and we can demonstrate how this was done by looking at pages from *The Federalist Papers*.

This first page is from "Federalist Essay No. 23," which is definitely by Alexander Hamilton. Looking at a randomly selected page, there are three occurrences of the word "upon." The first reads:

"It rests upon axioms as simple as they are universal, the means ought to be proportioned to the end ... "

Later on the page, he writes:

"As their requisitions are made constitutionally binding upon the states, who are in fact, under the solemn obligations to furnish the supplies ..."

Finally, at the end of the page there is a third instance:

"If we are in earnest about giving the union energy and duration, we must abandon the vain project of legislating upon the states in their collective capacities."

So, he used the word "upon" several times. Reading these three sentences, you will notice that in many instance, he might have chosen to just use the word "on." For example:

"As their requisitions are made constitutionally binding upon the states" he could have said "on the states." But Hamilton used the word "upon."

Let's look at an example that is known to have been written by James Madison. This is "Federalist Essay No. 39." In it, he has the following part of a sentence:

"We may define a republic to be—or at least may bestow that name on—a government which derives all its powers directly or indirectly from the great body of the people."

You notice that if you chose to use the word "upon" in that sentence, it would sound quite reasonable.

"We may define a republic to be—or at least may bestow that name upon—a government which derives ..."

So, perhaps Hamilton, who preferred "upon," might have used "upon" in that instance. Of course, in any individual case, it's completely inconclusive.

Now we'll turn to one of the disputed essays, which is "Federalist Essay No. 52." Here there are a couple of sentences in which the word "on" is used, where "upon" might be used instead.

"... under the federal system, cannot possibly be dangerous to the requisite dependents of the House of Representatives on their constituents."

The author might have said, "requisite dependents of the House of Representatives upon their constituents," which would read rather well.

Here's another example:

"The advantage of biennial elections would secure to them every degree of liberty which might depend on a due connection between their representatives and themselves."

That might have been written, "every degree of liberty which might depend upon a due connection between their representatives and themselves."

So, we see that in these examples, choices are being made by the author in each instance whether to use the word "on" or "upon," and Hamilton more frequently used the word "upon" than Madison did.

In this particular dispute, it was discovered that, in fact, the authorship of these papers—that is to say the word usage of meaningless words—corresponded much more strongly with Madison than with Hamilton.

So this was strong evidence from which it was rather persuasively concluded that, in fact, the disputed *Federalist Papers*—all of them were written by Madison. So, this is an example of an area in which it's not clear that statistical evidence would be pertinent whatsoever, and yet it can obviously be very helpful.

Another example of analysis of authorship is a paper entitled, "Did Shakespeare Write a Newly Discovered Poem?" by two statisticians. You might expect that it would be written by two English professors, but, no, this is written by two statisticians. In this paper, there's a different strategy by which these statisticians try to decide whether or not a poem was written by Shakespeare.

The method that they use in this case is the method of looking for unusual words. The previous strategy was to look for usual words, and how frequently usual words were used. This strategy is another statistical variant in which they look for unusual words.

Hamilton was fonder of the word "upon" than was Madison. In Hamilton's extant writing, he used "upon" at the rate of about six words per 1,000; that is, six occurrences of the word "upon" per 1,000 words in his writing, on average—whereas, Madison only used the word "upon" less than 1 time per 1,000 words, overall.

The kind of statistics that they presented were ones where they tried to claim that, among the words that Shakespeare used, very frequently he used words very few times.

In other words, his vocabulary included 31,534 distinct words that appear in the 884,640 total words in the Shakespearean canon. It's interesting that all of these things are so precise.

The concept here was to look at the words in a poem newly discovered by Gary Taylor on November 14, 1985. The question was whether this Taylor poem—as it's come to be known—was or was not written by Shakespeare. It had 429 total words, and the issue was how to distinguish whether or not this could be ruled out as a Shakespeare poem. It's more ruling out than asserting that it was, in fact, written by Shakespeare.

This is the basis on which this analysis is done. They discovered that unusual words are very common for Shakespeare. Two-thirds of the 31,534 distinct words occur three or fewer times in the entire Shakespearean canon. The effect of this is that you expect, even in relatively small samples of works from Shakespeare, you expect words that do not appear in the rest of the canon.

So, in this poem of 429 words, there is an expectation—and these statisticians developed a model—of how many words that they would expect to be new—words that did not appear elsewhere in the canon. In fact, there were nine new words that appeared in this poem, which are the following: admirations, besoughts, exiles, inflection, joying, scanty, speck, tormenter, and explain. Those words occurred nowhere else in the canon, which is sort of surprising.

By the way, a variation on a word counts as a different word in this counting. For example, "admirations" counts, although the word "admiration" appears 14 times in the rest of the canon. And "besoughts" counts as a new word, although "besoughted" did appear elsewhere in the canon. So using this strategy and a data analysis, these statisticians were able to educe evidence that, in fact, this poem was certainly possibly written by Shakespeare.

It can be troubling to a lot of people who study literature or history that decisive evidence in favor of one theory or another would not be based on expertise in the area in which this evidence is being educed. One wonders how experts feel about these kinds of arguments. But the evidence is very difficult to refute without further kinds of evidence.

Using data and statistical analysis is obviously a central part of our world today, but one can argue that it will become even more prominent in the future. The main reason is the computer and the continuing development of computer technology. With the computer, it's now possible to deal with large databases, and we can use techniques that were previously computationally impossible.

Some techniques, for example, involve simulation as a means to understand a collection of data, where you simulate things and see what happens. Often, these methods are computationally intensive.

Consequently, as we become increasingly able to have more computer power applied to them, then these methods become concomitantly increasingly valuable. ■

The preceding lecture was an excerpt drawn from The Great Course:

Meaning from Data: Statistics Made Clear
Course #1487

This course introduces you to a vitally important subject in today's data-driven society. In 24 half-hour lectures, you will explore the principles and methods that underlie the study of statistics. You have probably heard such terms as mean, median, percentile, quartile, statistically significant, and bell curve, and you may have a rough idea of what they mean. This course sharpens your understanding of these and scores of other statistical concepts and shows how, properly used, they can extract meaning from data.

Lecture Titles

Michael Starbird

Michael Starbird is a Professor of Mathematics and a University Distinguished Teaching Professor at The University of Texas at Austin. He received his B.A. from Pomona College and his Ph.D. in Mathematics from the University of Wisconsin.

Professor Starbird has won several teaching awards, most recently the 2007 Mathematical Association of America Deborah and Franklin Tepper Haimo National Award for Distinguished College or University Teaching of Mathematics.

If you would like to order this course, please contact us at:

Phone: 1-800-TEACH-12
Web: www.TEACH12.com
For more information on our pricing policy, see page 245.

Biology and Human Behavior: The Neurological Origins of Individuality, 2nd Edition
Course #1597
Lecture 18

Taught by: Professor Robert Sapolsky
Stanford University

Exploring Behavior in Context

Ethology is the study of the behavior of animals in their natural environments. Understanding how the brain responds to ethological sorts of signals and the world around it, and how the brain, in turn, produces those fixed-action patterns—that's neuroethology.

In order to approach that, we need to think about behavior, not rats in cages, but instead, this vast variability of animals behaving in their appropriate context, their natural setting; asking the number one question: What does the behavior look like? The fixed-action pattern, what does it look like? Number two, what's the adaptive value of the behavior? And rather than evolutionary models speculating about adaptation, actually going and doing the experiment to show what the adaptive value is.

It's in this realm that one needs to most definitely interview an animal in its own language, and, it makes no sense until you recognize that for a rat, most of its language is olfactory. If you take a rat and sit there and count the number of synapses going from the ears and the mouth and the eyes and the nose to the limbic system—you find that the nose has far more access to emotion in a rat. That's a realm in which neuroethology thrives, understanding how the brain is wired up in one species, dramatically different from another. Jeez, I wonder what that's about, because different species are paying attention to dramatically different things in the world, different releasing stimuli. Of course, the first question is: How do ethologists study this? Suppose you've got some bird and, as is the case with a lot of birds, there's some distinctive dot on its beak, and it's bright red. It looked as if, in some species, this was the thing that chicks would hone in on when they would peck on Mom's beak, and that would be a signal for Mom to give it food, or however things worked at that point. Of course, you come up with this ethological speculation: What is triggering this pecking behavior on the part of the kid? What is triggering this fixed-action pattern? What's the sensory information that triggers it? There would immediately be the speculation that it was the spot on Mom's beak. What would you do?

You would do all sorts of experiments. First version, you get some Wite-Out or something and you paint over the spot there, so you've now got a mom without that spot. Will the kids stop pecking at it? Then, you do the replacement, the substitution, the replication strategy. What you do here is now after you've whited it out, you paint back a little red dot there, and you see if the behavior starts coming back again. Okay, is it the redness of the dot or is it the size of the dot that matters? You put a dot that's blue; you put a dot that's checkered; you put a dot that's paisley—or whatever pattern—all over the beak; is it the "dotness" or is it simply having anything there? You see how much of the behavior you elicit, or you could give what they called a super stimulus. Instead of this little red dot, it would be this shining huge, fluorescent-red dot, and you would see if the chicks would now peck until the cows come home. You would begin to understand what the parameters are of the sensory information that would trigger this behavior.

These would be the classic experiments. These guys would do them once again, actual experiments showing what it is that triggers this. It's in this realm that you begin to see this whole universe of animals getting sensory information we haven't a clue about, we limited human primates. What you would find out is not only are there all different types of sensory communication, but, in different species, what the most salient type of information in the world around us is, can differ dramatically.

Let's look at some examples. Auditory information—there are all sorts of deer species that experience seasonal ovulation or induced ovulation. The female will ovulate if, and only if, there's an appropriate male around. How does she figure out there's an appropriate guy around? It turns out it's through vocalization. Males give this call or bellow that's heard for miles all over the woods of Minnesota, or wherever this occurs, and it's the sound that triggers the ovulation. For this species, the releasing stimulus, for a whole bunch of reproductive behavior, is auditory.

Meanwhile, there are electric fish, and they're going about courting each other, singing in electricity, and you get species-specific, animal-specific, electric songs. You get males competing with each other, this electrical competition, singing their electric songs, and jamming each other's frequencies, trying to block other's calls that way. You have a whole world that would make no sense at all unless you're thinking about interviewing an animal in its own language—an electric one in this case.

There's a gazillion species out there where the most important things in their lives are olfactory. Olfactory information—pheromones is the term we've been using at a number of points here—are odorants in the air coming from another member of your species bringing you information. In the world of rodents and canines, there's phenomenally subtle olfactory information, pheromonal information, telling you the gender of the other individual, their health, whether they're scared, whether they're stressed, whether they're ovulating, whether they have their testes, whether there is testosterone-derived molecules in their pheromones, whether there is estrogen-derived—all sorts of information like that. For a rodent, its world of releasing stimuli is overwhelmingly olfactory.

This approach also helped inform a much more subtle, much more landmark set of studies telling us about the releasing stimuli for something else. You ask what seems a mindless question about child development: Why do babies become attached to their mothers? You're a behaviorist, and you have the answer immediately—it's because Mom positively reinforces you. What is it that Mom provides for you? She provides calories and without calories you die, and you don't pass on copies of your genes. Positive reinforcement in a behaviorist viewpoint; you attach to this female, this organism, who is Mom because, when you're hungry, she makes the hunger go away. Great, I think I'm going to hang out around here. It's a perfectly obvious solution and the behaviorist explanation dominated throughout pediatrics in the early part of the last century.

Then, along came one of the most controversial scientists in all of psychology. A man named Harry Harlow, working at the University of Wisconsin, questioned this assumption and came up with, in some ways, an ethological experiment. It's a classic one that winds up in every single textbook out there, asking: Why is it that infants attach to Mom? This is this iconic picture that you always see. Harlow took baby rhesus monkeys and gave them two artificial mothers to choose from. One of them was made out of chicken wire, this chicken wire tube, and stuck on top was this Styrofoam head that kind of looked

Why do babies bond to their mothers? Behaviorist psychologists would say it's because mothers provide nourishment, but studies reveal a different reason.

like something with two eyes and ears and all of that. Out of that chicken wire Mom's torso came the thing that every behaviorist on Earth would want, which was a body filled with milk. Meanwhile, next to it was the other surrogate artificial Mom and, in this case, not giving milk. But the chicken wire torso was covered with warm felt, and what you wound up seeing was a very surprising answer—very surprising if you're B. F. Skinner, who would be there clutching the chicken wire Mom with the bottle. But what everybody else is able to guess, if they've had a baby, or if they ever were a baby at some point or other, is you don't attach to Mom because she gives you calories. You attach to Mom because she makes you feel safe, and warm, and enveloped, and all those things that chicken wire can't get you in a million years no matter how many of your calories it provides.

What Harlow showed was an astonishing finding that seems idiotically obvious now, but this was a time when mothers would be allowed to visit their children a half-hour a week if the child was hospitalized: "Oh, don't worry, we feed him three times a day and even put a blanket on him now and then and pat him on the head in the process." What is appropriate child development about? It didn't include concepts like warmth and physical contact, let alone something even more scientifically obtuse like the notion of love. Harlow absolutely revolutionized the field by showing it's got nothing to do with simple behaviorist models; it's got everything to do with different things releasing these behaviors, why it is you wind up loving an individual who is your mom. All of this wound up being really important in making sense of some other findings. These are some recent neurotological ones, really disturbing ones on first pass.

The amygdala becomes metabolically active in brain imaging scans when the person feels fear, anxiety, and aggression. Showing people pictures, often very fast demonstrations, subliminal, faster than you can consciously see, finding a certain picture, which in the first studies were reporting would make the amygdala suddenly get metabolically active. These were really unexpected, maybe expected, but really disturbing findings. What this first spate of studies showed was the amygdala would be activated when you would look at the face of somebody of a different race. Oh boy, did that stop everybody in their tracks and make them wonder what's going on? Are we looking at a hardwired fixed action of responsive xenophobia of people who are them versus us? All sorts of disquieting things, but what's emerged in more recent years is a more subtle literature showing that doesn't happen all the time. Straight out of our world of fixed-action patterns, it depends on who the face is. Celebrity faces don't evoke that, but it also depends on who you are and how it's framed.

There are some remarkably subtle psychological tests that can get at somebody's sort of implicit levels of racism, and how much they distinguish traits of people based on race, and the higher they score in that sort of scale, the more their amygdala activates. But in a brilliant study that was done by some psychologists at Princeton, primarily someone named Susan Fisk, showing if you frame the setting—if you frame the way the person looks at the face, if you make them think about the person as an individual beforehand, with some extremely subtle questions having nothing to do with race—if you force them to think about them as an individual, the amygdala doesn't light up anymore. So, what initially looked like a very disturbing bit of uh-oh, our brains may simply not be all that thrilled about people who look different from us—what you suddenly have instead is: It depends on the context; it depends on experience; it depends on not looking at any sort of neurotological inevitability. ∎

The preceding lecture was an excerpt drawn from The Great Course:

Biology and Human Behavior: The Neurological Origins of Individuality, 2nd Edition
Course #1597

When are we responsible for our own actions, and when are we in the grip of biological forces beyond our control? This intriguing question is the scientific province of behavioral biology, a field that explores interactions among the brain, mind, body, and environment that have a surprising influence on how we behave—from the people we fall in love with, to the intensity of our spiritual lives, to the degree of our aggressive impulses. In short, it is the study of how our brains make us the individuals that we are.

Lecture Titles

Robert Sapolsky

Robert Sapolsky is a Professor of Neuroscience at Stanford University in its Program in Molecular and Genetic Medicine.

His teaching awards include Stanford University's Bing Award for Teaching Excellence and an award for outstanding teaching from the Associated Students of Stanford University.

Dr. Sapolsky is a recipient of a MacArthur "Genius" Fellowship.

If you would like to order this course, please contact us at:

Phone: 1-800-TEACH-12
Web: www.TEACH12.com
For more information on our pricing policy, see page 245.

German goldsmith and printer Johannes Gutenberg invented the first Western printing press in the 1440s. For the first time, books no longer had to be scripted by hand.

LITERATURE

"The man who does not read good books has no advantage over the man who can't read them."

—Mark Twain

Moby Dick

In Herman Melville's *Moby Dick*, Ahab commands the *Pequod*, a Nantucket whaleship bound on a two-year voyage to the South Pacific.

Not long into the voyage, Ahab summons his entire crew to the quarterdeck, nails a bright gold Spanish doubloon to the mainmast, and offers it to the first man who catches sight of a white-headed whale called Moby Dick. Because Moby Dick chewed off one of Ahab's legs, Ahab has sworn everlasting vengeance on him. He tells the crew that his quest for vengeance must be theirs as well; that they must all swear to hunt and kill the great white whale.

This obsessive hunt for a single whale shocks Starbuck, the first mate of the *Pequod*. As a practical, reasonable, God-fearing man, he wonders how many barrels of marketable oil they'll get from a single whale. He's also alarmed by what he takes to be blasphemy in Ahab's quest for vengeance on a dumb brute—because such a quest implies that the whale deliberately maimed him; that behind those savage jaws of the whale lurked an evil intelligence, a malevolent mind. Once we credit a dumb beast with intelligence, we abandon the traditional idea that human beings surpass all other creatures on the Earth, and with it, perhaps, we might also jettison the idea that the whole universe is ruled by a wise, just, benevolent God.

Ahab doesn't give a damn. He doesn't care about traditional ideas or Starbuck's charges of blasphemy. All he cares about is hating and hunting the great white whale. In Moby Dick, Ahab sees "inscrutable malice" driving "outrageous strength," and that inscrutable malice is what he hates. The whale's white head is featureless, like a great blank wall or a pasteboard mask, but if the mask strikes Ahab, he will strike back. He will do everything in his power to penetrate its featureless exterior, to find and kill the malevolence lurking behind it—whether or not the whale is evil in itself, or merely the agent of some frighten-

Moby Dick is the story of one man's obsession for revenge against the great white whale that maimed him. The whale is often seen as a metaphor for nature, fate, and other facets of our life that are beyond our control.

ing, sadistic god. "Talk not to me of blasphemy, man," says Ahab to Starbuck. "I'd strike the Sun if it insulted me."

In this heated exchange between Ahab and Starbuck, in this passage so dramatic that it feels almost electrically charged, we find the beating heart of Melville's novel. Through the eyes of Starbuck, Ahab looks not only impious and blasphemous, but downright crazy, bent on sacrificing all other gain on this voyage for the sake of catching just one whale. And when Ahab says that he'd strike the Sun if it insulted him, he sounds really nuts. But Ahab speaks to something deep inside each of us.

Have you ever stubbed your toe on a rock and wanted to smash the rock to pieces? Have you ever cursed the clouds for raining on your picnic, your baseball game, or your outdoor party? If you've ever done any of these things, or even felt like doing any of them, then you know at least a little of what Ahab feels. Well, just imagine that feeling magnified. Imagine that instead of stubbing your toe or getting rained on, you had a leg ripped off. Imagine that every day of your life you had to live with a stump where that leg used to be. No way of forgetting—of ever forgetting—that traumatic loss. Now, you could of course accept the loss and adjust to it with the best artificial leg you could find. That would be the rational thing to do. But if you knew that a particular creature—dumb beast or not—had ripped off your leg, would you not feel the least prick of desire to track down that creature and kill it?

If you would, then you know how Ahab feels, and why he rouses every member of his crew to swear an oath of allegiance to his hunt for the great white whale. Even Starbuck feels obliged to comply—reluctantly. But there is no reluctance in Ishmael, the narrator of the novel. Even though he's a schoolteacher who has left his students for the sea, even though he's a well-educated, thoughtful, highly intelligent man, he feels the magnetism of Ahab's quest. He swears his oath with the rest of the crew; he shouts with them; paradoxically, he is galvanized by the very fearfulness of the beast they have sworn to hunt. "A wild, mystical, sympathetical feeling was in me," he says; "Ahab's quenchless feud seemed mine."

When Herman Melville started writing the epic story of this feud, he was just 30 years old, but already a well-known novelist. Born in New York City in 1819, he came of patrician stock. Grandson of General Peter Gansevoort, a hero of the American Revolution, he was the initially privileged second son of a merchant. But when his father's mismanagement of the business led the family deep into debt, they moved in 1830 to Albany, where Herman entered the Academy. When his father died two years later, the 12-year-old Herman had to leave school. After five years of work as a clerk and shoe salesman, he returned to the Academy for just one year; taught school near Pittsfield, Massachusetts; returned to Albany for a time; briefly studied surveying and engineering at nearby Lansingburgh Academy; read literature voraciously; published a couple of fragmentary stories in a newspaper; and then decided—in June of 1839, just before his 20th birthday—to work as a common sailor on a merchant ship bound from Manhattan to Liverpool. Thus began the seagoing adventures that he would re-create again and again in novels that made him famous.

When Herman Melville started writing the epic story of this feud, he was just 30 years old, but already a well-known novel-

A round trip across the Atlantic merely whetted his appetite for grander voyages. He returned from Liverpool in September, spent another year teaching school near Albany, and then briefly traveled west in a fruitless search for work. He went to New York in 1840, where he devoured Richard Henry Dana's *Two Years Before the Mast*. Written by a man just four years older than he, this book tells the story of Dana's life as a common sailor on a round-trip voyage from Boston to California, rounding each way the stormy, icy, treacherous Cape Horn. Fired in part, perhaps, by the words of Dana, Melville now

As a youth, Herman Melville led an eventful life at sea that became the source of his novels about maritime adventure.

decided to go to sea again—but this time on a whaleship bound for the Pacific in January 1841.

Quite possibly he sought to have the kind of adventures that would make a sensational book and thus make the name of its author. At sea he found a world of adventure—and cultivated his singular talent for storytelling. He sailed as far as the Marquesas Islands, a South Pacific archipelago where the sailors were warmly welcomed by a party of naked young girls. There he deserted the whaleship and spent several weeks with a savage tribe in the Typee Valley, thus gathering material for his first novel, *Typee*, published in 1846. Further adventures led to further books. Having left the Marquesas by joining the crew of an Australian whaler, he was jailed in Tahiti for his part in a mutiny, but escaped to spend some time on the island and gather material for his second novel, *Omoo*, which appeared in 1847.

Since *Typee* and *Omoo* both described the sexual favors freely offered by native women of the South Seas, Herschel Parker ventures to say that these two books made Melville "the first American literary sex symbol." Thus launched in the world of literature, Melville shortly wrote three more novels based on his life at sea: *Mardi* and *Redburn*, both published in 1849; and *White Jacket*, published early the next year.

By 1850, when *White Jacket* appeared, Melville had married Elizabeth Shaw, daughter of the

In writing Moby Dick, *Melville stretched his creative powers to the utmost. Though his most recent novels had been well received, he knew that he was still ... chiefly renowned as a man who had lived among South Sea cannibals.*

chief justice of the Supreme Court of Massachusetts. In the fall of 1850 they settled on a farm that he had bought near Pittsfield, Massachusetts, which he promptly named Arrowhead. There he wrote much of *Moby Dick* and cultivated his friendship with another novelist living nearby: Nathaniel Hawthorne, who in 1850 published his own best-known novel, *The Scarlet Letter*. The following year, on an afternoon in mid-November, it was to Hawthorne that Melville presented a brand-new copy of *Moby Dick* when the two men dined together at the Little Red Inn of Lenox, Massachusetts; and it was to Hawthorne that Melville dedicated the novel "in token of my admiration for his genius."

You may find this a little surprising, for it is hard to imagine two books more different than Hawthorne's novel of adultery in a tight little God-fearing, Puritan, New England town and Melville's story of a world-ranging, multiracial, God-defying quest for a great white whale. But a few years before *The Scarlet Letter* appeared, Hawthorne had produced a collection of stories called *Mosses from an Old Manse*, and it was these that roused the admiration of Melville. In August of 1850, during a brief stay with Hawthorne and his family, Melville dashed off a fragmentary essay that saluted Hawthorne for the "great power of blackness" in his stories, for their "Calvinistic sense of [man's] innate depravity and original sin," for their bold revelation of man's capacity for evil. You see, Melville's Hawthorne is not the cheerful, charming writer that many readers imagined him to be. And when Melville dedicates *Moby Dick* to a writer he most admires for displaying "the great power of blackness," you get some clue to Melville's ambitions for his own book.

In writing *Moby Dick*, Melville stretched his creative powers to the utmost. Though his most recent novels had been well received, he knew that he was still chiefly admired for the graphic colors of *Typee*; still chiefly renowned as a man who had lived among South Sea cannibals, ravished their women, and come home to tell the captivating tale of his adventures. But by the spring of 1851, Melville felt that he was far more than a storytelling adventurer. Reviewing his growth over the previous five years in a letter to Hawthorne, he wrote: "Until I was 25, I had no development at all. From my twenty-fifth year I date my life. Three weeks have scarcely passed, at any time between then and now, that I have not unfolded within myself. But I feel that I am now come to the utmost leaf of the bulb, and that shortly the flower must fall to the mould."

Fully developed, he was now caught up in a kind of adventure different from anything he had done before: an adventure in storytelling that was all at once nautical, scientific, psychological, and philosophical. When he wrote the words just quoted, he was completing an epic that would chronicle a doomed voyage taken halfway round the globe, dissect a living giant of the sea, and plumb the darkest depths of a human soul cut loose from all the comforts and constraints of land: a soul at war with all the inscrutable powers of the universe, with everything that threatens to crush, oppress, or annihilate mankind. ∎

The preceding lecture was an excerpt drawn from The Great Course:

Great Authors of the Western Literary Tradition, 2nd Edition
Course #2100

From Mesopotamia to Mississippi, from the anonymous writer of the *Epic of Gilgamesh* to William Faulkner writing 3,600 years later, many of the greatest figures of Western culture have been its writers.

This course is your guide to a rich sampling of their masterpieces, chosen, explained, and analyzed by five outstanding professors.

Under their guidance, you will explore the different strands of narrative in the book of Genesis, the complex allegory behind the medieval *Romance of the Rose*, the revolution in fiction wrought by Cervantes's *Don Quixote*, the ethical themes of Goethe's *Faust*, the indictment of colonialism in Conrad's *Heart of Darkness*, and many other facets of great works.

You will meet familiar names like Homer, Dante, Shakespeare, and Milton, and you will also discover geniuses who may be new to you.

James A. W. Heffernan

James A. W. Heffernan, Emeritus Professor of English and Frederick Sessions Beebe '35 Professor in the Art of Writing at Dartmouth College, earned his A.B. *cum laude* from Georgetown University and received his Ph.D. in English from Princeton University.

Professor Heffernan chaired the Dartmouth English Department from 1978 to 1981 and taught a range of courses at Dartmouth including European Romanticism, English Romantic poetry, methods of literary criticism, and the 19th-century English novel. For many years he also taught a senior seminar on Joyce's *Ulysses* that was regularly oversubscribed.

Professor Heffernan has received five grants from the National Endowment for the Humanities. He has published, among other books, *Representing the French Revolution: Literature, Historiography, and Art* and *Museum of Words: The Poetics of Ekphrasis from Homer to Ashbery*. The volume entitled *British Writers: Retrospective Supplement* includes his comprehensive essay on Joyce's work. He is the coauthor of *Writing: A College Handbook*, now in its fifth edition. He has also published nearly 50 articles.

Widely known for his work on the relationship between literature and visual art, Professor Heffernan has lectured at international conferences in Israel, Sweden, Austria, Ireland, Holland, and Germany, as well as in various parts of the United States.

Lecture Titles

1. Foundations
2. The *Epic of Gilgamesh*
3. Genesis and the Documentary Hypothesis
4. The Deuteronomistic History
5. Isaiah
6. Job
7. Homer—The *Iliad*
8. Homer—The *Odyssey*
9. Sappho and Pindar
10. Aeschylus
11. Sophocles
12. Euripides
13. Herodotus
14. Thucydides
15. Aristophanes
16. Plato
17. Menander and Hellenistic Literature
18. Catullus and Horace
19. Virgil
20. Ovid
21. Livy, Tacitus, Plutarch
22. Petronius and Apuleius
23. The Gospels
24. Augustine
25. *Beowulf*
26. *The Song of Roland*
27. *El Cid*
28. *Tristan and Isolt*
29. *The Romance of the Rose*
30. Dante Alighieri—Life and Works
31. Dante Alighieri—*The Divine Comedy*
32. Petrarch
33. Giovanni Boccaccio
34. *Sir Gawain and the Green Knight*
35. Geoffrey Chaucer—Life and Works
36. Geoffrey Chaucer— *The Canterbury Tales*
37. Christine de Pizan
38. Erasmus
39. Thomas More
40. Michel de Montaigne
41. François Rabelais
42. Christopher Marlowe
43. William Shakespeare— *The Merchant of Venice*
44. William Shakespeare—*Hamlet*
45. Lope de Vega
46. Miguel de Cervantes
47. John Milton
48. Blaise Pascal
49. Molière
50. Jean Racine
51. Sister Juana Inés de la Cruz
52. Daniel Defoe
53. Alexander Pope
54. Jonathan Swift
55. Voltaire
56. Jean-Jacques Rousseau
57. Samuel Johnson
58. Denis Diderot
59. William Blake
60. Johann Wolfgang von Goethe
61. William Wordsworth
62. Jane Austen
63. Stendhal
64. **Herman Melville**
65. Walt Whitman
66. Gustave Flaubert
67. Charles Dickens
68. Fyodor Dostoevsky
69. Leo Tolstoy
70. Mark Twain
71. Thomas Hardy
72. Oscar Wilde
73. Henry James
74. Joseph Conrad
75. William Butler Yeats
76. Marcel Proust
77. James Joyce
78. Franz Kafka
79. Virginia Woolf
80. William Faulkner
81. Bertolt Brecht
82. Albert Camus
83. Samuel Beckett
84. Conclusion

If you would like to order this course, please contact us at:

Phone: 1-800-TEACH-12

Web: www.TEACH12.com

For more information on our pricing policy, see page 245.

Taught by: Professor Peter Saccio
Dartmouth College

Shakespeare Then and Now

The plays of William Shakespeare are some of the most powerful works of art available in the Western tradition. They first filled theaters in London 400 years ago, and they continue to please, to move, and to enlighten many people today.

Thirty-eight plays of Shakespeare survive. They are not all that Shakespeare wrote; there's a sequence of 154 sonnets, some half dozen other poems, long and short. We know he had a hand in several other plays whose texts survive, and others whose texts are lost, apparently forever. Since he was the house playwright for a busy theatrical company, he probably also did lots of other writing, of which we have no record now, doctoring other playwrights' plays, putting in a scene here, a speech there. "Hey Will, we're doing this terrible old thing for kids next week. Could you put in some stuff to juice up the betrayal scene?"—That kind of stuff. That's what a house playwright does.

All this work was done in the space of about a quarter of a century, from about 1589, when Shakespeare was in his mid-twenties, to about 1612, as he approached the age of 50. If you have trouble remembering dates, perhaps an easy way to remember—this is four centuries ago—take the year 1600 as the midpoint; it is the midpoint of Shakespeare's career. It's the date of *Hamlet*; he was working 12 years before that and about 12 years after that. *Hamlet* is the great crossing place.

He was a productive man and was appreciated in his own time. About the year 1601, a Cambridge scholar named Gabriel Harvey scribbled some notes evaluating current English writing. Among his comments was the following, on a certain poet and playwright who had been gaining attention: "The younger sort takes much delight in Shakespeare's "Venus and Adonis," but his "Lucrece" and his *Hamlet*,

Prince of Denmark have it in them to please the wiser sort." Now, Gabriel Harvey was a vain and waspish man, the sort of nasty, argumentative shrew that gives academics a bad name. In fact, he was so quarrelsome, that he couldn't get a promotion even in his own university, let alone a decent job outside when he tried to do that. And you can see his condescension toward "the younger sort," who like love poems, amorous poetry like "Venus and Adonis." But his remark is also reassuring, the remark about *Hamlet*. A play that we find great now was appreciated in its own time by a demanding critic.

William Shakespeare was born and died in Stratford-upon-Avon. His life is a mystery. How did this country boy write words that have endured for centuries?

This is not to suggest that while he was still alive he was held in the extraordinary esteem that he is now. Now, he is a cultural icon, the biggest name there is in Western literature. But his plays were successful because they earned him both profit and credit in his own time. He was not a closet genius unknown to his contemporaries. And some of the ways the Elizabethan audience appreciated him continue now. The association of his work with English patriotism has continued to this day. The best known 20th-century use of Shakespeare for the building of patriotic morale has been the film *Henry V*, made by Laurence Olivier in 1944, to which the British government contributed some funding, and which Olivier dedicated to the British troops. It was a project in which Winston Churchill himself was deeply interested. He was aware of the value of cinema for public morale.

But Shakespeare had been many other things to his own time and to later generations, many other things than a patriot. He has been the source of livelihood to actors. The theatrical company of which he was part for most of his years in the theater became the most successful of his time. They were called the Lord Chamberlain's Men. When they were founded in the year 1594, their official patron was the Lord Chamberlain of the court of Queen Elizabeth I. When Elizabeth died nine years later and was succeeded by her cousin, King James I, there was a reshuffling of all the patronage at court, and a new patron of Shakespeare's company was the new King James himself. So they were called the King's Men, and under that name they lasted for another 39 years, until the Puritans closed the theaters in 1642.

The theatrical company of which he was part for most of his years in the theater became the most successful of his time. They were called the Lord Chamberlain's Men.

When the theaters opened 28 years after that, in 1660, after the Puritan interregnum, the old companies had, of course, long since fallen apart. But there were actors here and there who wanted to get back on the stage as soon as they could. Of course, nobody had been writing new plays; nobody writes plays if there's no chance of getting them produced. So for a while, the actors had to resort to the old repertoire, which meant Ben Jonson, Beaumont and Fletcher, and Shakespeare. This carries on into the 18th century, the next century, when Ben Jonson and Beaumont and Fletcher begin to be less interesting to current audiences, but Shakespeare goes on being revived again and again. Indeed, by the 18th century, English actors have come to be evaluated chiefly on their ability to perform Shakespeare's leading characters. Their portraits come down to us painted in the costumes and the scenes of his plays. We see Garrick as Richard III; we see Mrs. Siddons as Lady Macbeth. And it is still the case; English actors do many things besides Shakespeare, of course, but Shakespeare is where you achieve real distinction and fame. Dame Judi Dench, one of the really distinguished senior Shakespearean actresses currently at work, says "Shakespeare is known in our house as the gentleman who pays the rent."

Shakespeare is a source of livelihood to more than Dame Judi. He is a source of livelihood to Britain as a whole. Much of the Royal Shakespeare Company's audience at Stratford-on-Avon consists, of course, of overseas tourists: Europeans, Japanese, North Americans. The plays are a magnet that brings money, not only to the theaters, but to the restaurants, the hotel keepers, the airlines, the souvenir shops.

He has also become an educational staple. This began to happen in the 19th century, as the British, step by step, extended the franchise, the ability to vote, to more and more classes of people. As they did that, the British government realized they also had to expand the schools; these new voters from the lower middle classes and the working classes had to be educated. What should they learn? Well, working-class people cannot really be expected to learn Latin or Greek, like their upper-class betters, so English literature begins to replace the classics in the curriculum. If they can't read Julius Caesar in his original writing, they can at least read about Caesar in Shakespeare's play.

By the end of the century, English had become an acceptable subject of study in the universities as well as the schools, and that meant that research on Shakespeare—editing his plays, commenting on them (an activity which had formerly been in the province of private scholars and societies)—moved into the hands of academics. Players, shopkeepers, schoolmasters, college professors all have a heavy vested interest in Shakespeare. But beyond the economic argument, Shakespeare has assumed a massive centrality to English-speaking cultures, indeed to all the European-based cultures. There are, after all, Italian operas and Russian novels that make heavy use of Shakespeare, West Indian poets who rewrite *The Tempest*. Shakespeare gets quoted the way the Bible is quoted, to settle some important issue in human affairs.

Now, just what Shakespeare is wise about depends on the reader. In matters of philosophy, he has been enlisted on behalf of idealism; he has also been enlisted on behalf of nihilism. In matters of religion, he has been found in favor of Roman Catholicism; he has been found to favor Protestantism; he has been found to favor agnosticism and skepticism. In our own century, readers have found him particularly suggestive in political matters. The most influential scholarship of the 1940s and '50s argues that Shakespeare reflected what was called the "Elizabethan world picture." This is a strongly conservative view of the world; God created all things in a vast vertical order, the great chain of being; angels in their ranks at the top, then human beings, then animals, then plants, and then stones, and then down to the smallest mote of dust. Maintaining that order is essential to virtue—all sin can be defined as trying to get out of your place in that order. Influential scholars like E. M. W. Tillyard argues that Shakespeare's plays, particularly the history plays and the tragedies, show conflict to be the result of individuals breaking out of their places, and resolution to be possible only when they return to the proper order.

On the other hand, some of the most energetic criticism of the past 15 years is liberal and indeed radical in its direction, greatly concerned with the injustices perpetrated upon people through distinctions of race, gender, and/or class. Readers influenced by ideas of Marxism and cultural materialism point to passages that appear to sympathize with unprivileged classes rather than with kings and lords. Readers influenced by feminism stress the strength of some of his female characters, or stress the ways most women are marginalized or even silenced.

The point is a simple but big one. For many generations, Western culture, particularly English-speaking culture, has found Shakespeare important, found it necessary to relate to Shakespeare on those issues that seem to us to matter most: what we believe, what we find good or evil, how we should organize our relations with each other. Shakespeare is what the anthropologists call a culture-hero, a mythical figure who may or may not be based on a real person, a founder of the society, a lawgiver, a prophet. Such a figure each age must reinterpret according to its own needs. This applies not only to what is written by scholars, to be read in libraries, and what is said by teachers in classrooms, but also to productions of the plays in theaters and in films. When patriotism is needed in World War II, Laurence Olivier films a highly patriotic *Henry V*. When warfare becomes deeply suspect because of Vietnam and the Falklands, Kenneth Branagh films a skeptical and gritty *Henry V*.

The most extreme form of reinterpreting Shakespeare is to say that he was someone else, to deny that he wrote the plays at all. This is a famous topic; people who know nothing else about Shakespeare know there's been a dispute over this.

No one doubts that there was a William Shakespeare who was born in Stratford-on-Avon, went on to act in the London theaters, and eventually died back in Stratford. What is contested is whether that man wrote the plays that have come down under his name, and the people who contest it propose various different alternatives: Francis Bacon, the earl of Oxford, Christopher Marlowe, there's a long list under the blanket title of anti-Stratfordians. The one thing they agree on is it wasn't the guy from Stratford.

Anti-Stratfordianism is fascinating because it tells us a great deal about what people look for in a superlative writer. They see a wonderful poet, or a remarkable psychologist, or a great philosopher, or a man capable of expressing the views of an aristocratic class, or a man deeply concerned about the status of women and the oppressed, or any number of things for which there is some basis in the text of Shakespeare's plays. Then they note that the image they've constructed of the writer doesn't seem to cohere with a guy who was born the son of a country glover. The glover himself was probably illiterate, and the son never got beyond grammar school in Stratford, so it must have been somebody else.

There is no mystery here. There is no subject for debate. The facts of Shakespeare's life are as well recorded as anyone could expect—of his domestic life in Stratford, of his professional life in London. We'd like to know more, of course, but we don't know a great deal about the life of any person in his time, except for a few great figures of state and church, like the queen and the archbishops and the lords and generals, whose activities were naturally given a great deal of attention. We know as much about Shakespeare's life as we know about any other commoner of the time. The Elizabethans did not live filling out the records, keeping the forms the way we do. We do have documents that say, or that make sense only if you assume, that the actor from Stratford and the playwright in London were the same man. If they were not—if those documents are forgeries or lies—then quite a number of people would have to have been engaged in a great conspiracy, for which there is no positive evidence and no attested reason.

Anti-Stratfordianism is, in fact, just crazy if you know anything about how the theater works as a profession at all. Theater is a collaborative art, and people in the theater always know what other people in the theater are doing. Even now, in the much larger world of the New York theater, everybody in it knows everybody else. Everybody knows if someone is ghostwriting for someone else; everybody knows if a new director has been brought in to fix a play; everybody knows who's understudying such and such a play. Everybody knows who are sleeping together. In the much smaller world of Shakespeare's theater—in London of 1600, when probably no more than 200 people were trying to get a living out of putting on plays at any given time—it is unimaginable that three dozen successful plays could be written by someone other than the man to whom they were publicly attributed, without someone leaving some statement about the hoax.

Anti-Stratfordianism stems from false expectations. People expect that a great playwright would attract curiosity, that we would inherit diaries and personal reminiscences and the like, which we don't have for Shakespeare. But we expect that because successful playwrights today are celebrities. They are interviewed; they are invited to speak on college campuses. Elizabethan playwrights did not attract that kind of attention; they merely provided stage entertainment. If they were very good, they might have aroused the interest of what Gabriel Harvey calls "the wiser sort," or one's scribbled note in his study, but it would be the plays that would provoke interest, not the personality.

We expect, or at least some people expect, plays to reflect the personal experience of the writer. Specifically, it is assumed that plays about kings and queens and lords must have been written by an aristocrat. How else would he know how they behaved at court? Hence the suggestion that it was really Bacon, who grew up at court and became chancellor of the Realm; or Oxford, an aristocrat whose lineage goes back to the Norman conquest. But that is to mistake the nature of Shakespeare's art, which does not pretend to represent a realistic transcription of behavior in high places. No real king or duke ever spoke in spontaneous blank verse. And to suppose that a middle-class boy could not grow up to write tragedies about princes is sheer social snobbery. Most Elizabethan plays are about princes, yet none of the anti-Stratfordians ever suggested that the plays of Shakespeare's contemporaries were really written by lords.

We expect, or at least some of us do, that plays rich in literary allusions and classical references and historical knowledge, must have been written by a man with a university education. After all, we need a college education to understand them, or parts of them. Shakespeare did not attend a university; Christopher Marlowe did, so he must have written the plays. But education was different then. Grammar school provided a rich literary training: grammar, composition, rhetoric, poetry, figurative language, the classics. The universities, then, were like graduate schools; they were meant for specialized training in theology or medicine or law. From a good grammar school education, and the Stratford grammar school was good, a smart boy could have developed his verbal skills and also learned how to look things up, how to acquire specialized knowledge that he might want to use. Marlowe went to a university, true; so did other playwrights like Robert Greene. Ben Jonson did not; he taught himself, and he was the most learned playwright of the time. Thomas Kyd did not go to university, and Thomas Middleton went to Oxford but dropped out.

Anti-Stratfordianism is the extreme case of reconceptualizing Shakespeare to meet the interests or needs or expectations or fancies of the present. And some of it is really crazy in its methods. But however mad it may be, its fundamental impulse is one common to all readers of Shakespeare; confronted with enormously stimulating artistic achievement, achievement that encompasses a wide variety of human experience, those of us who are stimulated are bound to find something that speaks to our needs, our preoccupations. Those who fear a breakdown of social order find in his works a celebration of hierarchy and harmony. Those who desire to shake up the current establishment enlist him as a social critic on behalf of marginalized people. He writes with equal eloquence for the rulers and the oppressed, for women and men, for young and old. He can speak for each character with such authenticity that when it strikes a particular chord in us, we think we hear Shakespeare himself speaking.

Of course, it is all Shakespeare, and we all find in his riches something we need to stay in contact with him. ■

The preceding lecture was an excerpt drawn from The Great Course:

Shakespeare: Comedies, Histories, and Tragedies
Course #280

William Shakespeare: Comedies, Histories, and Tragedies introduces the plays of Shakespeare and explains the achievement that makes Shakespeare the leading playwright in Western civilization. The key to that achievement is his abundance, not only the number of plays he wrote and the length of each one, but also the variety of human experiences they depict, the multitude of actions and characters they contain, the combination of public and private life they deal with, and the richness of feelings they express.

Lecture Titles

Peter Saccio

Peter Saccio is Leon D. Black Professor of Shakespearean Studies at Dartmouth College, where he has taught since 1966. He received his Ph.D. from Princeton University. He has also served as a visiting professor at Wesleyan University and at University College in London.

At Dartmouth, Professor Saccio has been honored with the J. Kenneth Huntington Memorial Award for Outstanding Teaching.

If you would like to order this course, please contact us at:

Phone: 1-800-TEACH-12
Web: www.TEACH12.com
For more information on our pricing policy, see page 245.

Something New: A Modern Novel

To finish reading *Ulysses* is to find yourself in something of a daze. It ends with an almost intoxicating burst of lyrical affirmation, as Molly relives her ecstatic response to Bloom's proposal among the rhododendrons at Howth Head.

This sort of ending recalls not only the traditional ending of the fairy tale, but also the resolution of novels such as Jane Austen's *Pride and Prejudice*, where the heroine and her sister each marry rich and handsome young men.

Of course, *Ulysses* does not end with a couple poised on the happy threshold of marriage. It ends with Molly reviewing a marriage now riven by sexual estrangement and resentment and adultery. It ends with no clear resolution of the questions that seem to permeate the novel as a whole.

James Joyce used the stream of consciousness style of writing in many of his novels.

We don't know from the novel itself whether or not Stephen will become a great writer or just one more Dublin drunk. We don't know whether or not Bloom will ever see Stephen again. We don't know whether or not Molly is launching an affair that will kill her marriage or, paradoxically, revive it. On a lesser level, we don't know whether or not Bloom will persuade Alexander Keyes to renew his advertisement, whether or not he will keep up his furtive correspondence with Martha Clifford, whether or not he will revisit Gerty MacDowell on the beach.

Instead of answering these questions, Joyce leaves them open and unresolved because he has no use for conventional plotting.

Generally speaking, a novel is a narrative of events that are realistically situated in space and time and bound together by cause and effect. Conventional plotting requires clear-cut motivation and final, decisive answers to major questions. Take Charles Dickens's *Great Expectations*, for instance. Here, a poor English orphan named Pip is turned into a gentleman by a mysterious benefactor. He believes that he is destined to marry a beautiful girl named Estella, who is something like a fairy princess. When his benefactor turns out to be a criminal who is captured and hanged, Pip leaves England and gives up all hope of Estella, who marries another man.

The young women who married the rich and handsome young men at the end of *Pride and Prejudice* are themselves not rich at all. Much of the novel turns on what is called the "business" of matchmaking. Nevertheless, the novel ends with a glorious pair of weddings, like the plot of the fairy tale or the traditional romance.

Different as they are, these two novels dramatize two chief motivations: the desire for wealth and the desire for a mate, and by contriving to gratify those desires, if only imperfectly. Thus, each novel resolves nearly all of its conflicts and answers nearly all of its questions by means of marriage or by killing off some characters and marrying off others—the two most convenient ways of ending a novel.

Insofar as these two novels exemplify 19th-century English fiction, they help us to see how radically Joyce reconstructed the shape of the novel. Here is chiefly a story of characters who lack any clear motivation and achieve almost nothing specific by the end. Significantly, the only character who knows what he wants and gets it is Blazes Boylan, the villain of the piece.

By contrast, Stephen evidently plans to quit his teaching job, but he takes no specific steps toward any other profession. When he declines

Bloom's invitation, he does not even know where he's going to spend the night. He fits no recognizable template. He has rejected Bloom's plan that he launch himself into journalism and a quest for Miss Right. In other words, he's rejected the idea that he cast himself into the role of a traditional young hero of fiction.

Bloom himself could hardly say who he is when he tries to leave a message in the sand for Gerty—he comes out with just "I am a" blank. He does manage to meet Stephen and talk with him at length, but his plan to adopt Stephen as a would-be son or son-in-law goes nowhere. Nor does Bloom put his own house in order. We don't know whether or not he will ever again have sex with Molly. We find no evidence that he's driven off or vanquished, much less killed, the adulterous invader. Nobody dies in the course of this novel. Dignam is buried, and we hear from time to time of other people who died before Bloomsday began, but essentially the people in this novel just go on living.

Death is just one of many startling events that commonly occur in 19th-century novels but don't occur in Ulysses. *Great Expectations* begins on a note of terror and includes, among other things, one brutal beating and two violent deaths. Joyce eschewed such things. "A writer," he said, "should never write about the extraordinary. That is for the journalist." Except for the ghostly visitations of Stephen's mother in chapter 1 and the wild hallucinations of the "Circe" chapter, Joyce steers clear of violence, terror, horror, and bloodshed. Though his language is sometimes obscene, *Ulysses* offers nothing like the titillating, erotic sex scenes furnished by *Sweets of Sin*, the novel that Bloom buys for Molly, which is really Joyce's parody of 19th-century soft-core porn.

The closest we get to a titillating bedroom scene is the gloriously comic description of Gerty MacDowell roused by the spectacle of fireworks and the unbearably exciting knowledge that her undies are putting on a show of their own. Since that description comes within another parody, a parody of the sentimental novel, it exemplifies yet another feature of *Ulysses* that distinguishes it from earlier novels: its dazzling diversity of voices and styles.

Nineteenth-century fiction barely anticipates this diversity. Prior to Joyce, novels were largely dominated by a single, narrative voice. Regional dialects certainly make their way into the novels of George Eliot and Thomas Hardy in the later 19th century, but the narrator's voice in these novels is consistently educated and consistently in charge of the story, even when the story includes a great variety of characters and a multiplicity of plots.

Take George Eliot's *Middlemarch*, a superb, magnificent example of late Victorian fiction that in some ways looks forward to *Ulysses*. Its title, *Middlemarch*, refers to a fictional town in provincial England. It aims to recreate the life of that town, even as Joyce would later recreate the life of Dublin. To recreate the life of a town, George Eliot deploys and interweaves three different strands of plot and orchestrates a rich variety of voices, from the gentry right down to the peasantry. But all these voices and characters are supervised by a single third-person narrator who stays firmly in charge from the beginning to the end of the novel. We can see this kind of supervision at work in the fiction of the early 20th century as well, on both sides of the Atlantic and on both sides of the English Channel.

In novels such as Edith Wharton's *House of Mirth* and E. M. Forster's *Howard's End*, a single narrator steers the ship of the action. Before *Ulysses*, even the most pioneering French fiction preserved this consistency of viewpoint. In Édouard Dujardin's *Les Lauriers sont Coupes*, where Joyce discovered the interior monologue, a single character delivers an uninterrupted soliloquy. The whole of Marcel Proust's great *Remembrance of Things Past*, published from 1913 to 1927 and thereby overlapping the creation of *Ulysses*, is once again governed by a single narrative voice.

To set *Ulysses* beside any of these novels is to see that Joyce has virtually exploded the novel form—so much so that T. S. Eliot did not know whether to call *Ulysses* a novel at all. What should we call it? How do we classify a work of fiction that doesn't clearly motivate the major characters, that leaves major questions unresolved, that suddenly lurches from one narrative viewpoint to another, that apes in one chapter the layout of a newspaper, that parodies in another chapter every stage in the English language from Anglo-Saxon to high Victorian, that includes a gigantic play stuffed with hallucinations, that drives us through a seemingly endless sequence of questions and answers, and that ends with a soliloquy of a woman who seems absolutely out of control?

Is this anything more than an indigestible bowl of words or a bundle of random pages? Emphatically yes. It's much more than that. Let's start by recognizing that it offers in breathtaking or even overwhelming abundance what the novel is supposed to deliver: realism. If a novel is a narrative of events, realistically situated in space and time, then *Ulysses* most assuredly qualifies.

Think first about its locale. "If Dublin were suddenly destroyed," Joyce said, "it could be reconstructed from the pages of this book." Joyce thoroughly recreates the sights and sounds and smells of the city. He makes its streets, canals, bridges, churches, monuments, and tram cars integral parts of his fictional world. He makes us hear the many voices of its characters, from the courtly tones of Father Conmee to the peasant speech of the old milkwoman in chapter 1.

Joyce spared no effort to gather details. In November 1921, when the final chapter of *Ulysses* was already with the printers, he wrote his aunt, Josephine Murray in Dublin to ask this question:

> Is it possible for an ordinary person to climb over the area railings of no. 7 Eccles Street, either from the path or the steps, lower himself from the lowest part of the railings till his feet are within two feet or three of the ground and then drop unhurt[?] . . . I require this information in detail in order to determine the wording of a paragraph.

Joyce was thinking here about the "Ithaca" chapter and an aeronautical feat that Bloom performs to get into the basement kitchen of his house. Symbolically, this feat of flying links him for a nanosecond to Daedalus, father of Icarus, the fabulous winged artificer of ancient Crete whom Stephen invokes as his mythical father. But Joyce gives no wings to Leopold Bloom. Joyce is not writing fantasy. He's writing a work of fiction that keeps its feet on the ground. In this case, it tells us exactly—exactly—how Bloom dropped to the ground without getting hurt.

Joyce thoroughly recreates the sights and sounds and smells of the city. He makes its streets, canals, bridges, churches, monuments, and tram cars integral parts of his fictional world. He makes us hear the many voices of its characters.

Of course, the final chapter seems to leave the ground of Dublin when it enters the mind of Molly Bloom, lying in bed and reviewing her whole life, ruminating on her memories, desires, suspicions,

A rare photograph of the city of Dublin as Joyce would have known it.

fantasies, and fears. Here we seem to trade objective facts for subjective feelings, for an inner world where anything can be imagined. But once again, Joyce took pains to plant Molly's memories in the soil of realistic detail. In preparing to write this chapter, he read everything he could find about the island of Gibraltar, where Molly spent the first 16 years of her life. He then packed the chapter with so many facts about Gibraltar that when he later met a man who lived on the island, the man refused to believe that Joyce had never set foot on it.

If a novel needs not only a realistic setting but must also take place within a realistic length of time, this one resoundingly qualifies. If you think about the structure of a day, of all the things we do by habit in the course of a day, you can see how relentlessly and powerfully the times of the day govern the progress of this book.

How can a watch or even a grandfather's clock hold all of the stuff that Joyce packs into this novel? By themselves, the hours and minutes of the day cannot fully regulate the story we read, in part because Joyce now and then turns back the ticking of time to let us see that two or more things are happening at once.

If you think about the first six chapters, you see that they separately take Stephen and Bloom through the morning. Stephen talks to Mulligan, eats breakfast, leaves the tower, teaches his class, and takes the tram up to Sandymount, where he walks the strand and meditates. Meanwhile, Bloom talks to Molly, fixes breakfast for them both, goes out to collect a letter from Martha Clifford, and attends the funeral of Paddy Dignam.

In chapter 10, "Wandering Rocks," Joyce plays a still more elaborate game with time. To recreate a day in Dublin, he had to send his main characters through streets teeming with other characters, each with business of their own. As the clock ticks, many people make their way through the city at the same time. Out of their individual lives, Joyce weaves the fabric of the city they inhabit.

Besides turning back the clock now and then, Joyce also ruptures the flow of time in two chapters. The most dramatic examples come in the "Circe" chapter, where the hallucinations are essentially timeless—split-second ruptures in the otherwise realistic passage of the night. Less dramatic ruptures come earlier. In the "Cyclops" chapter, Joyce breaks up the conversation with parodies that recast the action in a wholly different time period, as if a chance remark about a phenomenon had become a scientific lecture, or the growl of a dog had become a poetry recitation worthy of an article in the newspaper.

Besides turning back the clock now and then, Joyce also ruptures the flow of time in two chapters. The most dramatic examples come in the "Circe" chapter, where the hallucinations are essentially timeless—split-second ruptures in the otherwise realistic passage of the night.

Throughout the book the reader wrestles with the glaring differences between Bloom and Ulysses, between the warrior king with the eternally faithful wife and the cuckolded advertising canvasser, between the lives of ancient Greeks and the life of modern Dublin, between the ancient epic of a 10-year journey and the modern novel of a single day, between fabulous monsters and all-too-realistic adversaries like the citizen. In bridging these differences again and again, in showing us how the citizen can be a monster and how barmaids can be Sirens, how a trip to the cemetery can be a journey to Hades, Joyce also reveals to us the timelessness of his story. It is timeless because its structure has endured, not just in carefully preserved manuscripts and learned editions of the Homeric epics, but in the very blood and bones of the human race. ∎

The preceding lecture was an excerpt drawn from The Great Course:

Joyce's *Ulysses*
Course #237

Joyce's great novel *Ulysses* is a big, richly imagined, and intricately organized book with a huge reputation. T. S. Eliot, bowled over by Joyce's brilliant manipulation of a continuous parallel between ancient myth and modern life, called it "the most important expression which the present age has found . . . [one] to which we are all indebted, and from which none of us can escape."

Ulysses depicts a world that many consider as fully conceived and vibrant as anything in Homer or Shakespeare. It has been delighting and puzzling readers since it was first published on Joyce's 40th birthday, February 2, 1922.

Lecture Titles

James A. W. Heffernan

James A. W. Heffernan, Emeritus Professor of English and Frederick Sessions Beebe '35 Professor in the Art of Writing at Dartmouth College, earned his A.B. *cum laude* from Georgetown University and received his Ph.D. in English from Princeton University.

Dr. Heffernan chaired the Dartmouth English Department from 1978 to 1981 and taught a range of courses at Dartmouth including European Romanticism, English Romantic poetry, methods of literary criticism, and the 19th-century English novel. For many years he also taught a senior seminar on Joyce's *Ulysses* that was regularly oversubscribed.

If you would like to order this course, please contact us at:

Phone: 1-800-TEACH-12
Web: www.TEACH12.com

For more information on our pricing policy, see page 245.

The *Odyssey* of Homer
Course #302
Lecture 1

Taught by: Professor Elizabeth Vandiver
Whitman College

Homecoming

Nostos, homecoming, is the main theme of the *Odyssey,* just as the concept of imperishable glory, *kleos* in Greek, was one of the main themes of the *Iliad.*

I n fact, some scholars say that the genre of ancient epic can be divided into *kleos* epic and *nostos* epic, into epic about glory and warfare and epic about adventures and troubles during homecoming; that these were the two main sub-genres, if you will, of ancient epic in the bardic tradition. Perhaps an equally valid distinction would be to say that we can divide epic into war epic and peace epic; because *kleos*—glory, what people say about you, your reputation—is still very important in the *Odyssey*. Odysseus and other characters are still concerned with their *kleos*, with what people say about them, with whether their exploits are known or not. The difference is that while in the *Iliad* what people will say about a warrior after his death is seen as the only kind of meaningful immortality he can seek, and in the *Odyssey* there is more of a focus on maintaining your reputation, keeping your *kleos* while you are yourself alive.

Like the *Iliad*, the *Odyssey* begins *in medias res*, in the middle of its subject matter. Because we are dealing with an epic that was composed in an oral tradition, by a bard working in an oral tradition, the bard is able to start the story anywhere he likes. The first thing he does is run through a little introduction, proem as it is usually called, in which he sets the scene. He announces to the audience who or what it is that he is going to sing about; he very rapidly gives a little summary of what's happened leading up to the point where he'll begin his story; and he focuses in on exactly where he wants his story to begin. The first 10 lines of the *Odyssey*, then, in English, are as follows:

> Tell me, Muse, of the man of many ways, who was driven far journeys, after he had sacked Troy's sacred citadel. Many were

they whose cities he saw, whose minds he learned of; many the pains he suffered in his spirit on the wide sea, struggling for his own life and the homecoming of his companions. Even so, he could not save his companions, hard though he strove to; they were destroyed by their own wild recklessness, fools who devoured the oxen of Helios, the Sun God, and he took away the day of their homecoming. From some point here, goddess, daughter of Zeus, speak, and begin our story.

Now, right away, in these opening lines of the *Odyssey* there is an attempt on the bard's part—and we'll see this again on Odysseus's own part—to get around an inherent problem in the story of the *Odyssey*. The *Odyssey* is Odysseus's story; for it to have full narrative power we need to see him coming home absolutely alone, having lost all his companions; and yet Odysseus is a leader. He took these men of Ithaka, his home island, off to Troy with him; he is the only one who makes it back alive. This is not exactly indicative of good leadership, or of what you would expect from a fine clever warrior and leader. There has got to be some way to explain how Odysseus could have lost all his men without making Odysseus seem blameworthy;

Like the Iliad, *the* Odyssey *begins in medias res, in the middle of its subject matter. Because we are dealing with an epic that was composed in an oral tradition, by a bard working in an oral tradition, the bard is able to start the story anywhere he likes.*

and right in these very opening lines, the bard addresses that. Odysseus was striving for his companions' homecoming but they, fools that they were, were destroyed by their own recklessness.

This is a theme that will be returned to many times in the *Odyssey*, the fact that Odysseus tried to bring his companions home but they were destroyed by their mistakes, their own foolishness.

You may notice that Odysseus is not named in the proem of the *Odyssey*. Unlike the first line of the *Iliad*, where the bard says, "Muse, goddess, sing the wrath of Peleus's son Achilles," the name Odysseus does not occur until line 21 of the *Odyssey*.

And yet Odysseus is established as the subject of the *Odyssey*, not just in the first few lines of the proem where we are told that this was the man who sacked Troy, but actually in the very first line; because

Odysseus is described, in the first line of the *Odyssey*, by the epithet, the essential adjective, *polutropos*. This is not his most common epithet in the *Odyssey*, but it is one of his most important epithets. The word *polutropos* is utterly untranslatable into one English word, but it means, literally, "many turns." So the *polutropos* man is the man of many turnings.

Now, what does that mean for Odysseus? There are two levels of meaning in this word. First off, he is literally a man of many turnings; he is blown back and forth on the sea, trying to get home to Ithaka. He keeps being turned off course, he keeps being blown back in the direction he has already come from. So literally, this word refers to his many wanderings. But it also refers to his cleverness; he is *polutropos* in his mind. He is able to think his way out of any situation, to think on his feet, to reason his way out of troubles, to come up with stratagems, clever ploys, to get himself out of any difficulty; and the word *polutropos* picks up on both of those aspects of Odysseus's story, his wandering and his cleverness. It is a very difficult challenge for a translator; right there, in the center of the first line of the *Odyssey*, is this word that is thematically of the utmost importance for the *Odyssey*, and can't be translated into one good English word or even one good English phrase. The above translation gives "The man of many ways," which is nicely ambiguous, but maybe a little too ambiguous; it doesn't quite get the punch of *polutropos* across.

> *Odysseus is literally a man of many turnings; he is blown back and forth on the sea, trying to get home to Ithaka. He keeps being turned off course, he keeps being blown back in the direction he has already come from.*

The very first word of the *Odyssey* is *andra*, which means "the man." So the first line of the *Odyssey* begins with the word "man," just as the first line of the *Iliad* begins with the word "wrath" or "anger." The first word of each of these poems sets its tone; when you hear the opening word of the *Iliad* you know that you are going to hear about anger, wrath, and a great quarrel. From the instant you hear the opening word of the *Odyssey* you know you are going to hear about one man, one individual, and his adventures.

And the *Odyssey* is first and foremost about Odysseus's struggles to get home. The first 13 lines include the word *nostos*—homecoming, or return, or a derivative of it—no less than three times in just 13 lines. In line 5, already he is longing for or striving for the *nostos* of his companions. In line 9, we are told that the Sun God takes away his companions' *nostimon êmar,* the day of their homecoming, the day of their *nostos.* In line 13, perhaps most importantly of all, we are told that Odysseus is longing for his *nostos* and for his wife—the two things that he wants, the two things that he is striving to regain in the *Odyssey,* his homecoming and his wife, Penelope. So very clearly, from the opening of the *Odyssey,* the idea that this is the story of Odysseus's struggle for his *nostos* is set up right from the very beginning.

After identifying Odysseus by summarizing his adventures, the bard asks the Muse to start the story "from some point." We have been told we are going to talk about Odysseus; we are going to hear a story of Odysseus's return home. But where is that story going to start? It could start anywhere. It could start right after the sack of Troy; it could start the day before Odysseus arrives back on Ithaka; anywhere in that whole 10-year time period that he spent trying to get from Troy to Ithaka the story could start. Our bard says to the goddess, to the muse of poetry, the muse who inspires him with the story, "pick it up at some point; from some point begin the story."

The bard then implies that the *Odyssey* will start in the 10th year after the Trojan War. He very quickly runs through a little resumé of what has happened to everybody else, and to Odysseus. He tells us that the other heroes have all either made it home or died; everyone who didn't die at Troy or get shipwrecked at sea is now home again. Only Odysseus is still missing, and the bard tells us that Odysseus is being held prisoner by a nymph, or a goddess, named Kalypso, on her island in the middle of the sea. As the *Odyssey* opens Athena—Odysseus's primary patron deity—beseeches the great god Zeus, the king of the gods, to send the messenger god Hermes to tell Kalypso that she must let Odysseus go.

So it seems as though we are going to start right at the point where Odysseus is freed from his seven years' captivity on Kalypso's island and is allowed to go home to Ithaka; Athena says to Zeus, "Send Hermes to tell Kalypso she must let Odysseus go."

But then, after giving us this false lead, in effect, this belief that we are going to immediately go to Kalypso's island and see Odysseus there and move on to Ithaka, the bard suddenly changes direction and goes off on a side story.

Athena says that while Zeus is sending Hermes to tell Kalypso it is time to let Odysseus go, she, Athena, will go to Odysseus's home island of Ithaka and visit his son there. And so we suddenly take this detour; we go off to Ithaka, and spend the first four books of the *Odyssey*—and that would be about four hours of performance time—not with Odysseus at all, but rather following the adventures of his son, Telemachos. Odysseus only shows up in person in the *Odyssey* in Book V.

So the narrative structure of the *Odyssey*, already from this beginning point, is extremely complicated and anything but straightforward.

In books I and II of the *Odyssey* we see Telemachos at home on the island of Ithaka. In books III and IV of the *Odyssey* we see Telemachos traveling to visit Nestor and Menelaos, two of Odysseus's old comrades-in-arms, two characters from the *Iliad*. So, the first four books are taken up with Telemachos.

Books V through VIII introduce us to Odysseus himself, and take up his story as he leaves Kalypso's island and journeys to the land of a people called the Phaiakians, who will show him great hospitality and help him on his homeward journey.

So you would expect then, after Book VIII, if the Phaiakians are going to help Odysseus home, Book IX should take him to Ithaka, right? Well, it doesn't. Books IX through XII—the heart of the *Odyssey*, the most famous section of the *Odyssey*—are actually a flashback section, in which Odysseus narrates in the first person his adventures from leaving Troy up to arriving at Kalypso's island.

Then finally, in Book XIII, the bard changes to a straightforward chronological sequence; and books XIII through XXIV show Odysseus's homecoming to Ithaka, all the way through his killing of the suitors of his wife, Penelope, and regaining of his status and power in Ithaka.

So, a purely chronological arrangement of the *Odyssey* would have to put books IX through XII first, followed by books V through VIII, followed by books XIII through XXIV. And the first four books, the adventures of Telemachos, really don't fit at all; they take place in the same time frame as books V through VIII, when Odysseus is traveling from Kalypso's island to the land of the Phaiakians.

Now, this extremely complex structure has struck some critics, over the centuries, as a blemish on the *Odyssey*, or even as an indication that the *Odyssey* is a not-very-skillfully assembled collection of shorter poems, that somebody put together rather carelessly.

Other scholars think that the complex structure is quite the opposite, is one of great beauties and glories of the *Odyssey*, that it adds immeasurably to the *Odyssey*'s power.

We do not see Odysseus for four full books; instead, we go to Ithaka and see Odysseus's family and country in his absence. Odysseus has been gone for nearly 20 years at this point, and this has caused immeasurable problems both for his wife and son and for his society.

In any culture, one of the most heartwrenchingly tragic things that can happen to a family is to have a member of that family be missing in action, to have someone go off to war, never return, and you don't know what happened to them.

That is terrible for any family, in any culture; but for Odysseus's family, in the culture portrayed by the *Odyssey*, it is even more terrible than perhaps would immediately be obvious to a modern audience. Penelope, Odysseus's wife, is caught between two absolutely conflicting duties, with no way of knowing which one she should follow.

If she is still a wife, it is her absolute unquestioned duty to remain loyal to her husband. If Odysseus is still alive, Penelope must protect his household, must not remarry, and must keep his goods, his family, and his home intact for him until he returns.

This is a society in which there is no possibility of divorce in absentia, no way to have someone declared dead after a certain number of years have passed—not that those are easy things to do, emotionally speaking, but they do at least allow someone in Penelope's situation to finish that episode of her life and figure what to do next. Penelope has no such possibility.

Also this is a culture, the culture of the *Odyssey*, that has no place for an unmarried woman. Penelope needs to be married; there is no role in this society for an independent, unmarried woman.

So, if Odysseus is still alive, Penelope's absolute unquestionable duty is to remain loyal to him.

On the other hand, if he is dead—since this is not a society that accepts unmarried women as contributing members of society—she has no less absolute a duty to remarry; to turn Odysseus's household over to her son, Telemachos, and to go off with a new husband and make a new life elsewhere.

So Penelope is caught in an agonizing dilemma; she has no way of knowing what her status is—is she a wife or is she a widow? Her duty is absolutely clear either way; but those duties are absolutely conflicting, and she has no way of knowing which applies to her.

Telemachos is in a similar situation, not knowing his status. Is he guarding the kingdom for his father, or is this his own kingdom and his own household that he should claim as a grown man for himself? And so Penelope and Telemachos are both left in a kind of limbo, in which their proper course of action is unclear and in which they have no way to figure out what their proper course of action is.

Odysseus's absence also causes great problems for his society. Like all the societies reflected in the Homeric epics, Ithaka is a monarchy. It seems never to have occurred to anyone on Ithaka that you can have

In the *denouement* of the *Odyssey*, Odysseus slaughters the suitors of Penelope revealing himself to be the true king of Ithaca and a hero of epic proportions.

any form of society except a monarchy. Ithaka, therefore, is a monarchy whose monarch has been missing for 20 years, and the disorder this causes in society is vast. There is no proper working of Ithakan society while its king is gone.

The focal point for these troubles, in both family and society, are the suitors of Penelope, young men of Ithaka who are trying to marry Penelope and by so doing to take over Odysseus's household and take over the rule of Ithaka. These suitors assume that by marrying Penelope they would be able, in fact, to take over the kingdom; they assume that Telemachos is still so immature that he would not be able to stop them.

So the suitors are threatening Odysseus's marriage; we know that, because we know that Odysseus is still alive. They are threatening Telemachos's inheritance; in their wanton disregard of the proprieties, they force themselves into Telemachos's house; they destroy his goods and his livelihood; they bother Penelope, who doesn't want them around—they are very clearly not acting as suitors ought to act. Their wanton disregard of the proprieties can been seen as a result of the disordered state on Ithaka.

So, Homer starts the *Odyssey* not at some random moment, and the focusing on Telemachos for the first four books is not an unmotivated digression. Rather, Homer starts the *Odyssey* at the precise moment when the situation on Ithaka is coming to a head, at the exact moment when the situation has become desperate. ∎

The preceding lecture was an excerpt drawn from The Great Course:

The *Odyssey* of Homer
Course #302

Keats compared discovering Homer to "finding a new planet." What is it in Homer's great works—and especially the *Odyssey*—that so enthralled him? Why have readers before and since reacted the same way?

The *Odyssey* tells of a long-dead epoch that seems utterly alien to us. Indeed, the Bronze Age Aegean was a distant memory even to the original audiences of these works. But age seems only to have burnished the luster of this epic. It may be precisely because of its very strangeness and distance that generation after generation of readers have come to love it so much.

By joining award-winning classics professor Elizabeth Vandiver for these lectures on the *Odyssey*, you can get answers to these and hundreds of other questions.

Lecture Titles

Elizabeth Vandiver

Elizabeth Vandiver is Assistant Professor of Classics at Whitman College in Walla Walla, Washington. She was formerly Director of the Honors Humanities program at the University of Maryland at College Park, where she also taught in the Department of Classics. She completed her undergraduate work at Shimer College and went on to earn her M.A. and Ph.D. from The University of Texas at Austin.

In 1998, The American Philological Association recognized Professor Vandiver's achievements as a lecturer with its Excellence in Teaching Award, the most prestigious teaching prize given to American classicists. Her other awards include the Northwestern University Department of Classics Excellence in Teaching Award and two University of Georgia Outstanding Honors Professor Awards.

If you would like to order this course, please contact us at:

Phone: 1-800-TEACH-12
Web: www.TEACH12.com
For more information on our pricing policy, see page 245.

The "fine" in fine arts describes the pur
of the discipline rather than the qualit

FINE ARTS AND MUSIC

"Music is the universal language of mankind."

—Henry Wadsworth Longfellow

Back to Bach

We understand the Baroque era as going from 1600 to 1750. It's in 1600 that opera is invented and this celebration of the individual human emotion, which is what opera is all about, is a great way to start this era of extravagant emotionalism.

I n 1750, Johann Sebastian Bach dies in Leipzig. Now in 1750 few people knew that Bach had died and fewer people cared, but with the hindsight of history we realize what an important date 1750 was, bringing the High Baroque, or at least Johann Sebastian Bach's take on the High Baroque, to its conclusion.

The word "Baroque" comes from the Portuguese word *baroquo*, meaning a pearl of irregular shape and/or irregular color. It became a slang usage for anything gross and bizarre or in bad taste. The original application was a pejorative—a reference to art, architecture, and music that was overly extravagant, detailed, and fussy in its design. For example, around the year 1750, the well-traveled Charles de Brosse complained that the facade of the Pamphili Palace in Rome was redone with a kind of a filigree ornamentation more suitable "to tableware than to architecture." Given to colorful language, de Brosse referred to the facade as Baroque.

Now, by the 1920s, the term Baroque had come to refer to the flamboyant, decorative, and, again, detailed art and music of the period from about 1600 to 1750. So it's a word we don't really start using for the period until the 20th century. Please, there is no single Baroque style, although the notey, brilliant, and superbly crafted of the late Baroque composer, Johann Sebastian Bach, has come to epitomize this era for the listener. Baroque music can best be described by two groups of adjectives, adjectives that either describe the brilliant, busy, and note-filled melodic surface of the music, or adjectives that talk about the steadiness of the beat, the sense of order and logic and control that overwhelmingly seem to be operative in the piece. There's so much detail, very fussy, notes everywhere one looks. Joyful, extravagantly joyful, brilliant instrumental music.

If music is indeed a mirror, then this music, and these adjectives, should also be a reflection of larger societal trends. So with the understanding that on the one hand Baroque music had a tremendous amount of detail and brilliance, and on the other hand a very steady beat and a sense of order and control, let us step back and investigate some of the general trends—philosophical, scientific, and intellectual—of what we call the Baroque era.

History books tell us that the Baroque era was an era of increasing secularization, scientific investigation, and rationality. The era sees rational thought and logic as transcendent. It is an era of great scientific observation and codification. The Baroque is the era of Hume, of Locke, of Descartes, of Malthus, of Bacon, of Leibnitz. It's the era that sees Galileo observe the heavens, develop his theory

Bach achieved an unprecedented fullness of artistic realization for every musical form in Western music of his day.

of heliocentricity—by which, he said, the Sun is the center of the solar system, not the planet Earth. It was the era of Johannes Kepler, who developed a complex mathematical formula by which one could predict the elliptical orbits of the planets. Something that would have seemed alchemical in a previous time is now an intellectually understood process.

This is the era of Anton von Leeuwenhoek, who looked through his primitive microscope and observed micro-organisms; it's the era of William Harvey, who put forth the doctrine of continuous blood circulation; and, perhaps most importantly, it's the era of Isaac Newton and his works in optics, gravity, physics. Newtonian physics, this world-view as espoused by Newton, is in many ways an almost religious vision of the cosmos. Newton said, essentially, that underneath the complexity, the visible chaos of our known world, is systemic order, and all we need to know are the formulas by which this seemingly complex and chaotic system works, and we can understand the past, the present, and the future. God was seen as a great watchmaker and the cosmos was God's own watch. Everything is systems-controlled, and we simply have to understand the systems to understand the universe.

During the Baroque, rational thought defeats supernatural explanation. God's not out of the picture, but there's got to be a better explanation than just a supernatural one. This is not a religious age; however this is not a nonspiritual age, it's just an age that demands that logic and thought be present in any explanation.

So, there is an attempt to explain the physical world that imbued the Baroque era with a love of symmetry and order-controlling complexity. For example, if we look at an illustration of a Baroque palace surrounded always by what were called parks or gardens, we will be aware of two things. We will be aware of an amazing amount of detail. When we call something Baroque—when we call furniture design Baroque, or architecture Baroque—we're talking about an infinitely detailed style filled with gewgaws, filigree, and ornamentation. When we look at Baroque

It's just an age that demands that logic and thought be present in any explanation. So, there is an attempt to explain the physical world that imbued the Baroque era with a love of symmetry and order-controlling complexity.

landscape architecture, we see again a tremendous amount of detail where nature is shaped by the hand of the landscape architect. But what holds all of this architectural—both building and plant—architecture in shape? What holds it all together? What keeps it from flying off into visual anarchy? Symmetry. Symmetry, balance. Baroque ceiling painting, no matter how many cherubs and angels and colors and clouds, everything is balanced. What we see on the right is reflected on the left; what we see on the bottom is reflected on the top—symmetry, logic, and control—controlling the exuberant detail.

In Baroque music you hear music that plumbs ever greater emotional extremes and melodic extravagance, always carefully, symmetrically, systematically, and intellectually controlled. The same sort of symmetry and control sought by scientists in the physical world was being sought by artists in the artistic world.

Bach wrote his B Minor Mass when he was 60 years old; and if we see paintings of Bach at this age, we see a rather portly, wigged man with a rather strict look on his face, a bit of a grimace. He looks like an old guy, but this is a bad image of Bach. Bach's a rock 'n' roller, he's a player! We hear terrific energy in this music. He fathered 20 children; someone old and stale won't do that. Bach was an action character and you hear it in his emotionally extravagant music that has an unre-

Often copied but never equaled, the palace at Versailles of Louis XIV is perhaps the ultimate expression of the Baroque style. At the time of its creation, it was the largest palace in Europe and was noted for its striking symmetry.

strained joy, almost physical in its power. If you listen to his B Minor Mass you will hear an incredible variety of different instrumental and vocal textures and, most importantly, a personal and energized affirmation of Bach's own brand of religious faith. Someone who didn't believe utterly in a glorious and joyful God could not have written music that sounds like his does.

Henry Purcell's Baroque opera, *Dido and Aeneas*, has a very famous aria called "Dido's Lament." A little background about the opera and the story of Dido and Aeneas: Aeneas is a survivor of the sack of Troy; he and a small band of Trojans go sailing about the Mediterranean. Ultimately, the gods have determined they will go to Italy and found Rome. But on the way to Rome, they stop at Carthage—in what today is Tunisia—and the queen of Carthage, Dido, falls in love with this handsome young man. Dido and Aeneas have a torrid love affair, but eventually

Louis XIV represents the epitome of the absolutist monarch. His huge and perfectly Baroque palace at Versailles was built to celebrate that monarchy.

the gods tap Aeneas on the shoulder and tell him he has a job to do in Italy. So, much to his sorrow, he informs Dido of his impending departure, packs up, and leaves. Dido, of course, is heartbroken. Having finally found love at the end of her life, she now gives it up. So, like every good operatic heroine of the Baroque, she decides the only way to honorably deal with this is to pierce her bosom with the sharpest blade she can find. "Dido's Lament" is the aria that she sings just before this self-destruction, and she sings: "When I am laid, am laid in Earth, may my wrongs create no trouble, no trouble in thy breast," as she's singing this directly in her mind's eye to Aeneas. "Remember me, remember me, remember me, but forget my fate." It's suicidal despair and this must be projected by the music. The music descends sadly, almost funereally; a very quiet and introspective aria, the darker side of the musical palette; a tempo that is very slow, it's as if we're hearing her funeral march even as we listen to her sing of her impending death. Everything in the music is to reinforce the feeling beneath the words. The emotional impact is profound. When we listen to Dido, we feel for her. We know where she's coming from. Having had our hearts broken, we hope we would not go to such extremes, but she's a person we can identify with, an individual.

This is infinitely different from the nature of expression and the emotional impact of the Renaissance madrigal. A madrigal evokes generic, approximate emotions that are illustrated via word-painting. Opera evokes specific, often extreme, individual emotions pointed directly at us, the individual listener. Many late Renaissance composers and aestheticians grew dissatisfied with the madrigal's inability to project the individual emotion, and that is why opera came into being around the year 1600. The difference between madrigal and opera reflects the difference between the sober, more calculated restraint of the Renaissance and the exuberant, pointed emotionalism of the Baroque. The Baroque is also the age of the absolute monarch, that monarch who claimed to rule by divine right. And the ultimate of these absolute monarchs was Louis XIV, who reigned from 1643 to 1715.

He was a huge patron of the arts. An incredible amount of art, architecture, and music was created to celebrate the magnificence of Louis' monarchy. Perhaps the ultimate example of Baroque extravagance is the palace Louis built for himself in Versailles, with over 1,300 rooms. Versailles, aside from being a residence, was a political statement, built on a scale that stupefies and subdues: If this is the power of the French king, you don't want to mess with the French king. But for all of its incredible size, the impression one receives when looking at Versailles is that despite its size, the symmetry holds everything in place. Everything is balanced, logically controlled by the hand of the landscape architect and the building architect to create a symmetrical and, in that way, balanced entity. The overall effect of the buildings and grounds, despite their size, is one of control and order.

A specific genre of music, and an important genre of music, evolves as a result of the pomp and extravagance of Louis' court, and that specific genre of music is called the French overture. An overture, a musical overture, is an instrumental work that precedes a stage work. Now a French overture is something more than that. Invented around 1660, the French overture is a royal and magnificent orchestral work designed to create a festive atmosphere for the stage event to come and to welcome the king to the theater. The king, of course, would have been Louis XIV, the so-called Sun King, who reigned for an extraordinary 72 years.

Louis XIV was the most powerful monarch in Europe in his day, and he was intent that everyone should know it. Pomp and ceremony at his court were carried to absurd lengths. Louis' court composer was a man after Louis' very own heart, Jean-Baptiste Lully—who was as cutthroat, as politic, as power-hungry, and as opportunistic as his regal boss. Lully, an Italian by birth, came to France at the age of 12. Through equal parts talent and scheming, and very possibly also assassination, Lully climbed the musical ladder, becoming ultimately the master of all music at the French court. One of Lully's most enduring contributions was the French overture.

A French overture consists of two sections of music. The first is a slow pomp-filled opening followed by a faster second section, magnificent music meant to reflect the magnificence of its patron. Such was the influence of Louis XIV's court, and such was the fame of Lully that the French-style overture became ubiquitous, written by composers of every nationality for the next 100 years, if not more. George Frederick Handel, a German-born, Italian-trained composer, began his English language oratorio, *Messiah*, with a French-style overture—as a footnote, Jean-Baptiste Lully smashed his foot with his heavy conducting staff during a performance, contracted gangrene, and died. This is a testament to the power of sustained group thought—20 years of orchestral musicians hoping for just such a thing to happen.

A wonderful anecdote about Handel's *Water Music*. Handel was born in Germany in 1685, just weeks and miles apart from Johann Sebastian Bach. He trained in Italy, and in June of 1710, at the age of 25, Handel went to work for the elector of Hanover in Germany. Now in the autumn of 1712, he obtained permission from the elector to visit London. On the permission slip this is what was written: "on the condition that he return within a reasonable time." Well, 1714, two years later, still sees Handel in London. We can't blame him. Nothing wrong with Hanover, but if you had your choice between Hanover and London, especially London at this time—London was the center of the Western world at the beginning of the 18th century—you'd be in London, too.

Anyway, August 1, 1714, Queen Anne of England died and was succeeded by the elector of Hanover, now George I, Handel's old boss. Now according to legend, the truant and chastened Handel, afraid to appear at court, was reconciled to his master by the ingenious diplomacy of his old friend, Baron Kielmansegge. When the king and his court took an excursion by barge on the Thames, Kielmansegge organized a second barge containing musicians under Handel's command, whose music so captivated the monarch that he pardoned the delinquency and restored Handel to favor. True or not, it's a great story.

In conclusion, Baroque art is characterized by a wonderful and most interesting duality: extravagant, expressive content and careful, logical control. It is a mirror of a larger artistic and intellectual community attempting, as it was, to logically understand and control the extravagant chaos of God's own creation. ∎

Born in Germany in 1685, Handel moved to England in 1712 and lived the rest of his adult life there. He had emigrated without the permission of his patron, the elector of Hanover, but found a place at the court of Queen Anne of England. This became a problem a mere two years later, when Anne died leaving no direct heirs. The next in line for the throne of England? Handel's former boss—George, the elector of Hanover, who became George I of England.

The preceding lecture was an excerpt drawn from The Great Course:

How to Listen to and Understand Great Music, 3rd Edition
Course #700

How can concert music—once it is understood—so move our lives? Professor Robert Greenberg explains in his introductory lecture: "Music—the most abstract and sublime of all the arts—is capable of transmitting an unbelievable amount of expressive, historical, and even philosophical information to us, provided that our antennas are up and pointed in the right direction. A little education goes a long way to vitalizing and rendering relevant a body of music that many feel is beyond their grasp."

This course can permanently enrich your life: With Professor Greenberg as your teacher, you will hear and understand an entire language of unmatched beauty, genius, and power.

Robert Greenberg

Robert Greenberg has performed, taught, and lectured extensively across North America and Europe. He is music historian-in-residence with San Francisco Performances, the city's premier presenter of chamber music, instrumental and vocal recitals, jazz, and contemporary dance.

Professor Greenberg received a B.A. in Music, *magna cum laude*, from Princeton University and earned a Ph.D. in Music Composition from the University of California at Berkeley.

Dr. Greenberg has served on the faculties of the University of California at Berkeley, California State University at Hayward, and the San Francisco Conservatory of Music, where he chaired the Department of Music, History, and Literature.

Professor Greenberg's awards include three Nicola De Lorenzo Prizes in composition, three Meet the Composer grants, and commissions from the Koussevitzky Foundation of the Library of Congress, the Alexander String Quartet, XTET, and the Dancer's Stage Ballet Company.

Dr. Greenberg has composed more than 40 works for a wide variety of instrumental and vocal ensembles. His work has been performed recently in New York, San Francisco, Los Angeles, Chicago, England, Ireland, Italy, Greece, and The Netherlands. His music is published by Fallen Leaf Press and CPP/Belwin and is recorded on the Innova label.

Lecture Titles

If you would like to order this course, please contact us at:

Phone: 1-800-TEACH-12
Web: www.TEACH12.com
For more information on our pricing policy, see page 245.

Incroyable! Napoleon III's Paris

Many of us, when we visit the city of Paris today, think that it has always looked like it does now, that it's essentially an ancient city filled with monuments built centuries and centuries ago.

While that's relatively true, the fact is that Paris is among the most 19th-century cities in the world. Virtually all of the important buildings that we now visit when we go on our tours of Paris, whether it's the Louvre or the Cathedral of Notre Dame, were extensively rebuilt and reconfigured in the 19th century. The whole city that we love, the city of boulevards, parks, cafés, and all of the romantic aspects of Paris, have their roots not in the distant past but in the 19th century. In many ways, Paris is no older than New York or Chicago. Its modernity and its transformations in the 19th century are something one has to understand before even being introduced to Impressionism.

The reason for the transformation has a good deal to do with French politics. When England and Germany finally conquered Napoleon, they split up the vast empire that was France's for a very short period of time. Afterwards there came a sense that the French nation was living in a constricted, narrow realm and that its greatness was in the past. There was a sense that France needed to redefine and modernize itself in order to become the great power that it had been under the kings of France. There was a sense of anxiety, of failing, of being a country and a nation that were in decline.

This notion was a very powerful one in the 19th century, felt throughout the country and in many social orders. Some people, like the aristocrats, felt that if only they could get their power back, there would be a sense of rebirth again. Other people, like the bourgeoisie, felt that if they could have control of money and be able to decentralize the economy, they could be stronger. Other people, like the proletariat, gained incredible strength, in political terms, after the French Revolution and thought that if there were individual liberty and if the people of France could lead the world in terms of justice and personal freedom, that would rejuvenate the French state. The tensions among those three particularly social notions of rejuvenation rocked the French state and its capital, Paris, throughout the 19th century.

In 1848, there was a revolution in France that toppled another monarchy and created a short-lived republic in which the French could elect a national president. The president they elected in 1849 was Louis Napoleon, the nephew of the Napoleon who had transformed France, who had made France great. And it was this sense that, through a newly elected president who had in his veins the blood of the greatest leader of the 19th century, that perhaps France could rejuvenate itself.

Louis Napoleon took on this idea of the mantle of his uncle very strongly, and he came to be called Napoleon III when he declared himself emperor in the early 1850s. In one of his first great acts, Napoleon III decided the way France could regain its luster and brilliance was to re-

Louis Napoleon was the nephew of Napoleon Bonaparte. During his reign, he oversaw the rebuilding of Paris.

build the capital city. As the 18th and 19th centuries continued, France continued to lose its way as a European economic power, ceding industrial power and wealth first to England and then to Germany, both of which had become richer and more powerful in the new capitalist economy than France. Both had created modern capital cities: Berlin, in one case, and London, in the other.

Louis Napoleon, Napoleon III, had, in fact, lived in London. He had lived in the St. James neighborhood in the center of London between the two great parks, and he was stunned by the modernity of London, by its systems for sewage, water, and light. It was a city in which one could drive. It was a city that was safe. It had nature and parks in it. It was a city that was, indeed, the opposite of his crumbling, ancient capital, Paris.

Napoleon III decided to completely transform Paris with the help

In order to create the famous Parisian boulevards, city planners knocked down huge swathes of apartment buildings.

of the Chamber of Deputies—the French legislative body—with a group of financiers whom he corralled, and a minister whose name was Baron Haussmann. Paris was the second largest city in Europe in the 1850s when this transformation began. It was growing by leaps and bounds because France was beginning to industrialize, centralize, and modernize. People were moving from the countryside into the city. The city was swelling with population, and there had been no planning to receive it. Napoleon III decided to do a comprehensive plan. The amount of money that was spent on the rebuilding, the reconstruction, and the refinancing and the rethinking of the city of Paris in the 1850s and the 1860s before Napoleon III's abdication in 1870 was so large that it's almost incalculable today. Probably more than a trillion modern dollars was spent on the city over a period of 20 years, a kind of urban investment that's absolutely unprecedented and that has never occurred since.

That kind of transformation of a capital is something that we have to remember in thinking about Impressionism, because the young men and women who became these artists didn't live in a defunct, grandiose, beautiful city of the past. They lived in a vast construction zone. The Paris that was inherited by Napoleon III and the Paris that was the childhood home of many of the Impressionist artists—Monet was born in Paris; Renoir lived his childhood in Paris—was a city that had no sewage system. Only 150 households in the entire city had a water supply. Water was in the streets in certain neighborhoods. There was no centralized transport system. Everything was kind of crumbling in a way, because there had been no infrastructure improvements in the city since the French Revolution. It was essentially a moribund city, with the exception of a few great building projects.

The city was transformed into a great imperial capital. Napoleon III thought about the city as a kind of set for parades, for extraordinary public events, for firework shows, for carnivals, for great supper parties, for the arrivals of kings and queens, for a kind of pomp and circumstance, of spectacle, that made one want to get out onto the streets and participate in urban life, rather than to be in one's neighborhood or one's house.

More than 100,000 people in Paris in the late 1850s and early 1860s were rendered homeless because their neighborhoods were razed to create the boulevards that we now think of as quintessentially Parisian. There was one boulevard in Paris when Napoleon III became the emperor of France. There were more than 100 by the turn of the century. That was the result of a process of urban reclamation which involved destruction and house-moving on a vast scale. That kind of destruction created an image of the city which was absolutely the opposite of the image that the court presented of itself.

One of the most interesting transformations of Paris in the 19th century involves the construction of housing. Most of us who live in American cities think of neighborhoods as divided into socioeconomic areas. The really rich live together. The middle-class people live together. The lower-middle-class people live together. They don't mix, because that ruins real estate values. That was largely true in Paris during the Second Empire. There was a sense of neighborhood segregation by income, with *rentiers* (shareholders) who rented flats and apartments to the lower classes, all of whose buildings were concentrated in certain areas, and those areas came to be associated with left-wing, revolutionary fervor and with sedition.

What Napoleon III wanted to do in rebuilding Paris was not only to cut modern boulevards through those traditional lower-class neighborhoods, which were the oldest and poorest sections of the city, but to create housing with vertical stratifications. On the lower floors you would have the shop and the kitchen, the things that nobody owns. In France the first floor is what we call the second floor, and there you would find the very wealthy, with nice chandeliers and moldings. You would go up another level and there, the ceilings would be lower, and there wouldn't be any moldings. There was a sense that as you would go up in the building you'd lose value because there were no elevators. The nearer the ground you were, the richer you were.

If this ideal system worked, then all of the populations of the city would live together, and there would no longer be neighborhoods of impoverished people and neighborhoods of very wealthy people. Everybody would live in a vertically stratified city, a completely new idea, which, as you can imagine, didn't work. But the theory of it was brilliant, and the theory of it created a whole new kind of boulevard architecture, which is very much the architecture of Paris as we think of it today and was very much the architecture celebrated by the Impressionists in their great exhibition pictures of the 1870s and the 1880s.

A typical boulevard of the "new" Paris with stratified apartments designed to eliminate slums and areas considered dangerous. In this new configuration, the bottom apartments housed the rich, the center apartments were home to the middle class, while the poor lived in the attics.

The second thing that Napoleon did, aside from the extraordinary boulevards, was really to think about the city in terms of nature and health. He was actively involved in creating water and sewage systems in the city. The boulevards were planted with trees, bringing nature directly into the most urban parts of the cities. For the first time in Paris, public parks, based on the London model, were created. These parks were extraordinary. The most imaginative one is a park called le Parc de Butte Chaumont, in the northeastern part of Paris in a working-class *arrondissement* or *quartier*. It's a park that brings in the railroad and lakes and all sorts of little bridges, and there's a grotto, and you can move around. It was an extraordinary piece of urban natural construction built in an old quarry from which the streets of Paris had been constructed.

Not only did Napoleon III build many parks—in fact, six major parks in Paris were opened and constructed in the 1850s and 1860s, creating places where people didn't have to leave the city to see trees and grass and flowers and to walk around and have natural exercise— but he was also very important in centralizing transport systems and in centralizing the markets in Paris. One of the most important buildings constructed during his reign housed the central markets of Les Halles. This steel-and-glass modern building was the place where everyone went to buy food and where all of the little shops all over the city bought their supplies. It was the first centralized market in any great capital city. Creating boulevards and parks and centralizing services were very important parts of Napoleon III's urbanism.

As he was doing all of those things, he began to think about the city as a historical museum, as a place you visited. Transportation in Europe was so much better that lots of tourists went from one country to the other increasingly in the 19th century. He wanted to detach the great symbolic monuments of the past from the urban fabric of the city and to renew them, to make them separate and symbolic. He created a city hall for Paris on the old Place des Grèves. He rebuilt completely the Louvre palace. We think of that great palace as one of the oldest urban palaces in France. Well, a small part of it is, but most of the building that we now visit as the Louvre was built in the 1850s and the 1860s under the direction of an architect named Visconti. He completely transformed the great palace into an administrative center for Napoleon III, and into the great museum that we know today, detaching it from the city. Renoir was raised in a slum, which was destroyed in the Second Empire, in the center of what is now the Louvre. More than 50,000 people lived in the 1840s and early 1850s in what is now the center of the Louvre, and that entire neighborhood was eradicated.

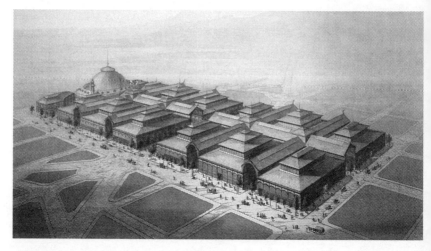

Les Halles was the first centralized market in all of Europe. Shops and markets were filled with the everyday ingredients necessary for French cuisine.

All of those people were forced to move for the glory of France under Napoleon III.

The same thing happened with Notre Dame. Notre Dame had been built with little shops and buildings all around it. It was part of medieval Paris, and it was turned into a symbolic monument in the 19th century. A park was built in the back. It was freed on all sides so you could see it from the water when you went on boat tours of the city. The plaza in front of it was newly created; it hadn't had a plaza before. Notre Dame was turned into a symbol of the greatness of the French religion, the French monarchy, and of the French church and history, just as the Louvre was the symbol of French power and regal authority.

Napoleon III was very involved with the creation of new symbolic buildings, the most important of which was l'Opéra. If France was the capital of artistic and leisure culture of the 19th century, the big new building that should be at the center of its urban experience was the Opéra. Designed by the great architect Garnier, it was built over a very long period of time, at enormous cost, for imperial usage, with areas for carriages to come in and out, and boxes for the emperor and the empress, and places for all of the members of the court. It had a kind of urban display associated with art and wealth and leisure. All the great sculptors of France worked on the decoration and buildings, the great furniture makers designed the cabinets and sets, and it was a kind of display hall to the excesses and extravagance of French Second Empire

Although it was built in medieval times, the grounds around Notre Dame were redesigned and updated during Louis Napoleon's reign.

taste. It was also a building that was completely modern. Underneath its stone façade was a steel structure that looked like a 20th-century or industrial building rather than an ancient building.

The sense of the modernity of the city and of its transformation is something that we absolutely can't forget in thinking about Paris as the subject for artists. Because the city that these men and women grew up in, or moved to when they were impressionable young people in their 20s, was a city that was essentially a huge construction zone. You had to move around. People of the lower classes, people who rented their houses, often moved three and four times in the course of a five- or six-year period because of the shifts in the city's construction, and it was sort of a set in construction for an imperial spectacle, always inventing itself as it moved along.

It was a place, therefore, that was as full of doubt and crime and problems and inconvenience as it was of prosperity and hope for the future. This sense of it as being a place that troubled its own citizens, a place that was inconvenient and a difficult place to live while preparing itself to be a great modern city, was a part of the anxiety of the Parisian experience in the 1860s and 1870s. It was also a place where it became a kind of sport to watch the city build itself and tear itself down and transform itself. There was the idea that the city itself was a work of art that could be controlled and planned by centralized authority and that it was the subject of the will and power of the nation itself. It was a place in which one lived with a kind of mixture of pride and awe

L'Opéra was Napoleon III's most important symbolic structure.

on the one hand, and on the other, of anger and inconvenience at the noise and the movement and all of the traffic problems and everything that's associated with urban reconstruction.

Today, when we look at photographs of the great monuments and the boulevards in the city of Paris, generally, we see the city when it's completed. But there were also hundreds, indeed thousands, of photographs taken of the city as a construction zone, as a site for transformation, as a place of inconvenience. The recording of the city as a place that was both building itself up and tearing itself down was of extraordinary importance in France in the 19th century. Napoleon III was the cause for that transformation and, whether you like Paris or don't, he is the most important person to make that city what it is today. ∎

The preceding lecture was an excerpt drawn from The Great Course:

From Monet to Van Gogh: A History of Impressionism
Course #7187

They appeared in a period of upheaval. They saw the rebuilding of Paris, the rise of industrialism, the ruin of the Franco-Prussian War. They displayed their works—paintings that were startlingly, even shockingly, new—in a series of exhibitions from 1874 to 1886. And by the 1890s this loose coalition of artists who rebelled against the formality of the French Academy had created the most famous artistic movement in history. "They" were the Impressionists, and Professor Richard Brettell is your expert curator and guide to a movement that created a new, intensely personal vision of the world.

Lecture Titles

?ichard Brettell

Richard Brettell is Professor of Aesthetic Studies at The University of Texas at Dallas. He earned his B.A., M.A., and Ph.D. from Yale University.

Dr. Brettell is the American Director for FRAME (The French Regional and American Museum Exchange), which links nine French and nine American regional museums in a consortium. He is the McDermott Director of the Dallas Museum of Art, the Searle Curator of European Painting at the Art Institute of Chicago, and the Senior Advisor for International Art at the National Gallery of Australia.

If you would like to order this course, please contact us at:

Phone: 1-800-TEACH12
Web: www.TEACH12.com
For more information on our pricing policy, see page 245.

Beethoven: The Piano Man

Beethoven published 32 piano sonatas. They span the length of his compositional career, having been written between early 1795, a few months after he turned 24, and January of 1822, a few weeks after he turned 51.

His 32 piano sonatas were, for Beethoven, particularly special works. You see, Beethoven was a piano player. The piano was his ax, his voice, his entrée to the greater musical world. He improvised for hours at the piano. He conceptualized essential musical ideas and compositional renovations at the piano. Literally, he spoke through the piano. Now, clearly, we can't hear Beethoven's actual speaking voice—as he was dead, 50 years before the invention of recorded sound—but we hear his voice, if we listen carefully to his solo piano music. We hear the

Though he played many in his lifetime, Beethoven never found a piano that satisfied him.

idiosyncratic nature of his musical "grammar" and pianism; the mercurial, often "stop on a dime" flow of ideas, the veritable flood of information, the manner in which his musical ideas take off in tangents—to be reconciled and explained further down the road, the juxtapositions of coarsely comic and deeply expressive and sometimes even tragically painful music—the sheer, breathtaking spontaneity of it.

Beethoven's piano music is his voice, emerging from his mind, through his fingers, to our ears and our hearts. Beethoven's piano sonatas are, more than any other of his amazing works, his personal testament expressed in his own voice.

The constantly changing technology of the piano affected the way Beethoven thought about, and composed for, the piano. His creative life corresponded precisely with the development of the piano from a small, portable, wooden-harped, five-octave keyboard instrument considered, still, something of a toys—in 1774, the great Voltaire referred to the piano as merely a "tinker's pot"—to the big, heavy, iron-harped pianos with which we are familiar today.

The two great innovations that, together, contributed to creating the modern piano—both occurred during Beethoven's lifetime, although we should note that Beethoven himself never actually had the opportunity to play pianos equipped with these innovations. The innovations were the French manufacturer Erard's double escapement action, introduced in 1821; and the Boston-based Alpheus Babcock's one-piece cast-iron frame, introduced in 1825.

Erard's action allowed for extremely rapid repetition of notes, and Babcock's cast-iron frame allowed for more and bigger strings, which produced a bigger and more sonorous sound. Beethoven would have loved the iron-framed piano, which was so much closer to his ideal instrument. He was never particularly happy with the instruments he actually owned and played, aware as he was of their limitations: their limited register range, their limited ability to get loud and soft, their limited ability to sustain, their relatively quiet tone, and their propensity to turn to kindling and chopsticks under his admittedly heavy touch.

The constantly changing technology of the piano affected the way Beethoven thought about, and composed for, the piano. His creative life corresponded precisely with the development of the piano.

The piano began to replace the harpsichord as the essential keyboard instrument of choice in the 1760s and 1770s, but did not completely replace the harpsichord until the early 19th century. Both Mozart, who was born in 1756, and Beethoven, who was born in 1770, first learned to play on the harpsichord, although Beethoven made the switch to the piano at a much younger age than did Mozart.

The sort of piano that Beethoven played as a kid would have been of German manufacture, very likely one built by either Franz Jakob Spath or Johannes Andreas Stein. It would have had 61 keys, a range of five octaves. It would have been double strung, meaning that most of the hammers would have struck two strings tuned to the same pitch, as opposed to modern pianos, which are triple strung. It would have used a mechanism that featured a very shallow key drop, and one that required an extremely light touch.

The music written for these pianos was but one step removed from harpsichord music. It was piano music that stressed brilliance, as we might find in the music of Wolfgang Mozart, but it did not call for big sounds, loud attacks, or long, sustained tones. When playing music like this one must sit upright at the center of the keyboard and play with a maximum of finger and wrist movement—and a minimum of arm, shoulder, and back movement, lest fine control be lost and the keys be struck too hard.

Beethoven's first published piano sonata, his Sonata in F Minor, op. 2, no. 1, was completed in 1795. This is not just brilliant music, but vicious music, and it demands a high degree of explosive percussivity and sonority that would have made a Viennese piano builder quake in his boots and the piano itself beg for mercy.

From the very beginning, Beethoven demanded a sheer volume and power from the piano as an instrument that no one before him had ever demanded, and I would point out something else. It is no more possible to play music like Beethoven's Sonata in F Minor sitting still at the center of the keyboard and using only the wrist and fingers, than it is to sumo wrestle using only one's tongue. That's full-contact piano music—style, elegance, and fine control be damned.

From the moment he arrived in Vienna, in late November or early December of 1792, Beethoven put the piano-crazed Viennese on their ears. Beethoven, whose first paying job back in Bonn was as an organist, was undoubtedly trying to wrest from the lightweight Viennese pianos of the time the same degree of power, of sonority, and of orchestral range of power that he could from a pipe organ. Good luck.

Beethoven's extraordinary approach to the piano helped develop his reputation as a piano virtuoso, but it did not endear him to everyone, in particular piano builders. For example, in his essay, "Brief Remarks on the Playing, Tuning, and Maintenance of the Fortepiano," the piano builder, Andreas Streicher, discussed two nameless pianists. According to Streicher, the first pianist—and here, he was undoubtedly referring to Muzio Clementi—is, and we quote Streicher: "A true musician, who has learned to subordinate his feelings to the limits of the instrument, so that he is able to make us feel what he himself feels."

The other pianist—undoubtedly referring to Beethoven—is, according to Streicher: "Unworthy of imitation. A player, of whom it is said 'he plays extraordinarily, like you have never heard before,' sits down (or rather throws himself) at the fortepiano. Already, the first chords will have been played with such violence that you wonder whether the player is deaf. Through the movement of his body, arms and hands, he seemingly wants to make us understand how difficult is the work he has undertaken. He carries on in a fiery manner, and treats his instrument like a man who, bent on revenge, has his archenemy in his hands, and with cruel relish, wants to torture him slowly to death. He pounds so much that suddenly the maltreated strings go out of tune; several fly towards bystanders who hurriedly move back in order to protect their eyes. He makes only harsh sounds … and we hear only a disgusting mixture of tones. … Is this description exaggerated? Certainly not!"

Streicher was not alone in his criticism of Beethoven as a pianist. In 1805, pianist and composer Camille Pleyel wrote:

"At last, I have heard Beethoven play a sonata of his composition. He has unlimited flare, but he has no schooling, and his execution is not polished—that is, his playing is not unblemished. He has a lot of fire but pounds too much. He manages diabolical difficulties, but he does not play them altogether precisely." The Italian composer and pedant, Luigi Cherubini, bluntly and simply said in 1805 that Beethoven's piano playing was, and we quote: "rough."

Muzio Clementi, himself one of the great pianists of his generation, commented: "Beethoven's playing was not polished, and was frequently impetuous, like himself."

Clearly, neither Andreas Streicher, Camille Pleyel, Luigi Cherubini, nor Muzio Clementi understood what Beethoven was all about, but some very influential Viennese were utterly fascinated by both Beethoven the man and Beethoven the musician. Wealthy musical connoisseurs, like Baron Gottfried van Swieten and Prince Karl Lichnowsky, who had a taste for difficult, serious music, actually encouraged Beethoven's predisposition toward musical experimentation and novelty. As result, once he settled in Vienna, Beethoven never had to appeal either to the conservatives or to the larger musical public.

The musicologist William Newman has identified 14 pianos that Beethoven owned or borrowed during his lifetime, and Newman notes that he may very well have owned others besides. What Imelda Marcos was to shoes, so Beethoven was to pianos: an inveterate consumer seeking, and yet never finding, the perfect instrument. Once he became famous Beethoven rarely, if ever, had to "buy" his own pianos, as piano builders vied with each other to lend him instruments. Like a contemporary professional athlete wearing a swoosh, Beethoven's use of a particular piano came to be considered a priceless endorsement. In 1802, Beethoven wrote, and we quote:

"The whole tribe of pianoforte manufacturers has been swarming around me in their anxiety to serve me. Each of them wants to make me a pianoforte exactly as I should like it."

In 1810, Beethoven wrote Andreas Streicher, asking for a piano. Now, this would be the same Andreas Streicher who had written the anonymous description of Beethoven at the piano 10 years before. By 1810, Herr Streicher had realized that whether or not he personally liked Beethoven's playing was immaterial. Business was business. By 1810, Beethoven was "da bomb." "Either Beethoven plays one of my pianos, or one of my competitors' pianos. Better he should play mine."

Anyway, Beethoven wrote to Streicher, and we quote: "You promised to let me have a piano by the end of October, and now we are already halfway through with November and as I have not yet received one—my motto is, 'Either play on a good instrument or not at all,' [I wait.] All good wishes, if you send me a pianoforte; if not, then, all bad wishes!"

The Streicher piano Beethoven asked for and received was considerably larger and more resonant than previous pianos. Bigger music, my friends, and a bigger piano on which to realize the conception of this big music.

It begs the "chicken or egg" question: Did Beethoven imagine his ever grander, more magnificent piano works because evolving piano technology made such works imaginable, or did Beethoven's music force piano manufacturers to build bigger pianos, instruments more appropriate to music he had already composed?

Well, I would suggest a little bit of each. Certainly, Beethoven was influenced by developing piano technology, but he was always four, five, or six steps ahead of that technology at any given point. This is especially true in Beethoven's most avant-garde piano sonatas. The final five, opus 101, opus 106, opus 109, opus 110, and opus 111, were composed after he was clinically deaf and no longer performing as a pianist. In these last sonatas, he was no longer composing for a contemporary instrument, if he ever had been, but, rather, for an idealized instrument, a pure piano, an instrument whose range, power, and sonority simply did not yet exist. ∎

The preceding lecture was an excerpt drawn from The Great Course:

Beethoven's Piano Sonatas
Course #7250

Beethoven was a revolutionary man living in a revolutionary time. He captured his inner voice—demons and all—and the spirit of his time, and in doing so, created a body of music the likes of which no one had ever before imagined.

"An artist must never stand still," he once said.

A virtuoso at the keyboard, Beethoven used the piano as his personal musical laboratory, and the piano sonata became, more than any other genre of music, a place where he could experiment with harmony, motivic development, the contextual use of form, and, most important, his developing view of music as a self-expressive art.

Lecture Titles

Robert Greenberg

Robert Greenberg has performed, taught, and lectured extensively across North America and Europe. He is music historian-in-residence with San Francisco Performances, the city's premier presenter of chamber music, instrumental and vocal recitals, jazz, and contemporary dance.

Professor Greenberg's awards include three Nicola De Lorenzo Prizes in composition, three Meet the Composer grants, and commissions from the Koussevitzky Foundation of the Library of Congress, the Alexander String Quartet, XTET, and the Dancer's Stage Ballet Company.

If you would like to order this course, please contact us at:

Phone: 1-800-TEACH-12
Web: www.TEACH12.com
For more information on our pricing policy, see page 245.

Yankee Doodle Cohan: Broadway Begins

No previous figure and no single figure in the entire 20th century comes close to Cohan in terms of the impact he made on audiences and the changes he introduced to Broadway.

C ohan danced peculiarly, he sang tunelessly, and wrote music and lyrics and libretto to every one of his shows, in addition to auditioning the cast and directing the shows. In an age when musicals were a patchwork of clumsy interpolations, Cohan's ego wouldn't let anybody else touch his work. As a result, Cohan's shows, though hopelessly dated, are closer to truly integrated musical theater than any other thing before *Show Boat*.

Cohan is the American equivalent of British playwright-actor Noel Coward, without Coward's sophistication. Nobody beats Cohan for sheer unadulterated self-assurance. Cohan always made sure his audiences knew how lucky they were to be in his presence. In his 1904 show *Little Johnny Jones*, young Cohan enters by strutting across the stage briskly and repeatedly acknowledging his admirers from the stage, he'd say "Hello, everybody!" No question, the star had arrived.

Cohan's show Little Johnny Jones *took as its model the career of Todd Sloan, a brazen, womanizing, American jockey whom everyone in the audience recognized, despite Cohan's calling him Little Johnny Jones.*

Cohan's songs captivated his audience; and while they weren't as sophisticated and harmonically complex as the later songs of Gershwin, Kern, and Rodgers, they were still as good as,

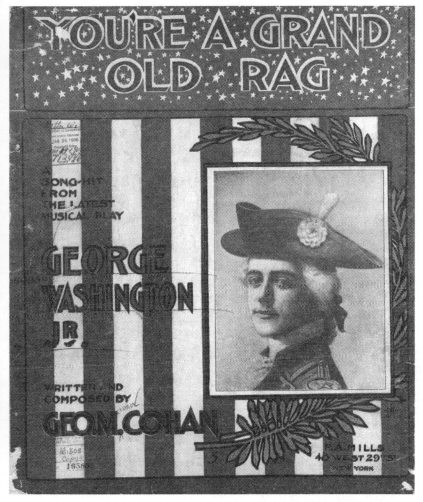

The sheet music of George M. Cohan's early Broadway hit, "You're a Grand Old Rag."

and usually better than, the best that Tin Pan Alley had thus offered America. His melodies, like Cohan himself, were snappy and unpretentious. And, his lyrics had a refreshingly conversational quality that made the singer seem all the more sincere.

Cohan's unique blend of patriotism and sentimentality captured the fancy of a public thrilled by the real-life exploits of another brash American battling for international respect, Teddy Roosevelt. "Cohan's genius," observed Oscar Hammerstein, "was to simply say what everybody in the audience was subconsciously feeling."

Cohan's libretti revolved around the all American character he created—brash, relatively honest, ambitious, athletic, and chauvinistic. Like Shaw's Henry Higgins, Little Johnny Jones and other Cohan protagonists are alter egos of their author. "Yankee Doodle Dandy" is sung by an American jockey racing in London. He's accused of fixing the race and so he launches into a musical defense, which simultaneously shows those uppity English that 100-percent Americans, like Little Johnny Jones, are not to be tampered with.

Cohan's show *Little Johnny Jones* took as its model the career of Todd Sloan, a brazen, womanizing, American jockey whom everyone in the audience recognized, despite Cohan's calling him Little Johnny Jones. He was as much a news item in 1904 as O. J. was in the 1990s or Michael Jackson was in 2005.

Sloan, a.k.a. Little Johnny Jones, had revolutionized horse racing by introducing the crouched-over-the-neck position that has since become standard in racing. The show, more integrated than any show that had preceded it, managed to displace what had become expected on Broadway—flowery sentimentality and stilted dialogue. The show was full of then-current events, and Cohan's idiom employed brash slang based on the latest talk in the street. In that sense, Cohan was a 1904-style hip-hop artist. Cohan's "Yankee Doodle Dandy," sometimes called "Yankee Doodle Boy," can seem an example of overcompensation because it had only been a few decades since there were signs all over New York City saying "No Irish Wanted." But Cohan, in this song, identifies himself with the heart of Americanism, and he even gives a little quote from the oldest popular song still around from the beginning of the American Republic, "Yankee Doodle."

Cohan's other hit song from *Little Johnny Jones*, "Give My Regards to Broadway," reads like a tour of central Manhattan:

> Give my regards to Broadway
> Remember me to Herald Square
> Tell all the gang at 42nd Street
> That I will soon be there.

Cohan got his start in vaudeville, and when he embarked on a musical theater career, totally ignored traditional formulas. Cecil Smith, in his book *Musical Comedy in America*, describes Cohan as "the apostle of breeziness"—in the brand-new optimistic 20th century—"the apostle of up-datedness, of Broadway brashness, and of (what was then) current slang." Of course, it's that very topical quality that makes Cohan unproduceable today. Shows that can be revived contain timeless elements.

But the songs have lasted. By the time he was 20, George was writing all the material for "The Four Cohans" vaudeville act—songs, comic skits, dramatic routines. In 1899, when George married Ethel Levy, the act became "The Five Cohans." In 1899, the year he was courting Ethel, right before they married, he wrote his first up-to-date national song hit. It was called "I Guess I'll Have to Telegraph My Baby."

Though 1904's *Little Johnny Jones* was Cohan's first hit Broadway show, he had written a less successful show in 1903 called *Mother Goose*. Though the show was not a "flag-waver" like *Little Johnny Jones*, nonetheless Cohan's most successful songs in *Mother Goose* were his patriotic ones.

Perhaps no other songwriter wrote as many patriotic songs as George M. Cohan. "You're a Grand Old Flag" was the hit song from his 1906 musical, *George Washington, Jr.* Surprisingly, this popular and enduring song was originally met with boos and jeers from his audience, and it was followed by castigating notes from local politicians. The controversy caused Cohan to quickly rewrite the song's lyrics. The song was originally called "The Grand Old Rag." Cohan's characters were always wise guys, but he'd gone too far this time writing "You're a Grand Old *Rag*." The disrespect for the flag brought him a great deal of negative attention immediately after the show premiered. Now he had to rewrite the song and make it "You're a Grand Old Flag." Meanwhile, the sheet music was already in music stores all over New York City. Cohan had to run to every music store, grab the music, bring it back, and burn it, and then bring back the rewritten sheet music. Today, there are probably only a half-dozen copies of the original song left, so if you open your piano bench and you find a copy of "You're a Grand Old Rag," don't throw it away—it's worth a lot of money.

As of 1906, Cohan is American musical theater's most important figure to date. Like Cohan himself, his songs had spirit. They're brash, they're noisy, they're aggressive, they're patriotic, they're oriented to the age in which they were created, and they're usually, but not always, devoid of sentimentality. They're not mushy, at least. They're full of the early modernist spirit of America on the brink of a brand new century.

After Cohan's peak years, on the day in 1917 when America declared war on Germany, Cohan wrote what was to become the most popular song of World War I. He heard a bugle call in his head and built the song around this bugle call. The biggest selling recording of this song was by Nora Bayes. The second biggest selling recording, which sounds like it's in Italian but isn't, was by Enrico Caruso. The song, of course, is "Over There."

George M. Cohan's popularity continued after his death. The movie *Yankee Doodle Dandy*, which premiered in 1942—a short time after Cohan's death—brought James Cagney the Academy Award® for his portrayal of Cohan. It's one of the few film biographies of the '40s that presents a pretty accurate picture of its protagonist without overly romanticizing him. If the stereotype of the broiling, brawling Irishman is resented by some of the Irish, it became a point of pride with others. If Cohan and Cagney were to be reborn as canines, the only appropriate breed would be the pug. Their very stature and the look in their eyes told you, "I can be a merry fellow, but don't cross me!" Nobody could have been better cast for the Cohan role than Jimmy Cagney. And, conversely, the failure of the 1968 Broadway musical, *George M.*, rests on the shoulders of its talented star Joel Grey, who could sing and who could dance and who could act with the best of them, but could not communicate that pugnacious intensity, combined with a raffish sense of humor that made George M. Cohan Broadway's biggest star. Cohan may be no Rodgers and/or Hammerstein, but it's questionable whether there could have been a Rodgers and Hammerstein without Cohan laying the groundwork for all who followed him.

On one hand, Cohan advanced musical theater by writing songs that grew out of his plots and by speaking in a voice that was closer to the real voice of the streets than any of the highfalutin' songwriters who'd preceded him. But on the other hand, shows like *Little Johnny Jones* were showcases for Cohan's unique talents and his unique personality—an impossible model to emulate for most actors. Therefore, the Cohan shows were doomed not to be revived in later years. George M. Cohan deserves the bigger-than-life statue that graces Times Square where, today, thousands wind around the square from one end to the other waiting in line for half-price theater tickets. Cohan's shoulders still support the century that followed him.

Paradoxically, musical theater depended on stereotypes, but at the same time, it exploded them. The Irish pride of George M. Cohan didn't stop him from marrying Ethel Levy and taking equal pride in her Jewishness by continuing to bill her as Ethel Levy, not as Ethel Cohan, though the audience knew they were husband and wife. America was the great melting pot and at least it gave lip service to being the great leveler. Nowhere did that leveling come closer to reality than in the make-believe world of George M. Cohan's Broadway. ∎

The preceding lecture was an excerpt drawn from The Great Course:

Great American Music: Broadway Musicals
Course #7318

"Give my regards to Broadway ..."
Is it possible to read those lyrics, let alone hear them, without mentally filling in: "Remember me to Herald Square"? Have you begun to hum or sing it to yourself, with the words and notes carrying you back in time to the Broadway of George M. Cohan and the heyday of Tin Pan Alley?
For most people who've grown up with and shared America's musical heritage, such a phrase opens the floodgates to a wealth of memories and feelings because, after all, that's what great songs do.

Lecture Titles

1. The Essence of the Musical
2. The Minstrel Era
   (1828 to c. 1900)
3. Evolution of the Verse/Chorus Song
4. The Ragtime Years
   (c. 1890–1917)
5. The Vaudeville Era
   (1881 to c. 1935)
6. Tin Pan Alley
7. **Broadway in Its Infancy**
8. The Revue versus
   the Book Musical
9. Superstars on the Horizon
10. Transition into the Jazz Age
    (1916–20)
11. Irving Berlin and Jerome Kern—
    Contrasts
12. George Gershwin's Legacy
    (1919 to c. 1935)
13. Rodgers and Hammerstein Era
    (1940s)
14. Golden Age of Musical Theater
    (1950s)
15. Rock 'n' Roll Reaches Broadway
    (1960s)
16. Big Bucks and Long Runs
    (1970s–Present)

Bill Messenger

Bill Messenger studied musical composition, on scholarship, at The Peabody Institute of the Johns Hopkins University under Louis Cheslock. He attended a master's class in 1963 with Nadia Boulanger, the teacher of Roy Harris, Virgil Thompson, and Aaron Copland. Professor Messenger has two Master's degrees, both from the Johns Hopkins University. He has done additional graduate work in Musicology at the University of Maryland.

Professor Messenger has taught composition, music history, and music theory at Goucher College in Baltimore and a number of community colleges. He regularly lectures on American music at The Peabody Institute of Music and Towson State University Elderhostels.

If you would like to order this course, please contact us at:
Phone: 1-800-TEACH-12
Web: www.TEACH12.com
For more information on our pricing policy, see page 245.

The famous figures of the Caryatid Porch on the Acropolis in Athens

ANCIENT HISTORY

"Most of us spend too much time on the last 24 hours and too little time on the last 6,000 years."

—Will Durant

The History of Ancient Rome
Course #340
Lecture 48

Taught by: Professor Garrett G. Fagan
The Pennsylvania State University

Thoughts on the "Fall" of the Roman Empire

Cicero coined the great phrase that there are as many opinions as there are people. About the fall of the Roman Empire, there is no doubt that this dictum holds true.

This issue has been discussed for about 500 years or more and quite intensively since the 18th century and the publication of Edward Gibbon's masterful study, *The Decline and Fall of the Roman Empire*. There are a myriad of explanations, and I have classified some of the more popular ones and some that have garnered support among professional scholars.

There are general explanations that the Roman Empire fell because of broad patterns of behavior. For instance, the well-known, popular idea that people still ask me about is: Did the Roman Empire fall because the Romans liked to have too many parties, and they got more decadent as time went on? The answer to that is, manifestly, no. The Romans were as decadent when they were building their empire as they were when they were losing it.

Another idea that has been put forward and was favored by Gibbon was the undermining effects of Christianity. The turn-the-other-cheek doctrine and so on, in Gibbon's view, weakened the moral fiber and fighting spirit of the soldiers and ultimately brought the empire to its knees. Two major arguments would tend to suggest otherwise. First, Christians in later eras showed no trouble when it came to fighting spirit, whether it be among themselves or against foreign enemies, for instance, the Saracens. Within the 5th century itself, there is no evidence that Christians failed to fight aggressively. Secondly, the eastern half of the empire was even more Christian than the western half of the empire, and that did not collapse in 476. In fact, it continued to exist as the Byzantine Empire into the 15th century of our era.

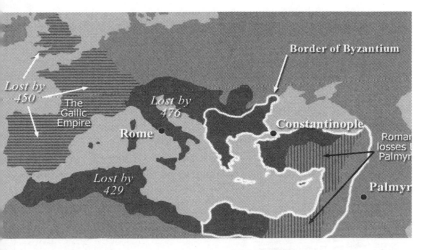

Beginning in 429 with the loss of North Africa to barbarian invaders, the western half of the Roman Empire began to slip from Imperial control. By 450, the lands of England, Gaul, and Spain had been taken, and in 476 Rome itself, having long ago ceded the title of Imperial capital to Constantinople, was sacked. The remaining eastern half of the empire, which we refer to as Byzantium, lasted until 1453.

Broad, general explanations are also sometimes provided by people who approach the subject with a theoretical position already in mind, such as Marxists. Marxists would consider the collapse of the Roman Empire as clearly a class war; the peasantry, crushed and oppressed by years of taxation and maltreatment at the hands of the evil central government, overturned the empire and joined the barbarians. There is little or no evidence to support such a proposition. Any theory of the fall of the empire that superimposes modern prejudices on ancient conditions is usually largely nonsense.

One class of explanation I call "catastrophic event theory" basically proposes something along the lines of massive climate change, depopulation, and the famous example of lead poisoning. The Romans all got lead poisoning because they used lead pipes and lead for their cooking. So, they all went completely insane and you had a Roman Empire full of insane people during the 5th century, and they could not withstand the Germans, who didn't use lead. There is the ecological depletion argument that the Romans simply raped the environment to such a degree that they could no longer sustain their population, so it collapsed. All of these theories also have little or no proof behind them, since, again, the people of the eastern empire also used lead. If climatic change affected the west, why didn't it affect the east? Were the people of the eastern empire who had survived any more ecologically conscious than the people of the western empire? If the environment was so destroyed by the behavior of the Roman Empire and the Romans, then how come the even more rural and rustic kingdoms of the barbarians that succeeded managed to work the land quite effectively and survived for generations? All such arguments, upon closer inspection, tend to fall through.

An explanation that was popular for a long time—quite an obvious one—is that the Germans killed the Roman Empire. The barbarian invasions are to blame for the collapse of the Roman Empire. They came in. They took the land of the Romans, and they simply beat out the Romans and conquered the Roman Empire. This argument as well has been generally considered by most people to be insufficient, since the eastern empire succeeded in beating the barbarians off. If the barbarians were so formidable, how come it was that the east could deal with them and the west could not? The argument would be that it is something about the west that must be at fault or the barbarians would have just destroyed the whole Roman Empire, rather than just one half.

As Rome's borders became easier to penetrate, barbarian groups took advantage and began to prey on the urban centers of Roman wealth.

Right now the Transformationist school is, beyond a shadow of a doubt, the most dominant view of the so-called fall of the Roman Empire. This Transformationist school suggests that there was no fall of the Roman Empire; that the world of the later Roman Empire simply changed into the barbarian world of early medieval Europe. It was not a process of cataclysmic fall and decline. It is not that you can say that in 476 the Roman Empire was over and in 475 it wasn't. Rather, the process was one of gradual change and transformation. The Roman Empire, cocoon-like, evolved into something different. ∎

The preceding lecture was an excerpt drawn from The Great Course:

The History of Ancient Rome
Course #340

Rome's span was vast. In the regional, restless, and shifting history of continental Europe, the Roman Empire stands as a towering monument to scale and stability.

Lecture Titles

Garrett G. Fagan

Garrett G. Fagan has taught at The Pennsylvania State University since 1996. He was born in Dublin, Ireland, and educated at Trinity College, Dublin. He received his Ph.D. from McMaster University, Hamilton, Ontario, and has held teaching positions at McMaster University, York University (Canada), The University of North Carolina at Chapel Hill, Davidson College, and The Pennsylvania State University. In all of these institutions, students have given very high ratings to his courses on the classical world. He has also given numerous public lectures to audiences of all ages.

If you would like to order this course, please contact us at:

Phone: 1-800-TEACH-12
Web: www.TEACH12.com
For more information on our pricing policy, see page 245.

The High Middle Ages
Course #869
Lecture 4

Taught by: Professor Philip Daileader
The College of William and Mary

Examining the Chivalric Code

Even before the emergence of the genre of chivalric romance, medieval clerics had attempted to use literature to reshape the medieval nobility. One of the most interesting precursors to the literary genre of chivalric romance was something known as the "courtesy book."

Courtesy books emerged in the first half of the 12th century. Their authors were clerics, and they were generally written for, and often dedicated to, high-ranking members of the medieval nobility. A courtesy book contained a list of advice for members of the nobility, especially advice concerning table manners and personal behavior, that the nobility was expected to adopt. Courtesy books asked medieval nobles, for example, not to stick such huge chunks of bread into their mouths that the crumbs went flying everywhere whenever they ate. They asked them not to speak while they ate, so that the food fell out of their mouths. They asked them to stop complaining about food that was served to them, to not stick fingers in the mustard, to not wipe their mouths with the tablecloth if there was one at hand, and not to blow their noses into the tablecloth anymore.

Most of this advice contained in the medieval courtesy books seems sound enough, but some of it seems rather peculiar today. My favorite example is the following. The nobles were told that, if perchance at a dinner party, they had itches on their faces, they should by no means scratch them using their hands. Rather, they should take a piece of bread, scratch the itch with the bread, and then eat the bread, to be polite.

Now, if you were at a dinner party today and witnessed such behavior, you would probably head for the door as quickly as possible. You would be well advised to do so, but there's a logic to this advice. In the Middle Ages, there were no individual dishes out of which people ate. Rather, there was one large, communal dish into which everyone dipped bread, and then ate whatever they could sop up. It was considered to be very bad manners to scratch yourself and then stick your hand into what was, after all, everyone else's dinner. It was much better to do the right thing; scratch it with a piece of bread, and then eat the bread yourself, so that no one else had to suffer as you were about to suffer for having to eat that piece of bread.

At a medieval meal guests shared food by dipping bread into one large, communal bowl.

Courtesy books were somewhat superficial in their attempt to reshape the nobility, and they were, more or less, a failure. They were a failure for a number of reasons, but primarily because they were nattering. They were simply list of things that knights and nobles should not do anymore. No one likes to be lectured at in that manner. They were written in Latin, and this was a problem as well. The nobility, certainly in the first half of the 12th century, did not know Latin, and for the most part, it did not know how to read any language whatsoever. Thus, the courtesy books were inaccessible to nobles, and even if they had been able to get at their contents, they would not have liked what they found there.

The chivalric romance on the other hand was vastly superior because of the manner of presentation. It consisted not of a list of things that you shouldn't be doing, but contained thrilling adventures—adventure after adventure after adventure—that chivalric heroes engaged in. It consisted of thrilling stories that could draw the listener, rather than the reader, in, because unlike the courtesy book, which was intended to be read, the chivalric romance was intended to be performed orally. The medieval nobles did not read *Lancelot* in the way that we would read the romance of *Lancelot* today. Their composition was also in the vernacular languages, which is to say old French, a language that was accessible at least verbally to the medieval nobility. Because they were great stories, and because the nobles could understand them, they were going to listen to the chivalric romances.

The first romances appeared around 1150, and the genre spread like wildfire between 1150 and 1200. Romances were being written left and right. They were being written in an increasingly greater geographical arca. Perhaps the most famous author of chivalric romances during this pioneering period was a French author by the name of Chrétien de Troyes. Chrétien was a court chaplain. He was attached to court of the Count and Countess of Champagne in France. Chrétien de Troyes wrote some of the most famous of the medieval chivalric romances. These included *Erec and Enide*; *Yvain*, which is also called *The Knight with the Lion*; and, most famously, *Lancelot*, which is also called *The Knight of the Cart*. In these romances, Chrétien crafted some of the most memorable chivalric heroes, and he explored the relationship between the knight's love of martial prowess and his love of fighting, and his relationship with a lady, as well—the ways these two might interfere with one another, and ways they might reinforce one another.

Some of Chrétien's romances are relatively straightforward. It's hard to miss the point. *Erec and Enide*, as well as *Yvain*, would both qualify as relatively straightforward romances. In *Erec and Enide*, a young knight named Erec is so in love with his young wife that he cannot tear himself away from his marital bed. Thus, he forgoes martial prowess entirely. He is too otherwise occupied to go out and fight as a knight should.

However, by neglecting his prowess, he loses his reputation. He puts in danger the love of his wife for him, and the rest of the romance consists of the adventures he must go through in order to regain his prowess, which equals the love of his wife, thus achieving the right balance in his life between his love of fighting and the love of the woman to whom he is supposed to dedicate himself.

Yvain, too, wrestles with the issue of how to find just the right balance between fighting and loving. It approaches it from a rather different angle, however. Whereas Erec neglects prowess for his wife, Yvain does the opposite. After marriage, he goes off and partakes of tournaments, and he is so wrapped up in jousting and fighting with others that he forgets to return home on time, and his wife dumps him. He goes mad, becomes a lunatic, a savage animal. Having lost the love of his wife, the rest of the romance is dedicated to his attempts to recapture the love of his wife, behaving as a chivalric knight should. Both *Erec and Enide* and *Yvain* deal with courtly love in the context of marriage; these are two married chivalric heroes. They both end happily.

The most famous romance that Chrétien de Troyes wrote, though, is much more ambiguous and much more complex, so that even today, people argue, and argue, and argue over what it was that Chrétien de

Troyes was trying to say: *Lancelot*. Lancelot is so complex because his love does not occur within the context of marriage. He is in love with the wife of King Arthur. He is in love with Guenevere. He is therefore in an adulterous relationship. He does not love Guenevere from afar, certainly not when he can help it. Theirs is, in fact, a consummated love, in fact, a rather heated love affair.

Lancelot's behavior is very, very odd during the course of the story. His devotion to Guenevere knows no bounds. He discovers a strand of hair, a single strand of hair on a comb. He is so overcome by love that he jabs himself in the eye repeatedly with it so that he can see it up close. Scholars wonder whether Chrétien was not mocking courtly love in this poem, mocking it because, in this instance, it was adulterous love that was not taking place in the context of marriage, and because that was consummated adulterous love; or whether Chrétien was quite serious in depicting Lancelot as the ultimate chivalric hero, someone who would go to any lengths, even though the love of his life was the wife of his lord. Perhaps it was because of this complexity that Lancelot remains a figure in popular culture today, whereas *Erec and Enide*, and *Yvain*, to be honest, are forgotten by all but medieval scholars.

Chrétien de Troyes was not the only important author of chivalric romances. One must mention the most important female author of medieval romances, Marie de France. Marie was also attached to the court of the Count and Countess of Champagne. She specialized in the writing of very short pieces, known as *lais*. These were short poems, and her stories tended to end rather unhappily. It has been suggested that as a woman, she had a rather different perspective on courtly romance: From a feminine perspective she saw that, for the woman involved, idealization was perhaps not all that it was cracked up to be by male authors.

Assessing the impact of all of this literature on real-life medieval knights is very, very difficult. One method that historians have devised to determine if knights changed the way they acted, and whether it was in response to chivalry, is the history of the tournament.

Tournaments were the favorite pastime of the medieval nobility. They loved taking part in tournaments almost as much as they loved hunting, which was their other favorite pastime. The tournaments, like hunting, allowed the nobility to keep its military skills sharp. The earliest documented tournaments to take place in high medieval Europe dated around 1100, took place in northern France, and much as the chivalric romance would do two generations later, became all the rage. Soon, tournaments were held throughout Europe, and knights and others couldn't get enough of these.

Now, tournaments, as they first existed, were very chaotic affairs. There were rules, but only a few. Before a tournament was held, invitations would be sent out to knights from various regions, often hundreds of knights at a time, inviting them to congregate at a certain time, and a certain place, announcing that a tournament was going to be held.

When the knights showed up, they were divided into teams, usually based on geography. There might be dozens, or even hundreds on a team. For example, the northern French versus the southern French knights, or the German knights versus the French. Boundaries were set within which the tournament would take place. Often, a single tournament would include acres and acres of land. Safety zones were designated, areas where knights could not be attacked. If you made it to your team's safety zone, other knights could not get you there.

That was pretty much it as far is the rules went for the early tournaments. They were fought using real weapons: real swords, real lances, with sharp edges to them. Almost anything went, in terms of what you could do to your opponent. Your goal was not to kill your opponent, but to unhorse someone, take the person captive, hold the person for ransom, take his horse, take his armor, and take as much money as you possibly could off of the person. If you accidentally killed a person, however, as you attempted to get hold of his armor or horse, well, those were the breaks, in an early medieval tournament.

In addition to using real weapons during the course of the fighting, the nobles would often wind up attacking innocent bystanders. The peasants who lived in the area suffered tremendously from early tournaments. They suffered because nobles would ride through their crops in pursuit of one another, trampling next year's food supply. Because it was not unknown for you to trap someone from the other team at a peasant's house, the best way to get the person out was to burn down the house, regardless of the fact that the poor peasant who owned the house had nothing to do with this particular tournament.

So violent were medieval tournaments that, rather early in their history, there were attempts to prohibit them. A church council of 1130 tried to forbid tournaments, and church councils would repeat this over, and over, and over again, without much success. In parts of Europe where royal authority was especially strong, where kings were able to restrain their nobles, not only did they forbid the building of private castles, they forbade tournaments as well, because they knew the harm that would be done to their subjects if the tournaments were fought.

The very violent, very realistic tournaments that one found earlier in the High Middle Ages had changed by the time 1300 arrived. They had become more subdued, more civilized, one might even say, and they resembled, more closely, the modern image of tournaments as we conceive of them now.

By the end of the High Middle Ages, certain ultra-violent practices had been banished from the tournaments. One practice that was gotten rid of was the use of kippers. Kippers were people on foot that nobles would bring to a tournament. The job of the kipper was to rush out on the field when you had dismounted someone, and to beat the person senseless with clubs, so that you could get the armor off the person more easily, and seize the person's horse. By 1300, the use of kippers was considered to be bad form, and you wouldn't find them at tournaments anymore.

The rushing around in peasants' fields, the uncontained roaming over acres and acres, too, had come to an end by 1300, and a different form of contest had become more popular. Jousting, a one-on-one contest, in which the violence, although considerable—if you were dismounted, you could still be killed in 1300—was at least limited to a specific geographic area.

Attempts were made to make jousting less violent, to make participation in a tournament less deadly. The use of real weapons was rare by 1300. Now, they used blunted weapons. There was no sharp point at the end of the lance. You simply tried to knock someone off of his horse. To prevent the very messy head-on collisions that sometimes occurred during jousting, the tilt was introduced. This was a railing that went down the middle of the jousting field, and contestants were to stay on opposite sides of the railing, so that there were no unfortunate collisions of two horses charging right into one another—an event that would often prove to be fatal for those who were riding on the horses.

People were still killed in tournaments in 1300. The church still condemned tournaments as of 1300, and kings, if they could, were going to try to keep the fighting in tournaments to a minimum. It was an unusual noble family during the High Middle Ages that could not point to at least one member who was killed in a tournament, who was trampled, or who fell badly off of a horse. Nonetheless, the bloodletting of the early tournaments had lessened.

Should these changes be attributed to chivalry, though, or are they independent developments? That's an especially tricky question. There is some reason to think that these changes should be attributed, at least in part, to the development of the chivalric ideal, to the notion that you should not display your prowess in frivolous pastimes, but only when you are doing good for someone who is defenseless.

By 1300, and especially in the Late Middle Ages, it became common for certain knights to be excluded from tournaments, knights who had spoken badly of women in public, because this violated courtly love; knights who had burned down peasant houses; who had inflicted violence on the defenseless; knights who had violated the chivalric ideal. Here, one can see the direct influence of chivalry on real behavior.

Some tournaments after 1300, it must be admitted, took the chivalric ideal to rather odd extremes. Some tournaments were organized as roundtable tournaments. In a roundtable tournament, different knights would pretend to be characters from chivalric romances. One person would dress up as Arthur, another as Lancelot, another as Yvain, and they would go around taking part in mock adventures, in imitation of what they had heard in chivalric romances.

On the other hand, one should not assume that by 1300, medieval nobility had been tamed completely. The fact that knights who burned down peasant houses, who spoke badly of women, who pillaged churches, had to be excluded from tournaments, tells you something. It tells you that there was still a problem with which Europe still had to contend. ∎

The tournament began as unstructured, violent horseplay and evolved into protocol-laden, highly stylized competitions. Jousting, a form of warfare using tipped lances wielded by knights on horseback, formed the central spectacle of these tournaments.

The preceding lecture was an excerpt drawn from The Great Course:

The High Middle Ages
Course #869

As the last millennium dawned, Europe didn't amount to much. Illiteracy, starvation, and disease were the norm. In fact, Europe in the year 1000 was one of the world's more stagnant regions—an economically undeveloped, intellectually derivative, and geopolitically passive backwater.

Three short centuries later, all this had changed dramatically. A newly invigorated cluster of European societies revived city life, spawned new spiritual and intellectual movements and educational institutions, and began, for reasons both sacred and profane, to expand at the expense of neighbors who traditionally had expanded at Europe's expense.

Lecture Titles

Philip Daileader

Philip Daileader is an Associate Professor of History at The College of William and Mary. He received his B.A. in History from Johns Hopkins University and earned his M.A. and Ph.D. in History from Harvard University.

Professor Daileader is the recipient of William and Mary's 2004 Alumni Fellowship Award for excellence in teaching. As a graduate student, he was a four-time winner of the Harvard University Certificate of Distinction in Teaching.

If you would like to order this course, please contact us at:

Phone: 1-800-TEACH-12
Web: www.TEACH12.com
For more information on our pricing policy, see page 245.

Reading the Rosetta Stone

Toward the end of Egypt's long history, 3,000 years of historic records, Egypt was conquered by many foreign armies—the Assyrians, the Libyans, the Babylonians, the Nubians, toward the very end the Greeks, and then finally the Romans. Because Egypt was eventually occupied by foreigners, the language died out. At one point Greek became the major language of

Then the Romans took over. So by A.D. 425 we have the last inscription written on a wall in a temple in ancient Egyptian. That is the last time that we know that anybody could read or write ancient Egyptian; it was probably a priest.

So after A.D. 425 no one could read ancient Egyptian records, and it remained a dead language for over a thousand years. Why? The answer is that everybody was making the same false assumption—that it was picture writing; that when you see birds it's talking about birds, and when you see snakes it's talking about snakes.

Ancient Egyptian was basically an alphabetic language like ours, but everybody was assuming it was picture writing, so nobody was deciphering it. Interesting, by the way, think about this: If it really were picture writing, wouldn't we all be able to read it? But no, it's not picture writing; it's mainly alphabetic. So for over a thousand years nobody could read or write it.

One Greek writer, Horapollo, wrote a treatise about ancient Egyptian hieroglyphs, but he couldn't read them. It's an interesting treatise. He got some things right, some things wrong. I'll give you an example. He says that when you see the hieroglyph of a duck, it was used by the ancient Egyptians to indicate someone's son. He was right. The reason he gave was, thinking it's picture writing, because the ducks fight so

The Rosetta Stone, an archeological discovery containing two languages in three scripts, provided the template for deciphering ancient Egyptian hieroglyphics.

fiercely for their offspring, the duck was associated with children. That was wrong. The duck indeed did represent a male child. But the reason the duck represented it was that the duck represents a sound, *sa*, and that was the ancient Egyptian word for son. So when an Egyptian looked at a duck, he was thinking about the sound *sa* and that meant a male child. There was an awful lot of speculation about what these sacred carvings meant, but nobody really knew.

The Rosetta Stone was found at Fort Rosetta. Napoleon's men were digging the fortifications, and buried into the wall of the fort was this stone, the Rosetta Stone. So whoever had built the fort originally took this old stone that was around—a good piece of building material—recycled it, and put it inside the wall. Bouchard, the lieutenant who found it, was an educated man, saw there was Greek on it, saw there was ancient Egyptian; he knew this was going to be the key. It was sent down to Cairo and the scientists started studying it.

Now, here's an Egyptological trivia question: How many languages are on the Rosetta Stone? I bet in high school you were taught three. That's wrong; the answer is only two. There are three scripts on the Rosetta Stone, but only two languages—Egyptian and Greek. Those are the languages. But the Egyptian is written in two scripts.

How many languages are on the Rosetta Stone? I bet in high school you were taught three. That's wrong; the answer is only two. There are three scripts on the Rosetta Stone, but only two languages.

We have printed letters—Latin letters, we call them—and cursive writing. That's what the Egyptians had also, they had different forms of writing, and on the Rosetta Stone are three different scripts. One is the hieroglyphic script. These are the symbols that are recognizable as ducks and birds. In addition the Egyptians had other scripts. One was called demotic. That's also on the Rosetta Stone. Demotic comes from the Greek, it means *demos*, "the people." This is the people's writing. Hieroglyphs, the sacred carvings, are used by the priests for religious texts and also used for official big statements by the pharaoh; when you put something on a temple wall about a victory, that was in hieroglyphs. But if you were writing, say, a laundry list, or a grocery list, or a receipt for goats, you did it in demotic, because it takes a long time to draw a bird and then a foot and so on, so they had a quick way of writing it, at the end of the Egyptian civilization, called demotic, that also was on the Rosetta Stone.

The third script and the second language was Greek, and that's one that scholars could read at the time. The key was the last sentence of the Greek. It says, "Written in sacred and native and Greek characters." In other words, that last line of the Greek inscription said, "We've written the same message three ways—in sacred, hieroglyphic; native, the demotic; and Greek." So it was the same message written three different ways in two different languages; this was going to be the key to deciphering it.

There is even one more script in Egyptian history, and it's going to be the key to the decipherment of hieroglyphs—Coptic. The Copts in Egypt, and they are there today—to this day you have Copts in Egypt—are the Christian Egyptians. In the 1st century A.D., St. Mark came into Egypt preaching the trinity. Now he was spreading Christianity, and the Egyptians adopted it very easily for two reasons.

One reason is that almost all the Egyptian gods come in threes, in trinities. For example, in the town of Memphis there was a trinity of the god Ptah; his wife Sekhmet, who was a lion-headed goddess; and they have a child called Nefertum, who was a lotus god. In Thebes, in the south of Egypt, you have Amun, who starts out as the hidden one; his wife Mut, who also has a lion head; and they have a child Khonsu, a ram-headed god.

So St. Mark comes in and says, "I'm preaching a trinity," and the Egyptians were ready. There is another reason why the Egyptians could adopt the Christian trinity. The Egyptians had a history of polytheism, belief in many gods. One of the things that people forget is that monotheism, the belief in one god, is divisive. If you believe in one god, then it's: I'm right, and those who don't believe are wrong. The Egyptians never felt they had to choose, to pick and throw out gods. So St. Mark

came in, and they adopted the trinity. These people who converted are called the Copts.

Now, their language is Coptic, but here is where it gets interesting. St. Mark comes in with Christianity, he says you can't use these pagan hieroglyphs anymore for our Christian religion. So the Egyptians—they are still speaking Egyptian, but they are not allowed to write their language in hieroglyphs—they need a new script. It happens at this time

Hieroglyphics were used by the state for religious and secular record keeping. Demotic script, also on the Rosetta Stone, was used by the rest of the population.

the Greeks had been in Egypt for many centuries; Greek was around as a language, and they chose to write their ancient Egyptian language in the Greek alphabet. So Coptic is really ancient Egyptian written in the Greek alphabet, just spelled out phonetically. That's the last script that we have of ancient Egyptian. Coptic, of course, doesn't appear on the Rosetta stone, but it is the key to deciphering hieroglyphs.

Now, the decipherment. Who deciphered the Rosetta Stone, and the hieroglyphic language, and Egyptian language in general is a bit of a conjecture. People argue still about it. The main decipherer, there is no question, is a Frenchman, Champollion. But he didn't do it by himself. An Englishman really started the job, Thomas Young. And the British like to say that Thomas Young deciphered the Rosetta Stone. So, here are their contributions, and you can decide for yourself.

Thomas Young was an amazing genius. He was a physician who also came up with a theory of light; but he loved languages most. He set it as his task to decipher ancient Egyptian language. When the Rosetta Stone was found, he started working. His first big leap was 1798. Someone had suggested that the kings in Egypt wrote their names in ovals. They had seen ovals carved on the walls with hieroglyphs inside; they couldn't read it, but it was long enough for a name.

So there was a suggestion that the kings' names were written in ovals. And they are called cartouches to this day, because of Napoleon's expedition. When the men saw these ovals they said they looked like bullets standing on their ends, and *cartouche*, that's the French word for bullet.

It had been suggested that the cartouches contained the names of the kings. Thomas Young figured names can't be picture writing. You can't have a picture, for example, of King Ptolemy. Now understand this: We have the Greek text on the bottom, and the first line of the Greek text, very first line, first two words, Ptolemaios Basilios, King Ptolemy. So the Greek let us know Ptolemy's name is on the Rosetta Stone. Young figured, in the cartouche those are going to be letters of Ptolemy's name. And he started thinking it out, there is a little rectangle, that's a hieroglyph; that must be the "P." There is a semi-circle; that must be the "T." There is a loop, like a lasso; that must be the "O." And he went through it and he worked out the name Ptolemaios, the Greek version of Ptolemy. So Thomas Young is one of the first ones to say, you've got an alphabet here, we can figure out the names.

Enter Jean François Champollion. His father was a librarian, and Champollion was used to playing in the stacks of books. And as he was crawling around, he was looking at different languages on the spines of the books, trying to understand what they were, and he became obsessed with languages. By the time he was 14 or 15 he knew eight languages. One of the languages that he knew was Coptic. Coptic had survived. You see, Copts still existed in Egypt and they have a church, the Coptic Church. And if you go to a Coptic church in Egypt and listen to the service, you're hearing ancient Egyptian. They've kept the language right through. So Coptic is really our connection with spoken ancient Egyptian, and Champollion knew Coptic.

Now, think about this: Thomas Young says it's an alphabet, great. We can look at the hieroglyphs and know how it sounded, but that doesn't tell us what it means. For example, you know the hieroglyph that everybody is familiar with, *ankh*. It's like a cross, and people often wear them as good luck symbols. Everybody knew that that was pronounced *ankh*; from the alphabet we can figure that out. But how do you know that the ancient Egyptians meant for *ankh* to mean the word "life"? The answer is, in the Coptic Church's liturgy; we know that *ankh* means life. So, by knowing Coptic, Champollion could look at the hieroglyphs, say it out loud, *ankh*, and then realize, "Ah, Coptic has that word, *ankh*, that means life." So that enabled Champollion to decipher hieroglyphs, not just phonetically, but get at the meaning of it. And he was the first one to translate the Rosetta Stone.

It didn't come easy, by the way. The Rosetta Stone, discovered in 1799 during the campaign, brought to England in 1801, was not deciphered until 1822. It was a long haul, but for the first time the records of ancient Egypt could be read thanks to Napoleon and Champollion.

Let me explain what was on the Rosetta Stone. First, the Rosetta Stone is a stela. A stela is simply a large stone, usually three, maybe five, sometimes nine feet high, shaped like a tombstone. And these were placed in front of temples, kind of like a bulletin board. If you wanted to announce something, if you wanted to say something great was done, you had a stela carved. And the Rosetta Stone, broken as it is, was originally from a stela erected in front of a temple.

It was erected during the reign of King Ptolemy V—a Greek who was ruling Egypt toward the end of Egyptian civilization. Ptolemy had done a couple of nice things for the priests. He said, you don't have to pay certain kinds of taxes, you don't have to make this trip that you always have to make to deposit your taxes. And the priests were very thankful. So they carved this stela in hieroglyphs because it was important, they carved it in demotic so that the people could read it, and they carved it in Greek so Ptolemy V could read it because he couldn't read Egyptian. The Greeks never learned to read Egyptian when they were ruling. The only Greek who ever learned ancient Egyptian language was Cleopatra. So the Rosetta Stone is basically a thank you letter

The Rosetta Stone was constructed by priests to honor Ptolemy V.

from the priests of Egypt to Ptolemy V, saying thanks a lot, you're a good guy.

Egyptian is the only language I know of that can be written either from right to left, or left to right, or top to bottom. And the reason is for artistic consideration. Let's say you're decorating a tomb and you want to have a religious inscription over the doorway. You want it to say, "May I have all the bread and beer and things good and pure that the gods live on." You could write it either from left to right, or right to left, or if you wanted to be really artistic and have it really symmetrical, you could start at the middle of the door and write one inscription from right to left, reading outward from the middle. You could start the same inscription in the middle going the other way, and you've got this beautiful symmetrical double rendering of this prayer. You know, Egypt is a very symmetrical land. You've got the Nile going down the middle; you've got the desert on both sides. They loved symmetry, they liked balance, and their language was done that way. Also, if you had a narrow space where you wanted to write something, you could write it from top to bottom.

To know how to read it, you always read toward the mouths of the birds. So if you look at the birds, you read it into the mouth, as if the bird is eating the direction it's going in. So you read always into the mouths of the birds, and that's what always tells you which way to do it. It's never confusing. I know that sometimes it sounds like it might be, but it never is. It's an amazing language. ∎

The preceding lecture was an excerpt drawn from The Great Course:

The History of Ancient Egypt
Course #350

Ancient Egyptian civilization is so grand that our minds sometimes have difficulty adjusting to it.
Consider time. Ancient Egyptian civilization lasted 3,000 years, longer than any other on the planet. When the young Pharaoh Tutankhamen ruled Egypt, the famous pyramids of Giza had already been standing well over 1,000 years.

Lecture Titles

Bob Brier

Bob Brier is an Egyptologist and Professor of Philosophy at the C.W. Post Campus of Long Island University. He received his Bachelor's degree from Hunter College and Ph.D. in Philosophy from The University of North Carolina at Chapel Hill.

Professor Brier has twice been selected as a Fulbright Scholar and has received LIU's David Newton Award for Teaching Excellence in recognition of his achievements as a lecturer.

If you would like to order this course, please contact us at:

Phone: 1-800-TEACH-12
Web: www.TEACH12.com
For more information on our pricing policy, see page 245.

Ancient Problem Solvers

Where and when do we start our study of the history of science? That can be a difficult question, but most historians of science tend to begin with ancient Egypt and ancient Mesopotamia, and there are good reasons for this.

The first reason is that those two cultures exerted influence on the ancient Greeks, and the ancient Greeks, in turn, created the fundamentals of Western thought and the fundamentals of Western history of science. Second, both the Egyptians and the Babylonians had the advantage of being literate cultures. Literacy makes a great deal of difference. It means there are historical records for us to examine.

The Babylonian civilization was one of several to develop in Mesopotamia. The word Mesopotamia comes from two Greek words which means "between the rivers," namely, the Tigris and the Euphrates, the so-called Fertile Crescent. Mesopotamia was the ancient site of the Garden of Eden and presently the site of the state of Iraq.

Babylonian culture was literate in extremely durable ways. The Babylonians wrote—or impressed, which is a better way of stating it—on clay. They used a stylus to make impressions in clay tablets. The stylus that they used left a wedge-shaped impression, and that gives us the name for their kind of writing. Using the Latin word *cuneus*, which means a wedge, gives us the name "cuneiform." The Babylonians were almost obsessive record-keepers. We have thousands and thousands of tablets from them. In terms of the history of science, the most important Babylonian activities were mathematics and astronomy.

Let's start, briefly, with their method of writing numbers, because their method of writing numbers is unique in the ancient world. In general, there are two different ways of writing numbers. The simpler method is by aggregation. You're probably all familiar with that in terms of Roman numerals. In aggregation systems, there's a set of

| 1 | 2 | 3 | 4 | 5 | 6 | 7 | 8 | 9 | 10 |

Cuneiform script was written on soft clay tablets with a wedge-shaped reed called a stylus. The writer could make a triangular indentation by sticking the stylus into the clay and could make a straight line by dragging the edge of the stylus through the clay. Cuneiform began as a pictographic form of writing but became more abstract as it advanced until the symbols no longer represented the original pictograms. Above you can see the cuneiform symbols for the numbers 1 to 10. Note the simple additive logic that produces the numbers 1 to 9 by adding wedges.

symbols which have a fixed value, and we add them up—aggregate them—to give us our total number. So, I is one in Roman numerals; II is two; III is three; X is 10; XX, 20; XXXII, 32.

The other system is theoretically much more complicated, and that is the place-notation system. We don't think about it as being more complicated because it's what we use, and so somehow it's familiar to us, but in place notation, not only are there symbols with specific values, but also, the position of those symbols relative to one another changes the value. Our system happens to be decimal. That is, in a three-digit number, for example, the first column on the right is the ones; the next, the first power of 10, or 10; and the next one, the second power of 10, or 100. If I write the numeral 1, that represents one, but two 1s does not mean two, it means 11.

Place notation, although it's more complicated, is much easier to use for large numbers in mathematical operations. If you don't actually believe me that it's much easier, let me give you a suggestion. Next year, when it's time to make out your tax return, try doing it in Roman numerals, and you'll see exactly what I mean.

Most ancient cultures use the aggregation system, but the Babylonians, curiously enough, used both aggregation and place notation simultaneously. Let's say we're Babylonian, and we're starting to write out our numbers for practice. The Babylonian would start out with a wedge-shaped mark pointed down, for one. Two of them would be two. Three of them would be three, and so forth. When we got to nine, instead of writing 10 little marks, we'd write a wedge-shaped mark pointing to the left, for 10. The aggregation system would work at this point. If we wanted to write 23, we would put two wedge-shaped marks pointing to the left and three pointed down.

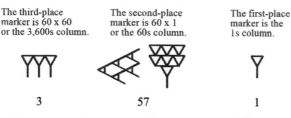

The sexagesimal place notation system invented by the Babylonians works on a base unit of 60, as opposed to our base unit of 10.

The third-place marker is 60 x 60 or the 3,600s column.

The second-place marker is 60 x 1 or the 60s column.

The first-place marker is the 1s column.

3   57   1

To arrive at the actual number written in this example you would multiply each number by the value of the place marker it holds, and add the products.

3 x 3,600   57 x 60   1 x 1

10,800   +   3,420   +   1

= 14,221

The numbering system of the Babylonians used a base of 60 instead of 10. Strange as this may seem to modern readers, we still use a base 60 in many of our measurements today, in hours and minutes, for example.

But something happens at 59. If the Babylonian wants to write 61, for example, he doesn't write six marks pointing left and one mark pointing down. He writes only two: one pointed down, a space, and another one pointed down, because it's at 60 that the Babylonian place notation starts to function. This is because their base was not 10, as ours is, but 60; it's a sexagesimal system. So a three-digit number in Babylonian would not have a ones, a tens, and a hundreds place, but rather a one, a 60, and a 3,600 place. It makes it very easy to write extremely large numbers in the Babylonian system.

What were the Babylonians lacking? Nothing. Literally nothing, and by that, I mean zero. They had no way to mark an empty place. If you don't think that's a problem, imagine this. Let's say we're reading along one sunny afternoon on a Babylonian cuneiform text, and we get to a single numeral. Let's say it's the wedge pointing downwards. What is that number supposed to be? Is it one? Could be. Is it 60? Could be. Is it 3,600? Possibly. Is it 3,600 times 60, whatever that actually happens to be? You don't know. In fact, it could even be one-sixtieth, because the Babylonians, again, unlike other ancient cultures, used the place notation to go to the right as well as to the left, and so were able to write fractions.

At any rate, the Babylonians developed quite sophisticated mathematics based on this system. There are, in fact, hundreds of mathematical problem texts that survive from ancient Babylon. In fact, they're a little bit disquieting because they're eerily familiar. They always make me a little bit nervous because they remind me of those word problems that we were all forced to do in the sixth, seventh, and eighth grade. Let me give you one example. This is actually from a text from the early part of the 1st millennium B.C. The only thing I've done is to convert the Babylonian units of measure and weight into modern ones. "A man earns two pounds of barley for one day of work. In one day, he can dig a trench four feet deep, two feet wide, and eight feet long. What will the cost be, in barley, and the time needed for eight men to dig a canal six feet deep, six feet wide, and 250 feet long?"

You might ask, "Why on Earth did the Babylonians choose a base of 60?" We can ask, "Why did we choose base 10?" That's an easy one. Anybody who has 10 fingers knows why a decimal system works, but why 60, unless the Babylonians were very strangely put together? There are a couple of reasons. One, 60 is full of factors. That means it's easy to take 60 and divide it by 2, 3, 4, 5, 6, 10, 12, 15, and so forth. You still get a whole number. Another possible cause may be that factors of 60 appear in astronomical phenomena. There are, more or less, 360 days in a year (6 times 60). In that same period, there are 12 lunar cycles (60 divided by 5). We don't know for sure which one of these, or both, it was.

I should mention, however, that as strange as the sexagesimal system seems to us, we do actually still use it. How many seconds are there in a minute? 60. How many minutes are there in an hour? 60. How many minutes in a degree? 60. Thank the Babylonians for that, because it's their sexagesimal system, handed down through the ages, that we still use for measuring angles, especially, for example, in astronomical calculations. It's quite remarkable to think that today's most modern telescopes are still pointed to coordinates in the sky marked out in degrees, minutes, and seconds, in a sexagesimal system that was handed down by the Babylonians first, and has constantly been used in astronomy for 4,000 years.

In fact, it was in astronomical matters that the Babylonians excelled and left us their most important legacy. The Babylonians compiled extensive observations of lunar cycles, of eclipses, of the movements of bodies through the heavens. Why? Really, there are two reasons. First of all, it was to regulate their calendar. The Babylonians used a lunar calendar, so their month began with the new moon. They needed to have observations, and they needed to know the length of the lunar cycle to regulate that. But their calendar wasn't just lunar because they were an agricultural society, as well. They needed to know when the seasons were—when to plant the crops, when to harvest them—so they needed solar observations as well. As a result of generations of astronomical observations, coupled with their very durable records, the Babylonians, certainly by 600 B.C.—probably earlier—had compiled very complex astronomical tables which allowed them to predict celestial events. For example, they were able to predict eclipses, the first appearance of the new moon, and such things.

Don't take that too far, because although the Babylonians could predict that an eclipse might happen, they were not able to say the exact time or whether it would be visible. It turns out that there's some evidence that priests were sent to various far-flung corners of the Babylonian Empire to watch to see if an eclipse happened, and they would report back on this. Again, they couldn't say exactly where an eclipse would happen, only that there was a possibility of it. What's interesting for us is that they had this predictive ability, apparently without any physical model of the heavens. That is, they don't seem to know what caused the eclipses. They didn't have any sense of how the heavenly bodies moved. It was purely a matter of recording repeating events that occurred again and again at regular cycles, and just extrapolating to the next event.

The second reason that the Babylonians were so interested in astronomy was for astrological purposes. The Babylonians, like most other Mesopotamian cultures, had a deep interest in astrology for predicting events. It's not just by accident that the Magi who come to Bethlehem are traveling from the east, because from the east of Judea are the Mesopotamian cultures, and by that point, Persian culture, all of whom were very interested in astrology and spent their time looking at the heavens, waiting for portents, and interpreting them. Please, don't confuse pre-modern astrology with the horrid fluff that shows up in the funny pages in the newspaper or the cheap little paperbacks in the checkout lines of grocery stores. It's a completely different subject. Pre-modern astrology required a substantial command of mathematical and astronomical knowledge. Moreover, it's very clear that the heavens influence us, isn't it? I'm not going to give you any examples now, but you just think about that. How do the heavenly bodies influence us? ∎

The preceding lecture was an excerpt drawn from The Great Course:

History of Science: Antiquity to 1700
Course #1200

For well over 2,000 years, much of our fundamental "desire to know" has focused on the area we now call science. In fact, our commitment to science and technology has been so profound that these now stand as probably the most powerful of all influences on human culture.

Lecture Titles

1. Beginning the Journey
2. **Babylonians, Egyptians, and Greeks**
3. The Presocratics
4. Plato and the Pythagoreans
5. Plato's Cosmos
6. Aristotle's View of the Natural World
7. Aristotelian Cosmology and Physics
8. Hellenistic Natural Philosophy
9. Greek Astronomy from Eudoxus to Ptolemy
10. The Roman Contributions
11. Roman Versions of Greek Science and Education
12. The End of the Classical World
13. Early Christianity and Science
14. The Rise of Islam and Islamic Science
15. Islamic Astronomy, Mathematics, and Optics
16. Alchemy, Medicine, and Late Islamic Culture
17. The Latin West Reawakens
18. Natural Philosophy at School and University
19. Aristotle and Medieval Scholasticism
20. The Science of Creation
21. Science in the Orders
22. Medieval Latin Alchemy and Astrology
23. Medieval Physics and Earth Sciences
24. The Middle Ages and the Renaissance
25. Renaissance Natural Magic
26. Copernicus and Calendrical Reform
27. Renaissance Technology
28. Tycho, Kepler, and Galileo
29. The New Physics
30. Voyages of Discovery and Natural History
31. Mechanical Philosophy and Revised Atomism
32. Mechanism and Vitalism
33. Seventeenth-Century Chemistry
34. The Force of Isaac Newton
35. The Rise of Scientific Societies
36. How Science Develops

Lawrence M. Principe

Lawrence M. Principe is Professor of the History of Science, Medicine, and Technology, and Professor of Chemistry at Johns Hopkins University.

In 1999, the Carnegie Foundation chose Professor Principe as the Maryland Professor of the Year, and in 1998 he received the Templeton Foundation's award for courses dealing with science and religion. At Johns Hopkins, Principe has won the Distinguished Faculty Award, the Excellence in Teaching Award, and the George Owen Teaching Award.

If you would like to order this course, please contact us at:

Phone: 1-800-TEACH-12

Web: www.TEACH12.com

For more information on our pricing policy, see page 245.

The Empire State Building is an architectural symbol of the modern age, completed in 1931, in the art deco style.

MODERN HISTORY

"The history of the world is but the biography of great men."

—Thomas Carlyle

155

The D-Day Gamble

Everyone in Europe understood, in the winter and early spring of 1943, that an invasion was coming. Fortress Europe was going to be assaulted by the Western Allies. The question was, where and when?

The Germans expected the invasion to come in the Pas-de-Calais 200 miles to the northeast. The distance across the Channel was only 20 miles at that point. It offered the shortest route both into France, and then a quick drive into the heart of Germany. The Germans clearly understood the goal of the Allied invasion was to get through France as quickly as possible, through the Low Countries and into Germany proper and particularly into the industrial heartland of Germany. An attack across the Pas-de-Calais would offer the most obvious, shortest route to that objective.

But for the Allies, the ports across the Channel from Normandy were larger and could handle the massive ship and troop concentrations that were going to be necessary. Normandy contained two important ports for resupply, Cherbourg and Le Havre, that were considered absolutely essential to any sort of sustained military operation on the continent. The projected landing areas lay to the east of the Cotentin Peninsula, which juts out into the English Channel and thus protects the beaches from the prevailing westerly winds. So for these reasons, the Normandy area suggested itself as the best place for this great undertaking, code named Operation Overlord.

The scale was absolutely awesome. This would be the largest amphibious assault in history, and Roosevelt, Churchill, and the Allied command felt that on its success hung the success of the Second World War.

U.S. troops exit their landing crafts at Normandy on D-Day. The mission was a huge gamble, and its results determined the fate of Western civilization.

The planning that went on through the winter of 1943 and into the early spring of 1944 was intense and secret, and was extraordinary in its attention to detail. The scale was absolutely awesome. This would be the largest amphibious assault in history; and Roosevelt, Churchill, and the Allied command felt that on its success hung the success of the Second World War. It would remain a well-kept secret—remarkably enough, given the number of personnel involved, the long run-up, and the planning. It was an extraordinary feat of security.

In early 1944 and right down to D-Day itself, the Allies did everything they could to convince the Germans that the invasion would indeed come in the Pas-de-Calais. The Allies created a dummy headquarters under Patton's command, with elaborate radio traffic, supply depots, railway sidings, inflatable tanks, and cardboard trucks. It was an extraordinary effort to confuse the Germans, who believed that no invasion would come without Patton, the hero of the American army as far as the Germans were concerned.

The British also created a dummy army in the north, also with radio

Moments before these soldiers were to deploy on D-Day, General Eisenhower talks to the troops, knowing full well that they faced high casualty rates in the days ahead.

traffic, with a whole series of ploys to make the Germans believe that the British were going to launch an attack in Norway. And although Hitler did not reinforce the German troops in Norway, the 13 German divisions that were stationed in Norway remained in place even as the spring approached and invasion season was upon the Germans.

Ultra, the Allied intercepts of German code traffic, reported that the Germans had indeed bought the deception. So the question of where was successfully disguised by the Allies. Everyone knew that the invasion would come sometime in the late spring or early summer, and the timing would be largely dictated by weather conditions. The Allies would need calm seas, they would need clear skies, if they were to take advantage of one of the great advantages they possessed, and that was air superiority.

Eisenhower, in planning, had set June 5 for D-Day, and the cumbersome loading process began on May 31. It's remarkable to think that this massive movement of troops—of vehicles of every sort, trucks, tanks, jeeps, artillery pieces—all of southern England, beginning on May 31, was simply in motion, moving by train, some by foot, some in convoys, to the ports from which they would load the ships. All along the route, British civilians were out waving at the troops. It was clear to anyone around that this was the big event; this was the long-awaited invasion. It was finally coming. And yet the Germans were in the dark about this.

By the evening of June 3, the assault waves of the Allied expeditionary force were loaded up, all prepared for the invasion on June 5. The ships assembled were extraordinary. There were 2,727 ships—battleships; destroyers; minesweepers; huge LSTs, landing ships to carry tanks, heavy supplies, troops, and so on. Nine hundred and thirty-one of these ships were headed for Omaha and Utah beaches, the two American beaches to be hit—the western naval task force. The eastern naval task force contained 1,796 ships bound for Gold, Juno, and Sword beaches, the code names for the British beaches. In addition, 2,600 landing craft, Higgins boats and other smaller vessels that were simply too small to make the cross-channel trip on their own, had been loaded up onto these giant LSTs so that, all together, an armada of 5,333 vessels had been assembled in the south of England to prepare for this enormous undertaking.

By June 3, all of the supplies, all of the men, had been loaded. And then, on June 4, a major weather front hit—howling winds, plunging temperatures, and rain falling in horizontal sheets. Still, the thousands of ships in the vast armada had begun to move out of their harbors and to form into convoys.

Eisenhower got more bad news at his weather briefing at 04:00. The situation, he was told by his chief meteorologist, who was a 28 year-old Scotsman by the name of J. M. Stagg—one thinks about the responsibility that this man shouldered in these days—told Eisenhower the situation was deteriorating rapidly, that the weather was going to get worse and, even more troubling, it was unpredictable. It was not at all clear if the weather would break, when it would break—that predicting the weather for more than 24 hours under these circumstances was almost impossible.

At 06:00 Eisenhower gave the order to put everything on hold. The troops in the ships were miserable. Caught in the storm out in the Channel, the seasickness was awful for the troops.

Eisenhower now was confronted with a choice. To postpone the invasion would mean putting things off until June 19. There were only three days in each two-week period in June when the two conditions he needed could be predicted; that is, when low tide and first light came together. Essentially, he had to have these conditions because of German defenses. They were concentrated in the tidal flats, so you wanted to be able to see them. The naval people bringing the boats in wanted to be able to see the underwater obstructions that would be obscured at high tide; and, also, the airborne operations required at least a half moon, and that reduced the availability of days to an even shorter period. If he postponed to June 19 and the weather were bad then, then one's talking about a postponement of an entire month—you'd lose a month of campaigning; the security might be breached. It was a nightmarish situation for Eisenhower.

Then at 21:30 on the evening of the fourth, at Southwick House, a weather briefing suggested that there might be a 36-hour respite after all, a brief break in the weather on the night and morning of June 5–June 6. A cheer went up from the gentlemen at Southwick House. As one person who was present said, he'd never seen so many middle-aged men cheer as vigorously at one time as when Stagg brought the news about this possible weather break. In fact, Stagg was quite certain about it.

The pressure on Eisenhower at this moment was intense. Leigh-Mallory, in charge of air operations, urged postponement. Air Marshal Tedder, Eisenhower's deputy commander, agreed. It was simply too dicey to undertake air operations if the weather was going to be this chancy. Eisenhower turned to Montgomery and asked him. And Montgomery, ever ready for this sort of thing, said, "I would say, go." Eisenhower paced the room and then decided. Overlord, the largest, most complex, and diciest amphibious assault in human history—an assault on which the outcome of the war would ride—would be launched on June 6 in weather conditions that boded only ill. It was a gamble of astronomical proportions.

When Eisenhower awoke at 03:30 on June 5, the wind was literally shaking his trailer. Rain fell in sheets, and the storm continued to rage. At a weather briefing, Stagg arrived with good news. He insisted, despite all of the conditions that Eisenhower and everyone present could see—the howling wind, the rain coming in sheets—Stagg absolutely insisted that the weather was going to break, and added a new note: It would only be a break, and then conditions would deteriorate again. The operation would have, at most—at most—48 hours of reasonably good weather.

Already the ship convoys had been forming up since midnight, and the men were forced to ride out the storm bobbing in the heavy surf. At this point Eisenhower could still have ordered a postponement, and, at a last briefing with his staff while the rain continued to pelt against the window, Eisenhower, supported once again by Montgomery, made the final decision. "OK," he said simply. "Let's go."

Eisenhower drafted a message to the troops of the Allied expeditionary force that is one of the most powerful and moving documents of the Second World War. This was to be given to all troops involved in the Normandy landings. "Soldiers, sailors, and airmen of the Allied expeditionary force, you are about to embark upon the great crusade toward which we have striven these many months. The eyes of the world are upon you. The hopes and prayers of liberty-loving people everywhere march with you. In company with our brave allies and brothers in arms on other fronts, you will bring about the destruction of the German war machine, the elimination of Nazi tyranny over the oppressed peoples of Europe, and security for ourselves in a free world. Your task will not be an easy one. Your enemy is well trained, well equipped, and battle-hardened. He will fight savagely. But this is the year 1944. Much has happened since the Nazi triumphs of 1940–41. The United Nations have inflicted upon the Germans great defeats in open battle, man to man. Our air offensive has seriously reduced

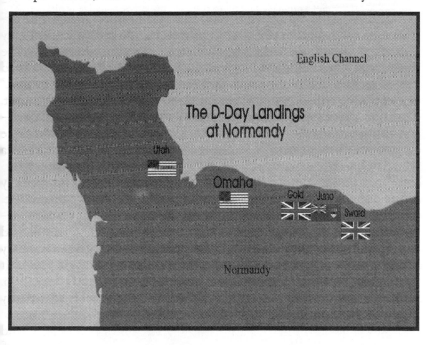

D-Day, June 6, 1944. The Allies aimed to punch holes in Hitler's "Atlantic Wall." Six Allied combat divisions penetrated the German network of traps and fortifications to open the continent for the massive invasion that was the beginning of the end of World War II. Americans stormed beaches code-named "Omaha" and "Utah," while the Canadians took "Juno," and the British handled "Sword" and "Gold" beaches. More than 200,000 troops took part to cut off the vital port of Cherbourg on the Cotentin Peninsula from the rest of Nazi-held France.

After the beachhead at Normandy had been secured, the Allies began moving massive amounts of troops, equipment, and supplies onto mainland Europe.

their strength in the air and their capacity to wage war on the ground. Our home fronts have given us an overwhelming superiority in weapons and munitions of war and placed at our disposal great reserves of trained fighting men. The tide has turned. The free men of the world are marching together to victory. I have full confidence in your courage, devotion to duty, and skill in battle. We will accept nothing less than full victory. Good luck, and let us all beseech the blessings of Almighty God upon this great and noble undertaking. Dwight Eisenhower."

Eisenhower, in these terribly tense moments on the eve of D-Day, also drafted a second message. He put it in his pocket. He wrote:

"Our landings in the Cherbourg–Le Havre area have failed to gain the satisfactory foothold, and I have withdrawn the troops. My decision to attack was based on the best information available. The troops, the air and navy, did all that bravery and devotion to duty could do. If any blame or fault attaches to the attempt, it is mine alone."

That was a message that he desperately hoped he would never have to print.

At 19:00 hours on the June 5, Eisenhower would visit the 101st Airborne units. They were to be among the first to land in Normandy. The die was now cast, the invasion was about to begin, the machinery was all in place, the ships underway. The great moment had at last arrived. ∎

The preceding lecture was an excerpt drawn from The Great Course:

World War II: A Military and Social History
Course #810

This course examines the greatest conflict in history, the Second World War. Between 1937 and 1945 approximately 55 million people perished in this series of interrelated conflicts. No continent was left untouched, no ocean or sea unaffected.

Lecture Titles

1. The Origins of the Second World War
2. Hitler's Challenge to the International System, 1933–1936
3. The Failure of the International System
4. The Coming of War
5. Blitzkrieg
6. The German Offensive in the West
7. "Their Finest Hour"—Britain Alone
8. The Battle of Britain
9. Hitler Moves East
10. The Germans Before Moscow
11. The War in Asia
12. The Japanese Gamble
13. The Height of Japanese Power
14. Turning the Tide in the Pacific—Midway and Guadalcanal
15. The War in North Africa
16. War in the Mediterranean—The Invasions of Sicily and Italy
17. Stalingrad—The Turning Point on the Eastern Front
18. **Eisenhower and Operation Overlord**
19. D-Day to Paris
20. Operation Market Garden and the Battle of the Bulge
21. Advance Across the Pacific
22. Turning Point in the Southwest Pacific—Leyte Gulf and the Philippines
23. The Final Drive for Japan—Iwo Jima, Okinawa, and the Fire-Bombing of Tokyo
24. War in the Air
25. Hitler's New Order in Europe
26. "The Man's Army"
27. Daily Life, Culture, and Society in Wartime
28. The Race for Berlin
29. Truman, the Bomb, and the End of the War in the Pacific
30. The Costs of War

Thomas Childers

Thomas Childers is Professor of History at the University of Pennsylvania, where he has been teaching for over 25 years. He received his Bachelor's and Master's degrees from the University of Tennessee and earned his Ph.D. in History from Harvard University.

Professor Childers has won several teaching awards, including the Ira T. Abrahms Award for Distinguished Teaching and Challenging Teaching in the Arts and Sciences, the Richard S. Dunn Award for Distinguished Teaching in History, and the Senior Class Award for Excellence in Undergraduate Teaching.

If you would like to order this course, please contact us at:
Phone: 1-800-TEACH-12
Web: www.TEACH12.com
For more information on our pricing policy, see page 245.

The History of the United States, 2nd Edition
Course #8500
Lecture 3

Taught by: Professor Allen C. Guelzo
Gettysburg College

Gentlemen
in the Wilderness

In 1606, a group of promoters in London and Plymouth obtained a charter from England's new king, James I, and organized itself under the title of the Virginia Company.

For their first settlement they chose the coast of modern day Maine at a place they called Popham, which, they supposed, had the same climate as England because it was on the same latitude. The winter of 1606 showed them just how wrong they were about the weather in Maine, and the settlement folded in 1608.

A second settlement, Jamestown, was planted at the same time by the company on the Chesapeake Bay along the James River—named in honor of the king. Because the Chesapeake lay along the same latitude as the Mediterranean, it was assumed that its climate would be as sunny and healthy as Italy's and that the Indians would be friendly and welcoming. Instead, the site of the Virginia Company's colony was marshy, humid, and fever-ridden; and the Powhatan Tribal Confederacy, which dominated the region, was already well-soured on Europeans.

On top of these surprises, there was a certain lack of focus as to what the purpose of Jamestown was supposed to be. Of the first 104 Jamestown settlers, more than half of them were classified as gentlemen. In other words, they were semi-aristocrats who thought that their chief purpose was to serve as the garrison of a military outpost intended for raiding the Spanish. This meant that, like any other military outpost, they expected to be supplied from England, or to supply themselves by "requisition" or theft from the Indians, but not to have to raise their own sustenance with their own hands. The problem was that the Indians were surly and uncooperative, and the Virginia Company was too under-capitalized to keep up adequate supplies.

Consequently, within the first year of Jamestown, disease, malnutrition, and Indian conflict had eliminated half of Jamestown's settlers. Only the arrival of the infrequent supply ships kept the settlement from starving, and only the imposition of draconian discipline on these gentlemen—who preferred loafing, prospecting for gold, and dreaming of the northwest passage to grubbing in the Earth to feed themselves—kept Jamestown from winking out.

Then, in 1622, the roof fell in for Virginia and for Jamestown. The Powhatan tribes staged a skillfully planned mass attack on Jamestown and the other English settlements along the James River, and the Powhatans came within an ace of wiping out the entire English population along the James. The blow destroyed the Virginia Company. Poor Virginia Company; it had never yet paid a single dividend to its investors, and in 1624, King James I revoked the charter he had granted them and declared the settlements under direct royal control.

Now, royal control does not mean what you might think it means. The king was more interested in punishing the Virginia Company than in rescuing Virginia, and he confined his attention to sending a royal governor to Virginia to manage affairs there or to wind them up completely. Characteristically, the king provided the governor with neither salary nor support, which meant that the governor had to call together the settlers in a general assembly of burgesses in order to weasel tax

Named for King James I, the Jamestown settlement was plagued by salty tidal river water unsuitable for drinking, mosquitoes, and little space to expand.

money out of them. Thus, entirely without planning, and entirely without intention, Virginia created the first legislature in America.

The crown also took no interest in reinforcing the Virginia settlements with drafts of new settlers. To the contrary, if the crown sent anybody to Virginia, it was usually assorted gangs of England's various criminals, unemployed and unwanted, and all of those categories in English life in the 17th century were vast. This form of benign neglect does not look, at first blush, as much of an improvement over the Virginia Company's incompetent attention. Because of this the imposition of royal control did not mean a whole lot; in fact, might have meant something less than control and direction from the Virginia Company meant.

What it did, however, turn out to mean was that royal control and benign neglect meant that things could happen in America that might not be able to happen in England. Therefore, Virginia and the Chesapeake Bay turned out to have an unanticipated attraction to a number of peculiar segments of English society, such as English Catholics. On paper, England was a Protestant nation, and all of its subjects were required under pain of law to be baptized into the Church of England and to subscribe to its Protestant beliefs.

But a number of English Catholics refused to abandon the old faith. That immediately made them subject to investigation and persecution. This was because loyalty to Catholicism was, in effect, loyalty to the identity of England's enemies. Clinging to Catholicism in 1600 was a little like broadcasting your allegiance to Communism or certain international terrorist organizations.

On the other hand, after some initial scares in the 1560s, Elizabeth—and her successor, James—preferred to take a "don't ask, don't tell" attitude toward English Catholics. This was better than outright persecution for the Catholics, but not by much. Given the even more distant attitude that the crown took toward the settlements in Virginia, it soon dawned on English Catholics that they might be able to get even greater freedom for themselves by planting a settlement on the Chesapeake Bay. There, benign neglect could be practiced by the crown toward the settlers' religion, as well as toward their survival.

In 1624, George Calvert, the first Lord Baltimore, converted to Catholicism and devoted the rest of his life to planting a settlement in North America, where his fellow Catholics could establish a colony, be true and loyal Englishmen, yet practice Catholicism freely out from under the watchful eye of Protestant officials. Calvert's first brief and unsuccessful effort at organizing a settlement was known as Avalon. He made the mistake of locating Avalon in Newfoundland, again on

THE THIRTEEN COLONIES
NEW HAMPSHIRE · MASSACHUSETTS · CONNECTICUT
RHODE ISLAND · NEW YORK · NEW JERSEY · PENNSYLVANIA
DELAWARE · MARYLAND · VIRGINIA · NORTH CAROLINA
SOUTH CAROLINA · GEORGIA

A map showing the boundaries of the 13 colonies. Some had been started as havens for religious groups persecuted in England, others as experiments in politics or charity.

the assumption that the climate of Newfoundland would be about like that of England. As anyone from Newfoundland can tell you, it isn't.

After that, the Calvert family obtained the charter for land on the Chesapeake. In 1634, Cecilius Calvert, the second Lord Baltimore, planted a settlement; they named it St. Mary's City, which eventually became Maryland.

Not only religious dissidents took courage from the opportunities offered by benign neglect. In 1625, King James I died and was succeeded by his son, Charles I, a bull-headed and unreflective monarch with a talent for outraging almost every part of English political life. In 1642, the English Parliament finally had enough of King Charles I, overthrew him, and briefly converted England into a republic. The republic lasted only until 1660 when, through mismanagement and uncertainty, a much-chastened Parliament agreed to recall Charles's son as king and revert back to a monarchy.

In 1632, George Calvert, first Lord Baltimore, sent his son Leonard and 300 settlers from their home in bitter Newfoundland in search of warmer land.

The taste of republican rule took the halo off kingly government, though. It set the most radical English political thinkers wondering whether monarchy was not, after all, handed down from God, but was simply another human-created form of political organization that could be taken down, reorganized, or set up according to how well it benefited the people.

No one had a very clear idea of what a working alternative to monarchy might look like. The indifference the crown continued to show to affairs in North America, however, suggested that—with enough financial backing—America might be a good place to experiment in new political arrangements.

In 1663—shortly after the restoration of King Charles II—a group of wealthy noblemen, looking for profits, joined hands with several well-placed political radicals and obtained a charter from King Charles II to organize a settlement south of Virginia, which they very prudently named, in honor of the king, Carolina; then, they set out to organize a colony that would be a political rather than a religious experiment.

Naming the colony Carolina was almost the last nod in the direction of monarchy made by the Carolina proprietors. For the political organization of their settlement, the proprietors hired the philosopher and radical political theorist John Locke to draw up the settlement's fundamental constitutions.

Now, it can't be said that what Locke devised looks like popular democratic government, but it also looked like nothing anyone had seen in England, either. Locke devised a three-tiered society for Carolina. At the top were the eight proprietors.

Below them were the gentry, who were actually classes of gentry with some very peculiar titles and names thrown in just to spice things up. At the bottom were the small landowners and the planters.

The proprietors, according to Locke's fundamental constitutions, would constitute what he called the Palatine Court. In other words, the proprietors would be both Supreme Legislature and Supreme Court all wrapped up into one. They would be assisted by a grand council whose job it was to compose all legislation, and to join with a popularly elected assembly who would have the power to veto the actions of the grand council. The Church of England would be the official church of Carolina, but anyone who believed in God, including Jews, would be allowed reasonably free religious practice.

In 1624, George Calvert, the first Lord Baltimore, converted to Catholicism and devoted the rest of his life to planting a settlement in North America.

In this way, Carolina came to life as an experiment, an alternative political theory. Think of it, if you will, as the 17th-century version of a counterculture. Nothing, however, in Carolina looked as strange as what developed in Georgia. If what we're seeing in the development of these colonies is—in the absence of crown interest and crown control—the growth of some very exotic experiments in politics, nothing in America matches Georgia.

Georgia was actually the last of the English North American settlements. It was not chartered until 1732, when it was founded by General James Oglethorpe, along with 20 others.

If Carolina was to be an experiment in radical politics, Georgia was intended to be an experiment in benevolence. Oglethorpe was an example of the new sensibility in English culture in the 1700s, the sensibility of social charity. Oglethorpe's plan for Georgia was to create what amounted to a gigantic poor farm for England's unwanted, homeless, debtors, and ne'er-do-wells. Oglethorpe's dream was that, once relocated to Georgia, these "unprofitables" would magically become prosperous and self-sufficient. In order to ensure that transition, however, these settlers would have to be not merely governed but managed.

Oglethorpe and his associates governed Georgia, not as proprietors, not as a legislature, not even as governors: They took for themselves the name of trustees. They banned the sale of liquor; they banned the sale and use of slaves. They even interviewed candidates for relocation to ensure that they were of the deserving poor, not just any one of the gutter low-lifes. It had to be those who deserved charity. Needless to say, there was no legislature in Georgia. Why would there need to be? The trustees already knew what was best for the people, and if that knowledge is fuelled by the best of intentions, who needs any second opinions from the people you're practicing it on?

Oglethorpe's plan for Georgia was to create what amounted to a gigantic poor farm for England's unwanted, homeless, debtors, and ne'er-do-wells. Oglethorpe's dream was that, once relocated to Georgia, these "unprofitables" would magically become prosperous and self-sufficient.

Well, this was, in its own way, as bizarre a departure from English practice as Locke's fundamental constitutions, as Calvert's Catholic colony, even the Virginia burgesses. To the surprise of all beholders, almost all of these settlements achieved some measure of success. In fact, in colonial North America, it was almost an inverse proportion between the oddity of the settlement and its likelihood for success. The more odd a settlement might be, at least by English standards, the more likely the colony would turn out successful.

I mean, Virginia, after all of its ups and downs, became the most successful colony of all by stumbling, very much by accident, onto the discovery that Virginia could grow an outstandingly fine strain of tobacco, which—in the 1600s—was another prime European luxury. Carolina discovered that its lowland climate was suited perfectly for the growing of high profit cash crops like rice and indigo. ∎

James Oglethorpe was an English general and the founder of Georgia. Appalled by the conditions of England's debtor prisons, he founded the colony of Georgia with the intention of populating it with England's poor.

The preceding lecture was an excerpt drawn from The Great Course:

The History of the United States, 2nd Edition
Course #8500

This is the story of a country in which immigrants of the late 19th and early 20th centuries huddled in cramped tenement apartments lit by hazardous kerosene lamps. And a country that, little more than a half-century later, a renowned economist described as The Affluent Society.
This is the chronicle of a nation that enslaved an entire race of people to perform its labor. And of a nation that fought a Civil War that freed its slaves, and outlawed segregation and discrimination.
This is history shaped by Revolutionary War and Vietnam, Thomas Jefferson and William Jefferson Clinton, Puritanism and Feminism, Booker T. Washington and Martin Luther King, Jamestown and Disneyland, Harpers Ferry and Henry Ford, oil wells and Orson Welles.
This is a review of the extraordinary blend of people, ideas, inventions, and events that comprise **The History of the United States, 2nd Edition.**

Allen C. Guelzo

Professor Allen C. Guelzo is Henry R. Luce Professor of the Civil War Era and Professor of History at Gettysburg College. He is formerly Dean of the Templeton Honors College and the Grace F. Kea Professor of American History at Eastern University. He holds an M.A. and a Ph.D. in History from the University of Pennsylvania, an M.Div. from Philadelphia Theological Seminary, and an honorary doctorate in history from Lincoln College in Illinois.

Professor Guelzo's essays, reviews, and articles have appeared in publications ranging from the *American Historical Review* and *The Wilson Quarterly* to newspapers such as T*he Philadelphia Inquirer* and *The Wall Street Journal*. In 2000, his book *Abraham Lincoln: Redeemer President* won both the Lincoln Prize and the Abraham Lincoln Institute Prize; and in 2005, his book *Lincoln's Emancipation Proclamation: The End of Slavery in America* won both prizes again, making him the first double Lincoln Laureate in the history of both prizes.

Professor Guelzo has received several teaching and writing awards, including the American Library Association Choice Award, The Albert C. Outler Prize in Ecumenical Church History, and the Dean's Award for Distinguished Graduate Teaching at the University of Pennsylvania.

Lecture Titles

If you would like to order this course, please contact us at:

Phone: 1-800-TEACH-12

Web: www.TEACH12.com

For more information on our pricing policy, see page 245.

Taught by: Professor Thomas Childers
University of Pennsylvania

The Rise of Napoleon

In 1795, a young military man by the name of Napoleon Bonaparte was ordered to put down the Parisian mob that was storming the Tuileries Palace. Napoleon, already in 1795, would demonstrate the combination of ambition and ruthlessness that would characterize his entire career.

As the mob advanced on the Tuileries, Napoleon, without blinking an eye, ordered his troops to fire into the crowd. The crowd quickly dispersed; this potential threat to the Directory, then the French government, was repulsed.

Where had this man come from? How had he arrived at this particular juncture in history? He had been born in Corsica, the second son in a gentry family, and following the traditional aristocratic pattern, the second son winds up with a career in the military. He had attended military academies in France. These somewhat humble origins would be one of Napoleon's great calling cards; Napoleon would become a great champion of the self-made man. He would become the idol of a great many people, commoners who saw in Napoleon the possibilities of what a man of talent, what a man blessed with ability, with ambition, could do if he were unfettered by the structures of the old regime.

He also, however, was a very savvy man politically. He married a politically well-connected widow, Josephine de Beauharnais, whose aristocratic husband had been killed during the terror. He was best known, however, for a string of very extraordinary military victories in 1796–97. In those years, he conquered all of northern Italy, forcing the Habsburgs to relinquish their territories there, and to seek control of the Netherlands as well. He also headed a military expedition to Egypt, seeking to weaken the British position there, and although his campaign in Egypt did not produce the results that he had hoped, he

Was Napoleon Bonaparte French or Italian? In 1768, France took possession of Corsica from Genoa. Napoleon's detractors declared him Genoese, stating his birth year as 1768, not 1769. No serious proof was ever delivered to the contrary.

did achieve a series of very striking military victories. This was given very great coverage in France. This was not only a military expedition; he took, in effect, what we now would think of as a public relations staff with him that monitored his every move.

These dramatic victories in Egypt and in northern Italy had made Napoleon a household name in France. By 1799, as the Directory continued to lose support and just was absolutely unable to inspire any sort of enthusiasm, Napoleon had become very well known and popular across all the country. In November of 1799, a number of the members of the Directory turned to Napoleon to help them establish some sort of stable government, capable of withstanding the recurrent threats of renewed radicalism and revived royalism. Two members of the Directory approached Napoleon and plotted with him and his brother Louis to overthrow the weak government and establish some form of stronger regime capable of charting a new course for France.

This coup would take place on November 9, 1799. The new government that was established called for power to be shared by three consuls. You already see terminology that's not harkening back to the French Revolution, nor even to the old regime, but consuls harkening back to the Roman Empire. Power was to be shared by a triumvirate, and Napoleon was to be first consul, *primus inter pares*—first among equals.

The Napoleonic Code would become one of the great achievements of his regime, implemented not only in France, but also in the countries of Europe occupied by the French armies.

Two things were already very clear about him at this point. One was his enormous ambition, and the other was his great charisma. One had seen this in his dealings with the troops—his troops in northern Italy, his troops in Egypt—and also, all sorts of contemporary evidence suggests that in dealing with people individually he exerted an enormous amount of charm, power, and charisma. It was hardly a mystery that he would very quickly outmaneuver his two partners in this triumvirate, as well as the legislative bodies of the regime.

In 1802, Napoleon had himself elected consul for life. And in a step that was really quite remarkable and was a preview of the way Napoleon wanted to reign, this step was to be ratified by a national plebiscite. The people were now called in to vote to ratify this step taken by the regime, taken by Napoleon. The outcome of the vote was 3,568,885 in favor, 8,374 against. One might suspect that there was a certain amount of manipulation and influence brought to bear on the outcome, but Napoleon was quite clearly very popular in France at this time.

In 1804, he used a trumped-up royalist plot to declare himself emperor. He claimed that there was a conspiracy to return the Bourbon monarchy, to overthrow the Revolution. Napoleon constantly talked about the Revolution, and even the Republic at times, and saw great danger. But he always tried to present himself on the one hand as a military man, a man of affairs, a pragmatist in some ways, but also as the legitimate heir of the Revolution. Once again, this step was ratified by a plebiscite, and the first line of this new constitutional document read: "The government of the Republic is entrusted to an Emperor."

What's interesting here are the resonances of the old Roman Empire. What sort of empire was this? What sort of state was this to be? Was he, as Napoleon claimed, the legitimate heir of the Revolution, or was he, as his critics certainly claimed, simply a military tyrant, reminiscent of the worst aspects of the Roman Empire? Or does his regime represent a really uniquely new political synthesis of both democratic forms and authoritarian control?

To answer these questions, we need to turn to the basic elements of the regime itself: its constitution, its administration, the domestic achievements of the regime. The Constitution of 1791 had been based on universal suffrage. In this sense, it's consistent with the Revolution, the Great Revolution, but elections were very indirect. There was universal suffrage to elect electors, who would then elect a final legislature. This was the usual kind of compromised solution. The use of the plebiscite was novel; it gave Napoleon's regime a patina not only of democracy, but of radical democracy, almost the general will speaking through the plebiscites. If one thinks about the period, this is absolutely a remarkable sort of phenomenon, of going directly to the people to say "Yea" or "Nay" to major matters of state.

Napoleon also insisted upon the codification of law; the Napoleonic Code would become one of the great achievements of his regime, implemented not only in France, but also in the countries of Europe occupied by the French armies. That new code imposed upon France a uniform system of justice. It called for equality before the law. This was a major step. One thing that equality before the law meant to the Napoleonic regime was that no one would be tax-exempt. All French citizens were now going to bear the financial burdens of state. Freedom of religion was guaranteed under the new constitution; Protestants would be able to practice their religion, and Napoleon took steps to emancipate the Jews. This had been done initially during the Revolution itself in the first constitution. Napoleon would take additional steps in this direction.

The new constitution also called for freedom of profession. This doesn't sound very revolutionary, but it was. It dealt the final death-blow to the old guilds, and it was a bow toward the new forces of commercial capitalism and industrialization in France. What it did was to signal to liberal economic elements that this was going to be a regime that would adopt policies that were favorable to business, favorable to trade, to commerce, to break whatever residual powers lingered of the old guild system in France.

What's also very significant about this is that Napoleon bothered at all even to have a constitution. For Napoleon, it was quite clear the genie could not be put back in the bottle; the Revolution had happened. Still, Napoleon believed you could not have a legitimate government, post-Revolution, without a constitution. His regime was built on a claim to popular sovereignty, embedded in the constitution, embedded in the elections, embedded in the plebiscites, all of which gave to this Napoleonic regime a very radical, progressive bent.

Napoleon also would continue a policy that had really been emphasized during the Revolution: an emphasis on education. Napoleon would create the system of *lycées* under close government supervision, and this emphasis was on educating people so they could read; so they could participate; so they could be citizens.

This was also part of one of the other great social claims of the Napoleonic regime. This was to be a regime in which careers were open to talent. It wasn't heredity, it wasn't connections, it was none of that. What really mattered was the man of talent, the man of ability, willing to take chances and to achieve.

His opponents claimed that Napoleon was really a dictator, if one with great popular support. Certainly the system was maintained by secret police and very strict censorship.

The regime also instituted a reform of the French administration. A rational, centralized administration was created under Napoleon. He created a very efficient system of taxation, not a very exciting sort of reform, but obviously, considering the history of France in the 18th century, it was absolutely essential. He returned France to a system of centralized administration, where local officials were appointed from Paris. In fact, under Napoleon, one sees the most centralized of all of the various French regimes of the 18th century and into the 19th century. In addition to these initiatives, though, and possibly one of the most important, if not the most important, in terms of sealing Napoleon's popularity at home, was his establishment of peace with the church.

After a decade in which relations between the various French revolutionaries and the church were strained, to put it mildly, Napoleon was determined to restore good relations with the papacy, to bring the church back into the mainstream of French political life. In 1801, he signed a concordant with the Vatican, with Pius VII, in which the Napoleonic regime recognized Catholicism as "the religion of the majority of French people." It was not to be the state religion; the constitution that would be drafted called for freedom of religion—but it acknowledged that Catholicism was the religion of the majority of the French people. This concordant with the Vatican was enormously popular in France.

These aspects of the regime certainly solidified Napoleon's hold on the population. But if these factors were consistent with the Revolution, other aspects of this Napoleonic regime were not. His opponents claimed that Napoleon was really a dictator, if one with great popular support. Certainly the system was maintained by secret police and very strict censorship. The number of newspapers in Paris shrank from 73 in 1799 to 13, and then down to four. They were closely censored by the regime. Secret agents supervised the press and the arts under Napoleon. Surveillance of enemies was common, and arrest of enemies or potential enemies was also commonplace. One also sees a somewhat chilling development here, which was that some opponents or potential opponents of Napoleon were arrested or taken into a kind of protective custody, and then sent off to mental institutions—not prisons, but mental institutions.

Still, for whatever oppressive qualities this Napoleonic regime displayed, the Napoleonic Empire was enormously popular in France, certainly down to 1812–13. Most of the population clearly believed that the regime had consolidated the most positive gains made during the Revolution. In addition to this, Napoleon had restored grandeur to France. Paris had once again become the center of Western civilization. The grandeur of empire, the military glory of French armies marching over the breadth of the European continent—all of these things cemented Napoleon's popularity in France. ∎

The preceding lecture was an excerpt drawn from The Great Course:

Europe and Western Civilization in the Modern Age
Course #820

Three lifetimes ago, Europe was a farming society ruled by families
of monarchs.
Modern European history began with two seismic tremors—capitalism and democracy—that shattered Europe's foundations.
In the decades after 1750, the Industrial Revolution in England
thrust aside the old economic order and introduced modern industrial capitalism. The French Revolution of 1789–99 swept away the
Ancien Regime in France and threatened entrenched elites everywhere in Europe.

Thomas Childers

Thomas Childers is Professor of History at the University of Pennsylvania,
where he has been teaching for over 25 years. He received his Bachelor's
and Master's degrees from the University of Tennessee and earned his
Ph.D. in History from Harvard University.

In addition to his position at Penn, Professor Childers has held visiting
professorships at Trinity Hall College, Cambridge, Smith College, and
Swarthmore College. He is a popular lecturer abroad as well, in London,
Oxford, Berlin, and Munich.

Professor Childers has won several teaching awards, including the Ira T.
Abrahms Award for Distinguished Teaching and Challenging Teaching
in the Arts and Sciences, the Richard S. Dunn Award for Distinguished
Teaching in History, and the Senior Class Award for Excellence in Undergraduate Teaching.

Professor Childers is the author and editor of several books on modern
German history and the Second World War. The first volume of his trilogy
on the Second World War, *Wings of Morning: The Story of the Last American Bomber Shot Down over Germany in World War II*, was praised by
Jonathan Yardley in *The Washington Post* as "a powerful and unselfconsciously beautiful book."

Lecture Titles

If you would like to order this course, please contact us at:

Phone: 1-800-TEACH-12
Web: www.TEACH12.com

For more information on our pricing policy, see page 245.

Taught by: Professor Kenneth Bartlett
University of Toronto

The Prince of Urbino

Of all the Renaissance principalities, Urbino really is in a category of its own. It is one of the most remarkable of all the Italian states, and one whose culture and experience resonates to this day.

And it's an improbable one because Urbino is a tiny, tiny principality—only 40 miles square, perched on the top of the Apennines—20 miles from the Adriatic. Almost inaccessible in the Renaissance, it is a strange place for a rich culture to develop.

Urbino is in the Marche, which formed part of the papal states. It was largely left alone by the popes because of the difficulty in imposing any kind of order on the powerful princes that ruled within them in these inaccessible mountaintop areas. The rulers of Urbino, nevertheless, were still papal vicars. They took their sovereignty from the pope, and they ruled in the pope's name. And it may have just been one of the many, many small principalities of Italy had it not been for the career of one family. Governed stably since the Middle Ages by the Montefeltro family, Urbino benefited from genius. And if the Italian Renaissance is the exercise of genius in an environment that is socially, politically, and economically structured to allow genius to take place, Urbino really was a perfect model of this cultural experiment.

The Montefeltro princes of Urbino were necessarily mercenary captains, *condottieri*, an occupation directly resulting from their geographical and social circumstances. The rocky soil of the Apennines could not produce sufficient agriculture to feed even a small population. It was impossible to get rich by trade because it was in the middle of nowhere. There were no natural resources, except for the strength, the resilience, the power of the citizens of this state. They were hearty mountaineers. They were tough, ideal soldiers; and they were committed and loyal to their prince, the Montefeltro.

As it happened, most Italian warfare took place during the Renaissance through *condottieri* and mercenary armies. The Italian states

High atop the Apennines lies the tiny domain of Urbino, where Renaissance painter Raphael was born. His work is featured prominently in many of Urbino's museums.

tended not to fight with citizen armies because it was not only inefficient, but it wasn't really the tradition of Italy at this time—at least north of the Alps. The mercenaries earned their living by fighting other people's wars, and doing so often with a degree of elegance and a degree of success. And of these, the Montefeltros were amongst the very best.

Federigo da Montefeltro, in a very long rule from 1444 to 1482, became known justly as the "Light of Italy," the greatest prince of his age. He was someone who took being a mercenary captain and the ruler of a tiny, obscure, poor principality and transformed it into a moment of great elegance and a moment of cultural history that still is with us.

As a *condottieri*, his necessary profession was to bear arms, and he was invincible. He never lost a single battle and always sought to preserve the lives of his soldiers. One of the curious things about mercenary warfare in Renaissance Italy was that hardly anyone got hurt. Since battles were fought by mercenaries, if your soldiers were killed, there went your capital. You had nothing to fight with and became impoverished and extremely exposed. So, mercenary captain fought mercenary captain in a way so that nobody really got hurt. It was more choreography than warfare.

The whole point was to be left in control of a field. The army that was forced to withdraw was the loser; the army that held the field was the winner. But it was done largely without much loss of life, which happened occasionally and usually accidentally.

The Duke and Duchess of Urbino perfectly complemented each other. Both were highly educated with a keen interest in the pursuit of the arts and an appreciation for civil affairs.

Federigo was not only a brilliant military captain, he was also a man of unimpeachable honor, a man of integrity in a profession where there was virtually none. He was honest. He refused to betray a client by switching for higher pay. And this was another way that mercenary warfare took place. Rather than fight your enemy, you simply outbid him and offered more money to the *condottieri* fighting for your enemy so that he would switch sides, leaving him without an army.

Now, this kind of economic warfare was engaged in by almost every mercenary captain except for Federigo. There's a very famous story that the Republic of Venice, at a particularly dangerous moment, feared that this might happen and unilaterally offered him a higher wage. Federigo sent it back, saying that his honor was worth more than all of their gold. He also charged huge fees—enormous fees—more than any other mercenary captain. As a retainer, if you simply wanted to make sure he would not fight against you, you paid him 65,000 ducats a year. If he actually fought on your behalf, 165,000—a huge amount—but you knew if you had Federigo on your side, it was a sure thing.

He served three popes, two kings of Naples, two dukes of Milan, the Venetian Republic, the Florentine Republic, and never once betrayed his client. He was decorated with every military honor. The pope made him a Knight of the Ermine. He was given the decorations of almost every Italian state and principality. Even the king of England gave him the Order of the Garter, something he wore proudly in the official portrait by Berruguete or Justus van Ghent.

Federigo also realized what war was. He was a professional soldier, and so one of his main policies—one that he never compromised—was to not let war get anywhere near his beloved Urbino. Part of the protection of the state was not just the topography but also the fact that Federigo made it clear that Urbino itself was not to be attacked.

He also took care of his army, his soldiers. If a soldier should get injured or killed, he made sure that the daughters of that family would be provided with dowries so they could marry honorably. When he was in the city, he was a model prince. He spent every morning walking unarmed and unattended through the city, stopping in its shops and asking about the state of the economy and whether there was something he could do better; whether there was something he needed, in fact, to do. This provided a sense of unity and commitment on the part of the people to the prince, and a commitment on the part of the prince to his people.

He spent the afternoons sitting in his garden, always available to solve disputes: both high-level disputes amongst important citizens and simple squabbles between neighbors. All citizens, regardless of rank or wealth, regardless of their importance to the prince, were treated equally.

He demanded, for example, that a merchant whose bill he simply forgot to pay, sue him. And he served the writ upon himself as an example for others, saying that not even he who was the law was above it, and that all citizens should remember their duty, a sense of responsibility that they owe to one another. In times of surplus, he purchased grain so that he could then distribute it at cost during times of famine. He was greatly beloved, and was seen as almost the perfect prince.

Although he knew he was destined for a military career, he still had the advantage of a superb humanist education. He studied with the greatest schoolmaster, Vittorino da Feltre. He knew his classical sources extraordinarily well. His academic interests were particularly history—because he saw that history was the example of great men that he would have to emulate, if not surpass—but also philosophy. He loved abstraction, and he was sufficiently flexible to enjoy both Aristotle and Plato together. He was a remarkable man, especially for a professional soldier.

His love of ideas, his love of culture, and his love of history drove him to create one of the great libraries of the Renaissance. Books were his great passion, and he fulfilled this passion using the profits he made from war. The library that Federigo amassed in his palace of Urbino was the greatest outside of Florence and Rome. He engaged the very finest copyists to go out and to find the very best examples of classical works, and then copy them so that he would have these excellent models in his library.

When he was first establishing the library, he kept 30 copyists employed for 14 years, copying the very finest Greek and Latin manuscripts then known. He also loved beautiful bindings, and these books were bound in ways that we can still appreciate through the portrait left of him. He had the bindings with his coats of arms on them so that everybody thereafter would know that this beautiful book was made for him. And he appreciated books that were beautiful in themselves.

One of the most beautiful books that survives to this day, often displayed in the Vatican library where it is now, is the Urbino Bible. This enormous two-volume collection of the Old and New Testament was written in purple and gold. It has miniatures by the workshop of the Ghirlandaio. It is a splendid and magnificent book with all of the attributes of ducal rule: the purple and the gold, the illustrations, the binding, and this in the book that he found most important, the Bible.

One of his favorite portraits depicts him in his library with his young son, in full armor wearing the Order of the Garter, but reading a book. It is, in fact, a curious image of a mercenary captain, one whose mind is engaged not in war, and plunder, and the possibility of power, but in the expansion and cultivation of his mind. It was appropriate that Federigo have a place to not only celebrate, but to indulge in his wonderful life of the mind and life of culture when he wasn't working as a mercenary captain outside of Urbino. He needed a grand palace, an appropriate place to house his library and his court, which was becoming larger and more sophisticated.

He began to build a huge palace in 1468 on a promontory in the Apennines in the center of Urbino, where it stands to this day, virtually—on the outside anyway—unchanged. It seems to grow from the very rock on which it's situated, and it becomes a pinnacle, both of power and also almost a kind of Platonic mediation between heaven and Earth. He engaged a fortress architect named Luciano Laurana to build it. And it's a strange building the first time you see it because of its cylindrical towers and its small windows, almost a *condottieri* fortress, which you would expect from a mercenary prince.

But then if you look more closely and you look at the deep recesses of the balconies and the elements of decoration, you realize it's also a pleasure dome. The building is almost an outward and visible sign of his personality and character: *condottieri* military captain and—at the same time—cultivated, humanist scholar.

The interior is where he lavished most of his wealth and most of his interest, and it was spectacular. He took the elements of architectural decoration and turned them into splendid works of art. This is especially true of the doors, doorframes, and the fireplaces. He had the finest artists and architects make them. Indeed, the use of in laid wood is such that no less a figure than Lorenzo de' Medici sent artists to Urbino to copy them so he could enjoy them in his own library in Florence.

Federigo also filled the palace with things that meant a great deal to him on a personal level that helped to stimulate his intellectual interests. He was interested in art and painting, and very interested in mathematics. He invited northern artists such as the Fleming Justus van Ghent, and the Spaniard Pedro Berruguete, as well as great Italian painters, the most famous being Piero della Francesca, to come paint for him. He wanted his portrait to be a reflection of who he really was. There is absolutely no sense of him being flattered. Indeed, his image is a curious one. Early in his career, he was blinded in one eye during a tournament, and afraid that he would not have full use of his field of vision as a consequence, he had the cartilage removed from his nose. The result was the hooknose made famous by one of the great portraits of the 15th century. It's the double portrait of Federigo da Montefeltro and of his bride, Battista Sforza, now in Uffizi—painted by Piero della Francesca.

This famous double portrait not only reflects the image of the duke, warts and all, but also reflects the fact that he took the world as it was, and he knew his own limitations. But he also realized, given the perfection of the background and what's painted on the back, a better place. Because what Piero put on the back of these double portraits are the triumphs; in the case of his wife, Battista, the triumph of chastity and in his own case, the triumph of arms and victory.

Berruguete, the Spaniard, was brought in to paint a number of images of famous men from the past—not only the classical past, but also some of the medieval past—and also some of his own contemporaries. The purpose of these small portraits was to line the top of Federigo's small study. It was a place to which Renaissance gentlemen and princes retired—always tiny rooms because they had to be able to be serviced without the use of staff. In other words, he didn't want to have servants around him there. He wanted to be alone with his own thoughts and his books.

One of the most famous individuals to be produced by this artistic court was somebody who came about as a result of his father's employment. The court artist for Federigo was quite a talented second-rater named Giovanni Santi, or Sanzio. As court artist, he not only did some particular pictures, but also he designed the embroidery for the ladies to do in the evening, stage scenery, the sorts of things that one did if one were the official artist at court. His son, born in Urbino and trained there, was the famous Renaissance artist Raphael. He called himself Raphael of Urbino and associated himself with Urbino—not just as a place of birth, but because of its idea in how it's remembered.

In 1460, at the age of 16, Federigo was married to Battista Sforza, the niece of Francesco Sforza, Duke of Milan. Battista was everything that he would want in a wife: extraordinarily well-educated with great skill in administration. She was a true companion to Federigo and often ruled in his name while he was away in his military campaigns, but they despaired of an heir. Because of the uncertainty of all of the principalities, especially those in this rather difficult world of the Marche and the papal states, it was felt that he needed a male heir to ensure that the Montefeltro line would continue. Only the last of her eight pregnancies produced a son, and sadly, at the age of 26, she died during that pregnancy bringing forth Guidobaldo, the only son that Federigo and Battista had.

This world dominated by these two remarkable personalities became a school of culture. It attracted those who wanted to celebrate this world and who wanted to have a place where they could discuss topics of mutual interest—culture and military affairs—surrounded by those who knew these things best. It attracted young men, and some young women, who wanted to learn as well. Some of the most famous families in Italy, then, sent their sons to be educated there. Urbino became almost a Platonic court, with the very best and brightest attracted to share a kind of culture that was recognized as the finest there was to have. The most celebrated of these visitors was perhaps Pietro Bembo, the Venetian nobleman who ultimately became a cardinal. He is probably best remembered for canonizing the Italian vernacular language by determining that it was really the vocabulary of Dante Petrarch and Boccaccio that should be used, and that literary Tuscan should be the language of Italy itself.

Surrounded by this fame and glory, Federigo died after a reign of 38 years in 1482. He was succeeded by his only son, Guidobaldo. Although very intelligent and promising in his early years, Guidobaldo soon began to exhibit the disease that would waste his body. It's uncertain what it was—it could have been juvenile arthritis—but it made it very difficult and very painful for him to walk and, ultimately, began to work on his body, so that he spent most of his time in bed.

In 1488, the young man was married to Elisabetta Gonzaga of

the ruling family of Mantua, sister-in-law of the celebrated Isabella d'Este. From her wedding night, she knew that her invalid husband was impotent. However, she refused to make this canonically invalid marriage end. As far as the church was concerned, it was no marriage because it was never consummated. But, instead, Elisabetta chose to live with him as a sister, and indeed, seemed to greet the fact with a certain degree of relief. They were devoted to one another, and when Cesare Borgia, son of Pope Alexander VI, threatened the principality of Urbino and ultimately and faithlessly took it and sacked it, she shared all of her husband's humiliation and exile.

This crisis came in 1502, and it was completely reflective of the personality of Cesare Borgia and the ambitions of the Borgia Pope Alexander VI to create a Borgia kingdom under the states of the church. Cesare first reminded Guidobaldo that Urbino was a papal vicariate, and, consequently, sovereignty resided in the pope. And Cesare then did what he did best—he lied. He told Guidobaldo that he had complete faith in him as a papal vicar, and supported him completely, and asked to borrow his artillery so that it could be used in the papal campaigns. Guidobaldo, naively, believed Cesare; he turned over his artillery—at which point, then, Cesare attacked Urbino.

There was nothing that the people of Urbino could do. Guidobaldo was not his father. He didn't have the physical stamina or the ability to be a military leader. The people of Urbino rallied behind him nevertheless, yielding freely their personal possessions, melting their family jewels and their wedding rings in order to try and buy another mercenary army to attack Cesare from behind. None of this worked.

Cesare, ultimately, took the city; he drove Guidobaldo and Elisabetta into exile, and then he sacked the beautiful city that Federigo had built. The taking of Urbino was one of the great acts of infamy of the Italian Renaissance at the time of Cesare Borgia. The beautiful palace that Laurana had built for Federigo was sacked, and an army of brutal, violent, vicious soldiers led by Cesare was billeted there.

The situation in Urbino was desperate and the people were in a state of despair. But then what Machiavelli would call *Fortuna*, fortune, intervened. Alexander VI, the Borgia pope, died. He died of malaria at the same time his son Cesare was extremely ill with the same disease. This meant that in 1503 the Borgia attempt to create a papal kingdom disintegrated, allowing the people of Urbino to rise up and drive out the papal garrison, and to demand the return of their beloved Guidobaldo and Elisabetta. They returned to great rejoicing—establishing themselves once more in the palace of Urbino.

Despite this, it was a time of great danger. It was clear from that the

Cesare Borgia, son of Pope Alexander VI, exhibited such ruthless tactics in the taking of Urbino that he was the role model for Machiavelli's *The Prince*.

Montefeltros had no security because they had no male heir, and because of the unconsummated marriage of the duke and duchess, there would never be one. The decision was taken after the death of Alexander VI that Guidobaldo would adopt his nephew as his successor. It was a brilliant choice because this nephew, Francesco Maria della Rovere, was also the nephew of the new pope, "the warrior pope," Julius II.

This provided a moment of respite, a moment of what is often called the Urbino Twilight. It was the reflected glory of Federigo's regime in those years of quiet around his son before his own death. It was a time when the culture that Federigo had established could then be fulfilled, but with a different kind of melancholy perspective. That sense of confidence and the ability to do anything evidenced so strongly in the "Light of Italy" of Federigo was now a different world.

It was a world in which those who were in charge of the restoration of Italian liberty and the maintenance of Italian culture were seriously threatened by forces beyond their control. Under Guidobaldo after the expulsion of the Borgia, it was a culture of melancholy. It was a culture, nevertheless, that became structurally important for the cultural world of the Renaissance, fundamental even in our memory and understanding of the Renaissance ideal because amongst that court was perhaps the greatest of all of its denizens—Baldassare Castiglione. Castiglione was not only the greatest of all of the associates of Guidobaldo, but the producer of a book that took this place out of space and time and turned it into an ideal. Castiglione's work, *The Book of the Courtier*, celebrates an ideal that can still galvanize today. ■

The preceding lecture was an excerpt drawn from The Great Course:

The Italian Renaissance
Course #3970

When you think of the Italian Renaissance, chances are you think of what it gave us. The extraordinary sculptures of Michelangelo. The incomparable paintings of Leonardo da Vinci. The immortal written works of Petrarch and Machiavelli.

Dr. Kenneth Bartlett explains the fascinating history of the artistic, cultural and intellectual explosion in Italy in the 14th century.

Lecture Titles

Kenneth Bartlett

Kenneth Bartlett is Professor of History and Renaissance Studies at the University of Toronto, where he earned his Ph.D. in 1978.

Professor Bartlett has received the Victoria University Excellence in Teaching Award, the Students Administrative Council and Association of Part-Time University Students Teaching Award, and the Faculty of Arts and Science Teaching Excellence Award. In 2005 he was awarded a prestigious national 3M Teaching Fellowship.

If you would like to order this course, please contact us at:

Phone: 1-800-TEACH-12

Web: www.TEACH12.com

For more information on our pricing policy, see page 245.

Perhaps at no other time in history has it been more important to understand others' religions.

RELIGION

"Religion is the recognition of all
our duties as divine commands."

—Immanuel Kant

The New Testament
Course #656
Lecture 24

Taught by: Professor Bart D. Ehrman
The University of North Carolina at Chapel Hill

Do We Have the Original New Testament?

The answer may surprise you.

We do not have the originals of any of the books that were later canonized into the New Testament. What we have are copies of the originals or, better yet, copies of the copies of the copies of the originals—copies made for the most part hundreds of years after the originals themselves. These copies were all written by hand, which is the literal meaning of the term manuscript—written by hand.

Unfortunately, all of our surviving manuscripts contain mistakes. For that reason, in many cases it's difficult to know what words were in the original texts of the New Testament, and that's an important matter because it's impossible to interpret what an author meant if you don't know what he said. What happens is that copyists—especially untrained copyists as were most of the early Christians who served as copyists—copyists make mistakes. And a subsequent copyist will not only reintroduce new mistakes, but will reproduce the mistakes of the copy that he copies, and so on.

We have at present some 5,400 Greek manuscripts of the New Testament. The earliest manuscript of any kind from the New Testament that we have is a tiny scrap that's about the size of a credit card. It's written on the front and back. It originally came from a full manuscript of the Gospel of John. This little fragment contains a few lines from John, chapter 18, Jesus' trial before Pilate. This little fragment was probably produced in the early part of the 2nd century, within 30 or 40 years of John's gospel. Unfortunately, we don't have the whole manuscript, just this one little scrap.

Among all of these thousands of Greek manuscripts that we have, with the exception of the smallest fragments, there are no two that are exactly alike in all of their particulars; that is to say, they all differ in their wording in places. It's difficult to know how many differences

The Pharisees bring a woman accused of adultery before Jesus. Traditional law ruled that the woman be stoned to death, but Jesus challenges the law and the Pharisees. "He that is without sin among you, let him first cast a stone at her."

there are among our surviving manuscripts of the New Testament because nobody has been able to count all of the differences. Some scholars think that there might be 200,000 differences; others say 300,000 or more. It's probably easiest, though, to put the matter in comparative terms. There are more differences among our manuscripts than there are words in the New Testament.

The single most common mistake is completely immaterial for the meaning of these texts: Scribes misspelled words even more than most people do today. Scribes, of course, will be excused for this; they are living in an age before spell check—in fact—they are living in an age before there were dictionaries.

Sometimes scribes would inadvertently leave out words or entire lines. On occasion they would leave out entire pages. Scribes would be tired or they would be incompetent, or their attention would be distracted and so they would leave some things out.

Whereas there are some textual changes that are of no real importance for interpretation—for example, the misspelled words—others are highly significant. For example, the oldest and best manuscripts of the Gospel of John do not contain the famous story of the woman who has been caught in the act of adultery. They bring her to Jesus and they say, "The Law commands that we stone one such as this. What do you say that we should do?" And Jesus stoops down and begins writing on the ground, and he looks up and he says, "Let the one without sin among you be the first to cast a stone at her." It's a brilliant story filled with pathos, a story that was used throughout the ages to show that one should be merciful to sinners, even the worst of sinners.

Sometimes scribes would inadvertently leave out words. Sometimes they would leave out entire lines. On occasion they would leave out entire pages. Scribes would be tired or they would be incompetent, or their attention would be distracted and so they would leave some things out.

Unfortunately, the story was not originally in the Gospel of John. It's not found in the oldest and best manuscripts. Moreover, the writing style of this story isn't at all like what is found in the rest of the Gospel of John. The first church father to quote this text in Greek as appearing in the Gospel of John isn't until the 12th century. It was only in the Middle Ages that this story was added to John, and the manuscripts that did have this in John were the manuscripts that were used then by the King James translators, and so it entered into English translation.

Scholars trained in textual criticism devote themselves to examining the surviving manuscripts in order to see where scribes made mistakes, in an effort to reconstruct what the authors originally wrote. And sometimes these are passages of real significance for the interpretation of the text. There is no alternative to this situation and there never will be, unless by some unbelievable stroke of luck we discover the original texts themselves. ∎

The preceding lecture was an excerpt drawn from The Great Course:

The New Testament
Course #656

Whether you consider it a book of faith or a cultural artifact, the New Testament is among the most significant writings that the world has ever known.

Scarcely a single major writer in the last 2,000 years has failed to rely on the web of meaning contained in the New Testament to communicate. Yet the New Testament is also among the most widely disputed and least clearly understood books in history.

In these lectures Professor Bart D. Ehrman develops for you a carefully reasoned understanding of the New Testament.

Lecture Titles

Bart D. Ehrman

Bart D. Ehrman is the James A. Gray Professor and Chair of the Department of Religious Studies at The University of North Carolina at Chapel Hill, where he has been teaching for over 15 years. He completed his undergraduate work at Wheaton College and received his Masters of Divinity and Ph.D. from Princeton Theological Seminary. Prior to taking his position at UNC, Professor Ehrman taught at Rutgers University.

If you would like to order this course, please contact us at:

Phone: 1-800-TEACH-12
Web: www.TEACH12.com
For more information on our pricing policy, see page 245.

The Bhagavad Gita: The Struggle of Self

The Bhagavad Gita is probably the most popular religious text among Hindus. Although it is not the most sacred or most authoritative Hindu writing, the Gita is widely read and extremely well-known.

T he Bhagavad Gita, which is usually translated as the "Song of the Lord," was probably composed between 400 B.C.E. and 100 C.E. Its author or authors is unknown. Although it's usually read as an independent story, the Bhagavad Gita is actually part of the *Mahabharata*, which is probably the world's longest epic poem, with over 100,000 verses.

The Gita has been a great influence on Indian thinkers throughout its history. It has also impressed many intellectuals in the West, such as Ralph Waldo Emerson, Henry David Thoreau, and T. S. Eliot. It is probably the work of Indian literature with which Westerners are most familiar. Gandhi referred to it as his eternal mother, and despite its message urging the protagonist to war, he found in it support for his practice of nonviolence.

The Gita is essentially a dialogue between Vishnu in his *avatara*, or earthly manifestation, as Krishna and a warrior by the name of Arjuna. Their conversation takes place on the battlefield just as two grand armies are about to go to war. The combatants are the Kurus and the Pandavas. They're fighting over the right to rule a northern India kingdom.

The Kurus and the Pandavas are members of the same clan, making this a kind of family feud. It's precisely because the enemy numbers include his uncles, cousins, and teachers that Arjuna is so aggrieved. As the battle lines are drawn and the action is about to commence, Arjuna and Krishna, who serves as his driver, steer their chariot between the two armies, and then suddenly all the action is suspended.

It's as if time has stopped, like a moment of eternity placed in the midst of time. Arjuna surveys the scene and begins to get melancholy and philosophical. When he sees his family members across the enemy lines, he drops his bow, having lost his will to fight. Arjuna tells Lord Krishna that he cannot go to war. He has no desire to fight members of his clan whom he reveres.

Arjuna concludes that such a battle can only lead to chaos. The term he actually uses is *adharma*, or chaos. He sees no value in gaining wealth, *artha*, or earthly pleasure, *kama*, if having these traditional goods of life entail destroying his own family. Fear of ruining the family remains a tremendous influence of individual behavior in India today. In South India, bottles of beer actually carry a warning label that frankly tells the purchaser: "Drinking liquor will ruin the family."

Rather surprisingly, Krishna's first response to Arjuna's qualms is to try to shame him. He taunts Arjuna and questions his masculinity, and commands him to get up and fight. Krishna tells Arjuna that fighting is his *dharma*. As a *Ksatriya*, a member of the warrior class, there is no greater honor or glory than to do battle. When Arjuna still refuses to fight, Krishna tries another tactic. He tells Arjuna to think of what people will say. Krishna says: "People will tell of your undying shame, and for a man of honor, shame is worse than death."

Arjuna does not respond to these appeals. He's become much too thoughtful, too philosophical to be bullied or shamed into war. Arjuna's conflict is deep and genuine, and he is paralyzed until he can see his way clear. His inner conflict is a familiar one. It is the dissonance that one feels when competing values clash.

Our most poignant dilemmas are not those between good and evil, which are relatively easy to solve. The problems in life arise when we must chose between the "lesser of two evils" or the "greater of two goods." For Arjuna, the values he must negotiate are these: to refuse to fight and hence disobey his *dharma* as a warrior, or to go to war and thereby invite the negative consequences of *karma* including family ruin, social chaos, and then, of course, continued rebirth.

Arjuna's intellectual dissonance has become a teaching moment. He wisely asks Krishna to be his guru. When such a moment arises, one knows that a great opportunity for breakthrough has occurred. The student is prepared for insight. Krishna's first lesson recalls the teaching of the Upanishads.

Indeed, Krishna essentially paraphrases a famous Upanishadic passage. "He who thinks the self a killer, and he who thinks it killed, both failed to understand. It does not kill, nor is it killed. It is not born. It does not die. Having been, it will never not be. Unborn, enduring, constant, and primordial, it is not killed when the body is killed." Krishna's point is simply the logical conclusion of a philosophy based on the immortality of the soul. Life and death are ultimately meaningless.

Arjuna presses further. He is concerned with another matter now, the problem of *karma*. Perhaps it is true that one cannot kill the soul. But killing the body is still action, and all action generates *karma*. How does one avoid the negative karmic consequences? Arjuna is well-schooled in the idea that *karma* of any sort cannot bring one to ultimate salvation.

Krishna now responds with another lesson, acting without attachment or aversion. Krishna says it is not possible not to act, but it is possible to act without creating *karma*. One does this by performing all action without hatred or desire. Krishna says:

> "Be intent on action, not on the fruits of action. Avoid attraction to the fruits and attachment to inaction. Perform actions firm in discipline, relinquishing attachment. Be impartial to failure and success. This equanimity is called discipline [or *yoga*]. Arjuna, action is far inferior to the discipline of understanding, so seek refuge in understanding—pitiful are men drawn by the fruits of action."

Krishna maintains that the true effects of *karma* come from the heart and the will, not the action itself. Thus an equanimous disposition frees one from bondage to *karma*. Krishna says: "Action imprisons the world unless it is done as a sacrifice. Freed from attachment, Arjuna, perform action as a sacrifice."

When Arjuna asked how one might learn to perform *karma*-less action, Krishna tells him it takes discipline, and he proceeds to discuss, over the span of many chapters, the entire panorama of Hindu practices. Krishna discusses the value of asceticism, renunciation, study of the sacred Veda, the sacrifices of the Brahmins, fasting, prayer, meditation. One can get a comprehensive view of the entire Hindu world just by reading the Gita.

This discussion continues. Arjuna raises objections, and Krishna responds. At one point, Arjuna becomes terribly confused and frustrated. He complains to Krishna: "You confuse my understanding with a maze of words; speak one truth so I may achieve what is good." Like all of us, Arjuna longs for clarity and simplicity. He just wants to know what to do. That simplicity, however, is not forthcoming.

Krishna continues to spin a swirl of words as rich and as complex as Hinduism itself. This richness and this lack of clarity is one of the reasons for the Gita's vast appeal. Every Hindu finds something of value here, some wisdom that pertains to his or her place in life. The Brahmins find their sacrifices honored. The ascetics see their renunciation and asceticism valued. The warriors have their *dharma* affirmed. Always a genuine spirituality is embraced and accepted.

As the dialogue proceeds, Krishna's lessons begin to focus more and more on himself. Now the teachings become increasingly characteristic of the path of *bhakti*, or devotion to God. Krishna encourages Arjuna to focus his mind, his will, and heart on God and to let all else go.

> "Men who worship me, thinking solely of me, always disciplined, win the reward I secure. The leaf or flower or fruit or water that he offers with devotion, I take from the man of self-restraint in response to his devotion. Whatever you do, whatever you take, whatever you offer, what you give, what penances you perform, do as an offering to me, Arjuna! You will be freed from the bonds of action, from the fruit of fortune and misfortune, armed with discipline, the discipline of renunciation. You are self liberated. You will join me."

For *bhakti* practice, *what* is done is not as important as *how* it is done. All that matters is that one do all things with faith and devotion to the god. It doesn't even matter whether or not one is devoted to the god Krishna, by name. One can worship other gods as long as they do so with fidelity. "When devoted men sacrifice to other deities with faith, they sacrifice to me, Arjuna, however aberrant the rites." All paths performed in the right spirit lead to Krishna.

The tradition has come a long way from Vedic times, when the priests insisted that the *mantras* of the sacrifice had to be pronounced at just the right pitch and inflection. As the teachings continue to center more and more on the path of devotion, Arjuna feels his doubts melt away. In a climatic moment, he asked Krishna to grant him an extremely rare boon, the ability to see Krishna in his full glory as god.

Krishna gets Arjuna a divine eye with which to gaze on the god's form. The passages that describe this great vision are fascinating and memorable. The narrator tells us:

> "If the light of a thousand suns were to rise in the sky at once, it would be like the light of that great spirit. Arjuna saw all the universe in its many ways and parts, standing as one in the body

of the god of gods. Then, filled with amazement, his hair bristling on his flesh, Arjuna bowed his head to the god, and joined his hands in homage."

J. Robert Oppenheimer, the director of The Manhattan Project, said that when he saw the atomic bomb detonated in the desert of New Mexico, he immediately recalled the first two lines of this passage, comparing the light of Krishna to a thousand suns rising at once in the sky. Arjuna's response to this awesome vision is characteristic of such experiences, as reported in the history of religions.

Rudolf Otto called such events experiences of "the holy." Otto said the experience of the holy is marked by a highly ambivalent reaction, just as we observed in Arjuna. Arjuna is both terrified and fascinated. What Arjuna sees accents the absolute otherness of divinity.

> "I see no beginning or middle or end to you, only boundless strength in your endless arms; the moon and the sun in your eyes, your mouths of consuming flames, your own brilliance scorching the universe. You alone fill the space between heaven and Earth and all the directions. Seeing this awesome, terrible form of yours, Great Soul, the three worlds tremble. Seeing the many mouths and eyes of your great form, its many arms, thighs, feet, bellies, and things, the worlds tremble, and so do I."

Now Krishna speaks:

> "I am time grown old, creating world destruction, setting in motion to annihilate the worlds; even without you, all these warriors arrayed in hostile ranks, will cease to exist. Therefore, arise and win glory! Conquer your foes, and fulfill your kingship! They are already killed by me. Be just my instrument, the archer at my side!"

After his vision, Arjuna arises and goes to battle, claiming that his doubts have been dispelled.

It's not altogether clear what precisely resolves his misgivings. Has he been persuaded by Krishna's arguments or by the vision of Krishna in his manifest form? Is he convinced by seeing that Krishna embraces all things in life and death, and that ultimately from the perspective of eternity, whether one lives or dies does not really matter? What about Arjuna's initial uncertainty about fighting against his own clan? Has Krishna adequately set that issue at rest?

There are many who think that much in the Gita is left unsettled, despite the fact that Arjuna himself seems to have gained clarity. The war commences, and Arjuna and his brothers—the Pandavas—ultimately win. Significantly, the Gita itself ends before we know the battle's outcome. The question of who wins and who loses is not the issue in the Gita, nor does the Gita really solve the problem of war.

The two sides are not identified as good or as bad. There are no clear favorites here. War is, by almost any standard, tragic according to the Gita. Yet the context of war is significant in the Gita, because the battlefield is really a metaphor for the soul, the self, the mind and its struggle.

For ordinary Hindus wrestling with the issues of *dharma*, one's sacred duty is a much more present reality than the subjects of the Veda or even the Upanishads. As a metaphor for the self and its internal struggles, perhaps the Gita is a reminder that often there are no clear avenues of choice. Our decisions must be made in ambiguity and uncertainty. ∎

The preceding lecture was an excerpt drawn from The Great Course:

Great World Religions: Hinduism, 2nd Edition
Course #6104

What, specifically, do other people believe? How do those beliefs guide the way they lead their lives on a daily and yearly basis—how they dress, eat, work, pray, and raise their families? How do they view those who do not share their understanding of God?

Such questions are exactly the focus of this course, an authoritative and up-to-date survey of the history and nature of the world's five major faiths: Buddhism, Christianity, Hinduism, Islam, and Judaism. You will be given an insider's look at each religion by exploring the issues that are most meaningful to its adherents.

Mark W. Muesse

Mark W. Muesse is Chair of the Department of Religious Studies at Rhodes College in Memphis, Tennessee. He received a B.A., *summa cum laude*, in English Literature from Baylor University and earned a Masters of Theological Studies, a Masters of Arts, and a Ph.D. in the Study of Religion from Harvard University.

Before taking his position at Rhodes, Professor Muesse held positions at Harvard College, Harvard Divinity School, and the University of Southern Maine, where he served as Associate Dean of the College of Arts and Sciences.

Professor Muesse has written many articles, papers, and reviews in world religions, spirituality, theology, and gender studies, and has coedited a collection of essays entitled *Redeeming Men: Religion and Masculinities*. He is currently compiling an anthology of prayers from around the world.

Professor Muesse is a member of the American Academy of Religion and the Society for Indian Philosophy and Religion, and has been Visiting Professor at the Tamilnadu Theological Seminary in Madurai, India. He has traveled extensively throughout Asia and has studied at Wat Mahadhatu, Bangkok, Thailand; the Himalayan Yogic Institute, Kathmandu, Nepal; the Subodhi Institute of Integral Education in Sri Lanka; and Middle East Technical University in Ankara, Turkey.

Lecture Titles

Christianity
1. Christianity among World Religions
2. Birth and Expansion
3. Second Century and Self-Definition
4. The Christian Story
5. What Christians Believe
6. The Church and Sacraments
7. Moral Teaching
8. The Radical Edge
9. Catholic, Orthodox, Protestant
10. Christianity and Politics
11. Christianity and Culture
12. Tensions and Possibilities

Islam
1. Islam Yesterday, Today, and Tomorrow
2. The Five Pillars of Islam
3. Muhammad—Prophet and Statesman
4. God's Word—the Quranic Worldview
5. The Muslim Community— Faith and Politics
6. Paths to God—Islamic Law and Mysticism
7. Islamic Revivalism— Renewal and Reform
8. The Contemporary Resurgence of Islam
9. Islam at the Crossroads
10. Women and Change in Islam
11. Islam in the West
12. The Future of Islam

Judaism
1. What is Judaism?
2. The Stages of History
3. The Jewish Library
4. The Emergence of Rabbinic Judaism
5. Jewish Worship—Prayer and the Synagogue
6. The Calendar—A Communal Life-Cycle
7. Individual Life-Cycles
8. God and Man; God and Community
9. Philosophers and Mystics
10. The Legal Frameworks of Judaism— Halakha
11. Common Judaism— or a Plurality of Judaisms?
12. Judaism and "Others"

Hinduism
1. Hinduism in the World and the World of Hinduism
2. The Early Cultures of India
3. The World of the Veda
4. From the Vedic Tradition to Classical Hinduism
5. Caste
6. Men, Women, and the Stages of Life
7. The Way of Action
8. The Way of Wisdom
9. Seeing God
10. **The Way of Devotion**
11. The Goddess and Her Devotees
12. Hinduism in the Modern Period

Buddhism
1. Buddhism as a World Religion
2. The Life of the Buddha
3. "All is Suffering"
4. The Path to Nirvana
5. The Buddhist Community
6. Mahayana Buddhism— the Bodhisattva Ideal
7. Celestial Buddhas and Bodhisattvas
8. Emptiness
9. Theravada Buddhism in Southeast Asia
10. Buddhism in Tibet
11. Buddhism in China
12. Buddhism in Japan

If you would like to order this course, please contact us at:

Phone: 1-800-TEACH-12

Web: www.TEACH12.com

For more information on our pricing policy, see page 245.

From Jesus to Constantine: A History of Early Christianity
Course #6577
Lecture 19   **Taught by:** Professor Bart D. Ehrman
                    The University of North Carolina at Chapel Hill

The New Testament Canon

It seems logical to us that a major world religion would have a set of authoritative writings that it understands to be scripture. After all, that is true for all of the major Western religions: Judaism, Christianity, and Islam.

I t is striking, however, that in the ancient world, the idea of having a collection of sacred books at the heart of a religion was virtually unheard of in most pagan circles in the ancient Roman world. Contrary to what is sometimes said, the *Iliad* and the *Odyssey* by Homer were not the Bible of Greek and Roman religions. These books were read as classics, talked about, and reflected on, but they did not provide any kind of guidelines for faith and practice. There really was nothing quite like authoritative scripture for most people living in that ancient world.

Judaism was the one exception in that the Hebrew scriptures were accepted by Jews throughout the world as providing sacred tales and laws to govern the lives of God's people. Jews in Jesus' day largely accept the Torah—the first five books of what is now the Hebrew Bible: Genesis, Exodus, Leviticus, Numbers, and Deuteronomy—as authoritative texts coming from God. Some Jews accepted other writings, especially writings of the prophets as being scriptural. Jesus himself accepted the writings of the prophets and some other books, including the book of Psalms, along with the Torah, and he taught the Torah to his followers. Since his followers were the first Christians, Christians inherited a canon of scripture from the very beginning.

This remained true even after Christianity became predominantly Gentile. Since it started out as Jewish, with the Jewish Jesus and his Jewish followers, the Gentile Christians who came into the church inherited sacred books as their sacred authorities. It was not long before Christians started elevating other authorities as being on a par with the sacred writings from the Old Testament, as they began to call it.

When Christians began to appeal to other explicitly Christian writings as being on an equal footing with their scriptures, that was the beginning of the formation of a distinctively Christian canon. This began remarkably early in Christianity. Already during the 1st century, Jesus' own words were being granted sacred authority by the very earliest Christian author, the apostle Paul.

We find the same phenomenon relating not just to Jesus, but also to the writings of his apostles. Interestingly enough, the earliest author of the New Testament, Paul, is cited by the latest writing of the New Testament, by St. Peter, as a scriptural authority. This is a movement, then, that would continue on through Christianity, as the words of Jesus and those of his apostles are considered canonical.

Christians who believed that the writings of the apostles should be considered scripture had to decide which books to include. This was one of the biggest debates among the early Christian churches. Which books should have been considered for inclusion in the canonical authorities?

It appears that Marcion, the 2nd-century philosopher and theologian who was later condemned as a heretic, was the first to give a definitive canon of scripture to his followers. Marcion maintained that something like our Gospel of Luke and 10 of Paul's letters—the 13 in the New Testament, minus 1 and 2 Timothy and Titus—were canonical authorities. He apparently came up with an actual text of these 11 books that were circulated within the Marcionite churches, and used as sacred authorities for their perspective.

St. Paul was converted by a miraculous event on the road to Damascus.

Other Christians accepted other books as canonical. For example, some Christians accepted Matthew, Mark, or John. Some accepted the Gospel of Thomas, or the Gospel of Peter, and so forth. It may well be that Marcion himself provided the impetus for proto-orthodox Christian leaders to devise their own canon of scripture. There is some evidence to suggest that not only was Marcion the first to come up with a canon, but that he also gave the impetus that led, eventually, to

Irenaeus was an early Christian bishop in Roman Gaul, one of the fathers of the church.

the canonization of the 27 New Testament books.

What is this evidence? The evidence is that proto-orthodox writers of the 2nd and 3rd centuries, the writers who had the perspective that later became orthodox in the 4th century, had certain perspectives on the canon that appeared to develop over time. During Marcion's own day, the proto-orthodox author Justin Martyr, living in Rome, showed no concern at all for having a fixed set of scriptural authorities. We have three writings from Justin, two of which are fairly lengthy, his First Apology and his Dialogue with Trypho. In these lengthy writings, Justin quoted Christian authors and Christian texts, including the gospels, especially Matthew, Mark, and Luke, but didn't cite those as being part of the closed canon of scripture. He didn't call those books by their names, nor say how many of them were accepted as authoritative. When he quoted the Gospels, he referred to them as the "memoirs of the apostles."

The reason he called them the memoirs of the apostles was because the authority of these books resided in the fact that they come from apostolic tradition, not because they were part of a canon of scripture. Justin had a fairly loose understanding of Christian authoritative texts.

Some 30 years later, things had changed rather drastically. A heresy hunter named Irenaeus stood in the same theological tradition as Justin, but his writing showed that things had changed severely by the time he produced his works of heresy in 180 or 185. Irenaeus, unlike Justin, had a set number of authorities he cited as being scriptural. In his book, *Against the Heresies*, Irenaeus attacked heretics for not understanding that there were four, and only four, Gospels to be accepted. He pointed out that different heretics used different Gospels as their authorities. "The Ebionites used the Gospel of Matthew, and only Matthew. The Gnostics used the Gospel of Mark, and only Mark," he said. "Marcion uses Luke, and only Luke. The Valentinian Gnostics use John, and only John."

Irenaeus insisted that all of these groups were wrong because you couldn't simply take one gospel as an authority. If you did, you had a skewed vision of who Jesus was. You needed the full picture, provided by the four gospels. According to Irenaeus: It is not possible that the books can be more or fewer in number than they are, for since there are four zones of the world in which we live, and four principal winds, which, while the church is scattered throughout the world, and the pillar and ground of the church is the gospel and spirit of life, it is fitting that she should have four pillars.

Athanasius was an early Christian bishop of Alexandria. He is considered a doctor of the Church.

Get the argument? The four corners of the Earth, four winds that drive the Gospel everywhere throughout the Earth, and therefore, there also must be four Gospels, not more.

What drove this movement toward having a set number of Gospels? In Justin's day, when Marcion was just starting out, there didn't seem to be any reason to have set authorities. Thirty years later, Irenaeus did have a set number of authorities. What's the difference? The difference was 30 years' worth of Marcionite churches spreading their canon of scripture. That appeared to be driving the proto-orthodox to come up with their own canon of scripture that stood over against the Marcionites' canon.

The earliest canonical list that we have is a list of books that an author thought belonged to the Christian list for a Christian canon, called the *Muratorian Canon* after the 18th century Italian scholar who discovered it. The *Muratorian Canon* is probably a late 2nd-century Roman document, written in Latin, which lists 22 of our 27 books of the New Testament, but also includes the Wisdom of Solomon, and the Apocalypse of Peter, so that he had a 24-book canon. When you read through what the author had to say about why books should have been included or not, you find four criteria that he used that are the same four criteria used in other proto-orthodox of the canon.

How do you know which books should have been included? First, a book had to be ancient. If it was not an ancient book, it could not

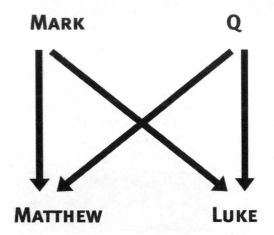

MARK　　　　　**Q**

MATTHEW　　　　**LUKE**

Similarity in word choices and event placement leads scholars to believe that there is a literary relationship between the first three canonical gospels of Mark, Matthew, and Luke. Most scholars now adhere to the two-source hypothesis, illustrated above. It states that, of these three gospels, Mark was written first and used as a source by both Matthew and Luke. Matthew and Luke also used a document lost to us known as Q, which seems to have been a record of the sayings of Jesus.

be a canonical book. Second, the book had to be apostolic, written by either an apostle or a companion of the apostle. Third, a book needed to be widely read and accepted among the proto-orthodox churches to be seen as canonical. Fourth, the book had to contain the correct theology, had to be orthodox. These were the four criteria to determine whether a book was canonical or not. A book had to be ancient, apostolic, widely accepted, and orthodox.

The debates over which books to include in the canon were long and hard. Even though Marcion began the process already in the mid-2nd century, it took centuries for it to be resolved. It was not until the year 367 that anyone of record listed our 27 books, and only our 27 books as belonging to the New Testament. This is the year 367, 300 years after many or most of these books had been written, so that the canon did not come into place right away but took centuries of debate.

In the year A.D. 367, the famous bishop of Alexandria, Athanasius, wrote his annual pastoral letter to the churches in Egypt, in which he told them which books were to be considered canonical scripture and used in the church. He listed our 27 books, and only our 27 books. This did not end the matter because, in fact, debates continued in certain parts of the church. But by and large, Athanasius's letter of 367 was used by other orthodox Christians to argue that only these 27 books, should be accepted, and they have become the canon for Eastern Orthodox, Roman Catholic, and Protestant churches down to today. ∎

The preceding lecture was an excerpt drawn from The Great Course:

From Jesus to Constantine: A History of Early Christianity
Course #6577

These lectures offer a fresh and provocative perspective on what are perhaps the most intriguing questions about Christianity: How could a movement originally made up of perhaps only 20 low-class followers of a Jewish apocalyptic preacher crucified as an enemy of the state, grow to include nearly four million adherents in only 300 years? And how would it eventually become the largest religion in the world, with some two billion adherents?

Lecture Titles

Bart D. Ehrman

Bart D. Ehrman is the James A. Gray Professor and Chair of the Department of Religious Studies at The University of North Carolina at Chapel Hill, where he has been teaching for over 15 years. He completed his undergraduate work at Wheaton College and received his Masters of Divinity and Ph.D. from Princeton Theological Seminary. Prior to taking his position at UNC, Professor Ehrman taught at Rutgers University.

If you would like to order this course, please contact us at:

Phone: 1-800-TEACH-12
Web: www.TEACH12.com
For more information on our pricing policy, see page 245.

Endgame:
The Apocalypse as Genre

There were a lot of apocalypses written about in the ancient world, and it was a common genre among Jewish and Christian thinkers.

W hen people today read the Book of Revelation, it seems very odd, very peculiar, unlike anything else they ever read. For many Christians this serves as an indication or a sign of its inspiration. But in the ancient world there were a lot of books like this that existed. In fact, it was an entire genre of literature.

We have a number of ancient writings from both Jews and Christians that are of this apocalyptic genre. In general, the characteristics of the genre are as follows:

First, most apocalypses are pseudonymous writings. They are written in the name of somebody who is famous, and so they are forged in the sense that whoever is writing them claims to be a famous person.

Second, the genre of usually pseudonymous writings consists of a narrated revelation given by God. God has revealed something to the person writing it, who is portraying himself as a prophet. That's why the genre is called an apocalypse. An apocalypse means "an unveiling" or "a revealing." It's the Greek equivalent of the Latin word "revelation." The words apocalypse and revelation are synonyms.

The third characteristic is the heavenly mediator. Revelation is given by God, and it is narrated by the prophet who is writing the text. This revelation is mediated by a heavenly mediator, for example, an angel will give the revelation and then explain it to the person who receives it.

Fourth characteristic: This revelation shows mundane realities on Earth that can be explained in light of the ultimate truths of heaven. So the revelation tries to make sense of what's happening here on

The word "apocalypse" now commonly refers to the end of the world. In Christian thought, much literature, paintings, and movies have been devoted to graphic descriptions of this event.

Earth in light of ultimate realities in the world above. Those are the characteristics of most apocalypses.

There are actually two kinds of apocalypses that we find in the ancient writings of both Jews and Christians. The first kind of apocalypse is one in which the prophet is shown a symbolic vision that mysteriously describes the future fate of the Earth when the forces of evil are overthrown and God's kingdom will come. An example of this actually does occur in the last book of the Hebrew Bible to be written, the Book of Daniel. In Daniel 7, the prophet has an apocalyptic vision of four beasts rising fast out of the sea, one after the other, to take over the world. The fourth is the worst of all, more terrible than all the beasts before him. Finally, the prophet sees coming from heaven "one like the Son of Man." Then the beasts are destroyed, the kingdoms are taken over and given the son of man, who then has rule, power, and dominion, for ever and ever. This is the first type of apocalypse, a vision of the future fate of the Earth.

The Apocalypse of Peter was discovered in the year 1886. Though unknown throughout the Middle Ages, it was mentioned by authors of the late 2nd century, some of whom thought that the Apocalypse of Peter should have been included within the canon of the New Testament.

A second type of apocalypse is one in which a prophet is actually taken up into heaven in order to see the heavenly realities that foreshadow the ultimate triumph of God here on Earth. This second type is found in the New Testament Book of Revelation, in which a prophet named John is taken up through a window in heaven and goes up to the heavenly realm. He ascends through this window and observes the throne of God, on which is sitting God himself; and then he has a vision of subsequent events that take place in heaven, reflecting events that take place here on Earth.

It's a highly symbolic and metaphoric vision that he has. He sees seven seals of a large scroll that are broken, and after each seal is broken a set of catastrophes happen on Earth. After the seventh seal is broken, instead of a final catastrophe on Earth, we're introduced to seven angels who blow trumpets. Each time an angel blows a trumpet, more disasters happen on Earth, until the seventh trumpet, after which there's a period of silence, followed by seven angels who appear with seven bowls of God's wrath, which are poured out on the Earth.

After all of these series of judgments, and persecutions, and oppressions, and wars, and famines that take place on Earth, finally the end comes, in which God sends Christ back to Earth from heaven to set up a perfect millennial kingdom on Earth. At the end of the book, the prophet sees a new heaven and a new Earth, a Jerusalem descending from heaven, a place where people who have followed God will live forever, where there will be no more tears because God will wipe away every tear. There will be no more sin or hatred or war or death. This then is the Book of Revelation, describing the future fate of the Earth by a prophet who has been taken up to the heavenly realm.

Both types of apocalypses—both those in which there is a vision given to the prophet and one in which the prophet is taken up into heaven—are concerned with the fate of the Earth and with people on it. They are theodicies, explanations of God's justice. They try to explain how it is there can be evil and suffering in a world created and maintained by an all-powerful and loving God. If God is all-powerful and all-loving, surely he can stop the suffering people are experiencing. Why, then, doesn't he stop it? According to these apocalypses, God is going to stop the suffering in this world. If people can hold on for just a little while, he will bring in his good kingdom.

Christians living somewhat later than the 1st century adopted this apocalyptic world-view over time. They eventually became less concerned with the salvation of this material world and became more concerned with the salvation of each person's soul. This was a shift away from the teachings that there was to be a real physical overturn of the forces of evil here on Earth. When that never happened, Christians began to transmute the original apocalyptic message of a future kingdom on Earth into a spiritual kingdom in heaven. Rather than thinking in terms of what would happen here in the future, people began thinking in terms of what would happen up in heaven when a person died.

The original expectation of the overthrow of forces of evil here in this world led Christians to emphasize the salvation of the individual soul in the world beyond. This is when heaven and hell became centrally important categories for Christian theology. You look in vain in most of the New Testament for any discussion of heaven and hell as we think of it today, as a place a soul goes when it dies. That's a development that transpires later in Christianity, as soon as the apocalyptic vision of the earliest Christians failed to materialize.

This transformation of emphasis—from a kingdom of God on Earth to heaven after you die and hell after you die—can be seen already in the Apocalypse of Peter. The Apocalypse of Peter was discovered in the year 1886. Though unknown throughout the Middle Ages, it was mentioned by authors of the late 2nd century, some of whom thought that the Apocalypse of Peter should have been included within the canon of the New Testament. There were debates over whether Peter wrote the account or if it was forged, and Christians ended up deciding not to include it in the canon. So the Book of Revelation is the only apocalypse included in the New Testament.

This account is very interesting. It begins with Jesus teaching his disciples on the Mount of Olives, when they ask him when the end is going to come. It starts with a kind of title: "The second coming of Christ and resurrection of the dead, which Christ revealed through Peter." This is a book that involves a revelation about the future, which is given in a mediated way through Jesus to Peter, who then is being portrayed as the prophet. This fits the categorization of what a genre of apocalypse looks like. It then continues:

"When the Lord was seated upon the Mount of Olives, his disciples came to him, and we besought and entreated him separately."

"We" because the author is going to be claiming to be Peter himself.

"We implored him, saying, 'Declare to us, what are the signs of your coming and the end of the world?'"

They want to know what the end is going to be like. Jesus then begins to tell them, in words that sound familiar to the New Testament. Jesus says: "Learn a parable from the fig tree. As soon as its shoots have come forth and the twigs grown, the end of the world shall come. ..."

And I, Peter, answered and said to him, "Interpret the fig tree to me. How can we understand it?"

The Master said to me, "Do you not understand that the fig tree is the house of Israel? Verily, I say to you, when twigs sprout forth in the last days, then shall come false Christs. They'll come, awake expectations, and say, 'I am the Christ who has come before the end of the world.'"

This is a very interesting passage. It's like what we find in Matthew 24, when Jesus describes the wars and the rumors of wars that will happen at the end of time, earthquakes, disasters in many places, and at the very end the Moon will turn to blood, the Sun will stop giving its light, the stars will fall from heaven. Then the Son of Man will come, send his angels to collect the people from every corner of the Earth at the end of time.

And the disciples want to know when this will be, and Jesus says, "Learn the lesson from the fig tree; when the fig tree puts forth its leaves, you know that summer is near. So, too, when you see these hings you know that he is near; he is at the very gates."

The book goes on to explain what will happen in the future judgment. What is most interesting is that the future judgment is concerned not o much with the fate of the Earth, although that does come into play ome. It involves, much more, the fate of the individual souls.

Christ shows Peter what it will be like in the afterlife for people vho have disobeyed God. He describes the glories of heaven and the orments of hell. As typically happens in these Christian descriptions f heaven and hell, the bliss of the saved is described in very glowing erms.

But there's only so many ways you can talk about somebody being 1appy. On the other hand, there are numerous ways you can talk about omebody being tormented, and so there are rather lurid and graphic lescriptions of what it will be like in hell. And we are given this de-cription:

> "Then shall men and women come to the place prepared for them by their tongues wherewith they have blasphemed the way of righteousness. They shall be hanged up, there spread under them unquenchable fire so that they shall not escape it."

So the people who commit blasphemy are hanged by their tongues orever over flames of eternal fire.

> "Again, behold, there were two women. They hung them up by their neck and by their hair. They shall cast them into the pit. Who are these women who are hanged by their hair? These are those who plaited their hair, not to make themselves beautiful, but to turn them to fornication, that they might ensnare the souls of men to perdition."

So women who have braided their hair to make themselves attrac-ive will be hanged by their hair over eternal fire. The men who lay with hem in fornication shall be hung by other bodily parts. Besides those ire others.

In another place full of filth they cast men and women up to their knees. These are ones who loved money and took usury. So if you lend >ut your money at interest, you end up in pits of filth.

> "There shall be another place very high. The men and women whose feet slipped shall go rolling down into a place where there is fear."

And again, while the fire that is prepared flows, they mount up and fall down again and continually to fall down. They shall be tormented forever. These are those who did not honor their father and their mother."

He describes how people will be punished for their sins, and in most cases the punishment corresponds to the sins they committed during their lives. This is what people can expect during the afterlife, according to the Apocalypse of Peter.

The four horsemen of the apocalypse are figures described in chapter 6 of the Book of Revelations in the New Testament.

There are several major points this author wants to make. One obvious point is that anyone who sides with God is going to reap a reward but anyone who opposes God will pay an eternal and horrific price Ultimately, appearances notwithstanding, this shows that God is in control of this world and all that happens in it. You may think that people are sinning, doing horrible things, oppressing other people killing, doing all sorts of harmful, hateful things and they are getting with it. No. According to this account, they are not. God, ultimately is going to have the last say. The last say, though, involves not just future kingdom on Earth. It actually involves the afterlife of heaven and hell.

These accounts, like the other earlier Christian apocalypses, are no meant merely to scare people into avoiding certain kinds of behavior They are also meant to explain how it is there is evil and suffering in this age, and how that evil and suffering will be resolved in the next age.

What happens here will be overturned there; those who are wicked now will pay an eternal price later, whereas those who suffer for doing what is right in this age will be vindicated forever—as God show once andd for all that he alone is sovereign over this world. ∎

The preceding lecture was an excerpt drawn from The Great Course:

Lost Christianities: Christian Scriptures and the Battles over Authentication

Course #6593

In the first centuries after Christ, there was no official New Testament. Instead, early Christians read and fervently followed a wide variety of scriptures—many more than we have today.
What did these other scriptures say? Do they exist today? How could such outlandish ideas ever be considered Christian? If such beliefs were once common, why do they no longer exist?

Lecture Titles

Bart D. Ehrman

Bart D. Ehrman is the James A. Gray Professor and Chair of the Department of Religious Studies at The University of North Carolina at Chapel Hill, where he has been teaching for over 15 years. He completed his undergraduate work at Wheaton College and received his Masters of Divinity and Ph.D. from Princeton Theological Seminary. Prior to taking his position at UNC, Professor Ehrman taught at Rutgers University.

If you would like to order this course, please contact us at:
Phone: 1-800-TEACH-12
Web: www.TEACH12.com
For more information on our pricing policy, see page 245.

Behavior and thought are both influenced by our ability to communicate effectively with others.

SOCIAL SCIENCE

"Language is a city to the building of which
every human being brought a stone."

—Ralph Waldo Emerson

Linguistics:
Famous Last Words

There were once creatures in this world that were much taller and bigger than buildings. We know them as dinosaurs. You can see the skeletons in museums.

There are times when you have to look at those skeletons, which are practically dwarfing the room, and think, "That lived. That had skin and muscles. It mated. It made noise. It messed things up. It had emotions. It went to the bathroom. That was a living thing." We can know a whole lot about dinosaurs based on finding those bones, and there are so many massively clever ways that we can reconstruct what these animals were like by extrapolating from those bones.

But a language is not like that. It's just a mouthful of air; if it's not recorded there's no way to recover it. If we find an ancient skeleton, we have no way to reconstruct what language it spoke from looking at its hyoid bone or the cut of its jaw or how its teeth were. So when a language is dead, it is dead.

The fact is languages have always died to an extent. Languages have died when all of their speakers were exterminated for some reason or, more frequently, when speakers of a language are subordinated by some group and gradually switch to the language of the dominant. In the Eurasian region alone, there are dozens of languages that we know have died; some of them recorded, but a great many of them not at all or in just, say, a word list or two or an inscription that says something like, "This is my sheep." But that doesn't give you a sense of what the whole language was like.

The process accelerated with the Neolithic Revolution. It used to be that human beings were small hunter-gatherer groups patching the globe, only knowing each other when they happened to be close to each other. But once we had certain groups spreading and taking over

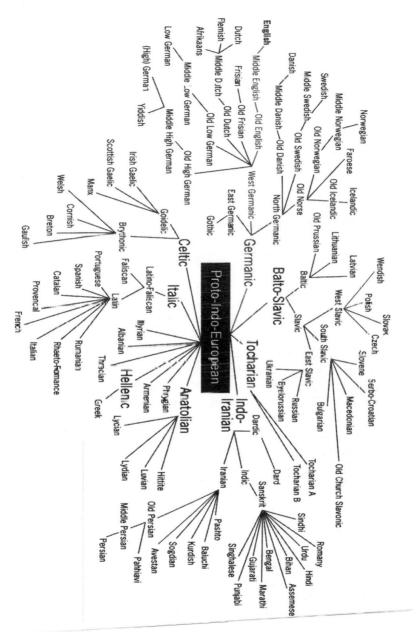

The Proto-Indo-European Family Tree. This diagram shows how Proto-Indo-European, a language spoken by the first Indo-Europeans, evolved into many of the languages we know today.

large portions of land and in the process of subjugating other people, then you had a situation where certainly a great many languages were being exterminated. There are estimates that there were probably tens of thousands of languages at a time in this original hunter-gatherer situation, and yet today we've got 6,000. If you look at the countries of the world and think that there must be 200 or 300 languages, when you read 6,000, that seems like a lot. But of course 6,000 is just a fraction of what could have been 50,000 or 100,000.

In general, migrators' languages tend to extinguish the languages of the people that they encounter. There are probably fewer languages today than at any other point in human history because humans have migrated extensively enough to more or less cover the planet. But the process today is occurring at a much more accelerated rate. An interesting statistic is that, today, 96 percent of the world's people speak one of the 20 most-spoken languages. In the vast majority of cases they also speak one of the many other languages, but they also are speaking one of the Big 20. The Big 20 are Chinese, English, Spanish, Hindi, Arabic, Bengali, Russian, Portuguese, Japanese, German, French, Punjabi, Javanese, Bihari (you probably won't believe that, because you probably haven't heard of it; most people haven't), Italian, Korean, Telugu, Tamil, Marathi, and Vietnamese. Those are the Big 20, and pretty much everybody on Earth speaks one of those, which is dangerous in terms of the others. Because, as life and reality tend to have it, if you're speaking one of the big ones, there is quite a chance that a generation that you sire, or a generation that that generation sires, is going to switch to only that one. That's especially the case the smaller your indigenous language is.

According to one estimate, we will have only 10 percent of the languages that we have today in the year 2100. So, in roughly a century we will lose about 5,500 languages as spoken ones. That is sobering. It has also been said that a language on Earth dies somewhere every two weeks. We're speaking English, and it keeps going. But imagine if this just vanished; if there were a 215-year-old woman, and she was the last speaker of English, and it had never been written down except for one shard of the Bible and something scratched on the back of a Bazooka Joe wrapper—which, of course, is redundant because the Bazooka Joe wrapper would be in English. But you take my point. Then she dies, her last breath, and her last word is something like "Bosco," and then that's it. That is happening to one language every two weeks. ∎

The preceding lecture was an excerpt drawn from The Great Course:

The Story of Human Language
Course #1600

Dr. John McWhorter, one of America's leading linguists and a frequent commentator on network television and National Public Radio, takes you on an in-depth, 36-lecture tour of the development of language, showing how a single tongue spoken 150,000 years ago has evolved into the estimated 6,000 languages used around the world today.

Lecture Titles

John McWhorter

Professor John McWhorter is a Senior Fellow at the Manhattan Institute. He earned his B.A. from Rutgers University, his M.A. from New York University, and his Ph.D. in Linguistics from Stanford University. Prior to taking his position at Manhattan, he held teaching positions at Cornell University and the University of California at Berkeley.

If you would like to order this course, please contact us at:

Phone: 1-800-TEACH-12
Web: www.TEACH12.com

For more information on our pricing policy, see page 245.

The Great Ideas of Psychology
Course #660
Lecture 43

Taught by: Professor Daniel N. Robinson
Georgetown University and Oxford University

On Being Sane in Insane Places

What do we mean by a mental illness? How do we define an illness that we regard in nonphysical terms, but mental terms?

We begin to answer that question by raising another question, and that is: Who has control of the labels? Who is it entrusted with the task of determining that Smith is manic or manic depressive or melancholic or that Jones is a witch—because, after all, that was yet another form of disturbance which for 300 years received a therapeutic intervention that was absolutely lethal.

Psychopathology, which these days is understood increasingly in genetic terms and biochemical terms, offers an example of the powerful influence of con-

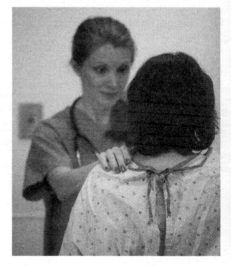

The sanity of a person is often judged on the basis of an initial diagnosis.

text, not only on behavior and judgment, but on judgment within settings that are quite professional settings. There's a very famous paper on this subject published many years ago by David Rosenhan, an article that he titled "On Being Sane in Insane Places."

David Rosenhan has for a long time been a distinguished professor of psychology at Stanford University, and many years ago he talked himself and some of his students and colleagues into a quite interesting experiment that would have them getting admitted to a mental hospital. In order to get admitted, they showed up at different times and they were in no apparent way related to each other, but they had to come in with certain sorts of vague presenting symptoms; they had to report certain psychological disturbances they were having, perhaps the occasional hallucinatory experience and nightmarish events and a kind of nervousness, a sense of suspiciousness, a difficulty getting along with people, a restlessness, and the like. They came in with this: They didn't quite know what was getting at them, but they needed some kind of help and got admitted.

Now the arrangement was this: Once admitted, they were to proceed to behave, daily, exactly as they would behave in life before the period of admission. So, nothing they were doing, once admitted, in any way would alert or alarm a clinical staff, a medical or psychiatric community, to the possibility that these were people in need of any kind of psychiatric treatment at all. Their behavior became quite normal. Interestingly, the diagnosis on admission was entirely unresponsive to any behavior they displayed after admission. There was no change in the diagnosis. In other words, the diagnosis on admission turned out to be a kind of typology. These people now were this type; that is, a type requiring psychiatric treatment. Subsequent behavior was largely ignored or irrelevant. They would have lengthy interviews with members of the staff in which they responded correctly and entirely normally.

One person in the group who happened to be an authority on the subject of depression, noticed that a patient in the ward who was being treated for depression was on a pharmacological regimen that this expert regarded as the wrong drug—it was not the drug of choice. He undertook a quite lengthy discussion on this subject with one of the attending psychiatrists, who, of course, regarded the interlocutor as a patient, but nonetheless engaged the interlocutor in this long discussion, with the chap pointing out that yes, he had made a study of depression, he did think he knew quite a bit about it, and he thought that in this particular case the medicine prescribed wasn't right for that patient.

So here's this long conversation going on—it might have been a conversation between colleagues—and what's written down on his chart once the conversation is over, is that he "suffers grandiosity." So, what he might have said for pay as a consultant or as part of a convention address that this very psychiatrist might have been pleased and proud to attend, constituted grounds for having his own medication increased because, after all, when somebody who's a patient says this, it can only mean one thing: He's quite grandiose.

Well, what is it like being sane in insane places? What is it like to be sane at all? What is it like being classified as a type, and namely as a type answering to the description psychopathology? Well, of course, what Rosenhan's study made quite clear is that once one is diagnosed as being an X, one is going to be treated as being an X, and it doesn't much matter how one behaves, what one says, what the contents are of one's perceptions and cognitions, what the affective tone of daily life is, because the setting now has established that you are an X, and you will be an X forever more.

There was some great concern about whether these people were ever going to be able to get themselves released; that is to say, one was not going to get released merely on the grounds that one was no longer symptomatic because, in fact, from the moment of their admission they ceased to be symptomatic. Indeed, had we been dealing with a scientifically developed mode of expertise, a scientifically developed mode of diagnosis, treatment, and the like, given the crowded nature of such facilities, the minute these people went into the second or third day of normal behavior, probably somebody would have sensed that there was a ruse going on.

The question that I always found very interesting and not answered by the research is: What is it that members of the staff were missing here? Should it not have been starkly obvious going into this clinic that some numbers of persons in the room were quite normal, just by way of a contrast effect?

Now, of course, what David Rosenhan would be fairly prepared to say—and has said—is that, of course, the reason why nobody noticed the stark contrast between the Stanford crowd and those who were there is that, in fact, there wasn't a stark contrast between the Stanford crowd and those who were there. It has been observed repeatedly, both before this research and after, that large fractions of clinical populations in mental hospitals only reveal themselves to be patients because of how they're dressed and how they're addressed and how they're treated or not treated.

This is not to say that there are not *bona fide* instances of serious disturbances at the level of cognitive and emotional life warranting hospitalization and treatment. It is to say, instead, that for the longest time the populations thus classified included only a relatively small percentage of people who manifestly, unequivocally, needed institutionalization and all of the treatments that go with conditions of so severe a nature. ∎

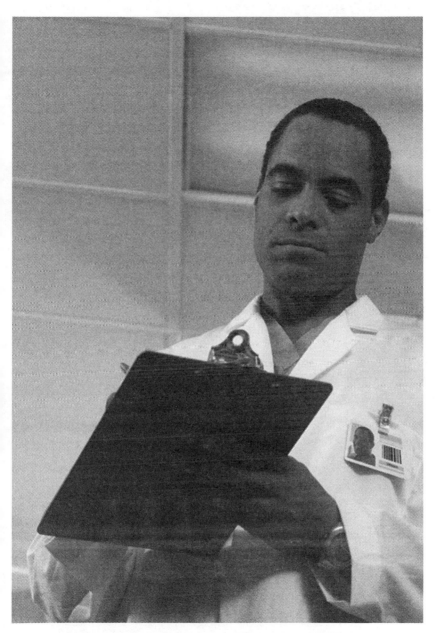

Rosenhan's study showed that once the initial diagnosis was made, no further evaluations of the patients' conditions were ever considered. Even though the patients behaved normally during their entire stay in the mental institution, they were treated, not on the basis of their behavior, but on the basis of their initial diagnosis.

Social Science

The preceding lecture was an excerpt drawn from The Great Course:

The Great Ideas of Psychology
Course #660

If you've ever wanted to delve more deeply into the mysteries of emotion, perception, and cognition, and of why people do what we do, this course offers a superb place to start.

As you hear these lectures, you hear the entire history of psychology unfold. And you learn that the subject most of us today associate with the names Sigmund Freud, Carl Jung, and B. F. Skinner really began thousands of years earlier.

In the hands of Professor Daniel N. Robinson, this course roams far and wide, encompassing ideas, speculations, and point-blank moral questions that might just dismantle and rebuild everything you thought you knew about psychology.

Daniel N. Robinson

Daniel N. Robinson is a member of the Philosophy faculty at Oxford University, where he has lectured annually since 1991. He is also Distinguished Professor, Emeritus, at Georgetown University, on whose faculty he served for 30 years. He was formerly Adjunct Professor of Psychology at Columbia University.

Professor Robinson earned his Ph.D. in Neuropsychology from City University of New York. Prior to taking his position at Georgetown, he held positions at Amherst College, Princeton University, and Columbia University.

Professor Robinson is past president of two divisions of the American Psychological Association: The Division of History of Psychology and the Division of Theoretical and Philosophical Psychology. He is former editor of the *Journal of Theoretical and Philosophical Psychology*. Professor Robinson is author or editor of more than 40 books, including *Wild Beasts & Idle Humours: The Insanity Defense from Antiquity to the Present, An Intellectual History of Psychology, The Mind: An Oxford Reader,* and *Aristotle's Psychology.*

In 2001, Professor Robinson received the Lifetime Achievement Award from the Division of History of Psychology of the American Psychological Association, and the Distinguished Contribution Award from the Division of Theoretical and Philosophical Psychology of the American Psychological Association.

Lecture Titles

If you would like to order this course, please contact us at:

Phone: 1-800-TEACH-12

Web: www.TEACH12.com

For more information on our pricing policy, see page 245.

Money—essentially worthless markers of paper and metals that represent actual value—has revolutionized human economic practices.

ECONOMICS

"Beware of small expenses; a small
leak will sink a great ship."

—Benjamin Franklin

234 The Federal Reserve and Its Powers

Money talks, and when the Federal Reserve Board speaks,
everyone listens. You can bank on the fact that this is the most
powerful financial institution in the world. Learn what this
means for you.

Economics, 3rd Edition
Course #550
Lecture 30

Taught by: Professor Timothy Taylor
Macalester College

The Federal Reserve and Its Powers

Here's a question for you: What is the most powerful individual economic actor in the world?

The United States has the largest economy of any country in the world, so you might think, maybe the president of the United States. But the president of the United States has a lot of control over foreign policy in a very direct sense, but all tax and spending bills have to go through Congress before the president makes a choice about signing them. Maybe it's someone like the leader of Saudi Arabia, for the amount of impact that person can have over world oil prices; or maybe it's someone in China, with its rapidly growing economy. But even in those nondemocratic countries, indi-

The Federal Reserve Bank in Washington, DC, was designed and completed in 1937. President Roosevelt dedicated the building.

vidual leaders are often constrained in various ways by the different groups to which they belong and owe allegiance.

Article 1, Section 8 of the U.S. Constitution gives Congress the power to coin money and to regulate the value thereof. In 1913, Congress created the Federal Reserve Bank and delegated these powers to the the Chairman of the Federal Reserve has great power over the money supply and interest rates; and on a day-to-day basis and a year-to-year basis, that power is not directly limited by Congress or by the president. In some ways, you can make a case that the head of the Federal Reserve, the head of the central bank of the United States, is the most powerful economic actor in the world.

The Federal Reserve, like most central banks, is run with a mix of public and private elements. In the jargon, we call it a quasi-public corporation—quasi-public meaning it's technically a private corporation, but it has some very strong public elements. Officially, the Federal Reserve Bank is a corporation, which is owned by all of the federally chartered banks. So while it's officially a company in that sense—a private company—it's not a company you can buy stock in. It's not listed on the Fortune 500, and you can't invest your pension in the Federal Reserve.

The Federal Reserve is a peculiar organization because of the way it mixes government appointees with representation and ownership, ultimately, of private-sector banks. At the national level, the Federal Reserve is run by what's called a Board of Governors. The Board of Governors consists of seven members. Each member is appointed by the president and then has to go through confirmation by the U.S. Senate.

The terms of the Board of Governors are structured in such a way as to create some political independence. The Board of Governors appointments are for 14-year terms, which means once you're appointed, you would outlast the president who appointed you. The terms are arranged so that one term expires on January 31 of every even-numbered year. So over 14 years, the entire board would rotate.

A person can serve only one full term on the Board of Governors. However, these 14-year terms are so long that Board members often leave before their term is completed. If a person is appointed to fill out the remainder of someone else's term, then that person could still be appointed to a full 14-year term of their own.

One member of the Board of Governors at the Federal Reserve is designated as the chairman. From 1987 up through 2006, the Federal Reserve chairman was Alan Greenspan. Greenspan was originally appointed in 1987 to fill out someone else's term, but then he was appointed to his own 14-year term in 1992, and that's why his term lasted through 2006.

The point of this structure is to ensure some degree of political independence. Yes, you have to be appointed by the president and confirmed by the Senate, but once you're in the Federal Reserve system, once you're a governor of the Federal Reserve, then on a day-to-day basis, you're quite insulated from day-to-day politics.

How does the Federal Reserve, or a central bank, in general, enact its monetary policy? In other words, monetary policy is the policy of expanding or contracting the money supply, of encouraging or discouraging a greater amount of aggregate demand or a lesser amount of aggregate demand in the economy. A central bank has three main tools for working with the web of banking and money to expand or contract how much money is out there. The three main tools are: reserve requirements, the discount rate, and open market operations. Let's walk through these three main tools one by one.

The first tool: the reserve requirement. The reserve requirement is that banks are not allowed to loan out a certain percentage of their deposits. What does that mean exactly? Banks lend out deposits to people; people deposit the money in other banks; those banks then have the deposits, and can lend the deposits out to other people; and this web of depositing and lending keeps going on and on.

Every bank is required to keep some of its deposits on reserve at the central bank. What that means is, in effect, they have to deposit money with the central bank. There's no payment of interest in exchange for that reserve requirement. It's just money that they have to hold aside as a safety reserve.

If this reserve requirement gets higher, then each individual bank has less money to lend out. If each individual bank has less money to lend out, the quantity of loans available in the economy diminishes, and one would expect that interest rates will rise. The price of borrowing money would get somewhat higher.

On the other side, if the reserve requirement is reduced, then all the banks in the economy can hold less money with the Federal Reserve. Banks have more money to lend out; they can expand the supply of lending and aggregate demand in the economy. As more funds become available to lend out and the supply of loanable funds expands, then the interest rate should decline a little bit.

In 2003, just to give you a sense of how this works, the Federal Reserve required that banks hold reserves equal to three percent of the first $41.3 million deposited in checking and savings accounts for the bank as a whole. For any amounts deposited above $41.3 million, the bank had to hold reserves equal to 10 percent of that amount. That was the reserve requirement in 2003.

Now, almost every year, small changes are made in the reserve requirement. For example, that $41.3 million dividing line is sometimes bumped up by a few million dollars, or bumped down by a few million dollars. Of course, banks are always inventing new kinds of accounts, and so the question of whether something is in a savings account or a checking account, or exactly how these different accounts work, requires some different technical rulings. But, changes in reserve requirements that have a large effect on bank reserves are actually quite rare. This tool of monetary policy, at least in the United States, is not used all that often.

There's a second way the Federal Reserve could think about controlling and encouraging banks to lend or not lend out money. Imagine a situation where the bank has loaned out most, or perhaps all, of the funds it can possibly loan out, right up to the edge of the reserve requirement.

Of course, banks can't be sure at the very end of the day, if they're right on the edge, if they've gone a little too far in lending, or not quite far enough; or what if someone comes, and gets deposits, and pulls some money out? Then unexpectedly, they might find that they don't have enough deposited with the central bank to meet the reserve requirement. In that situation, the reserve requirement has to be met. In the short term, if the bank gets into the situation where they're right on the edge, they borrow from the central bank. They borrow short term, just long enough to get their accounts straightened out, to adjust their balance of loans and deposits, so that they have enough money stored for the reserve requirement.

When you borrow from the central bank, the interest rate that is charged to an individual bank for borrowing from the central bank is called the discount rate. That discount rate is the second big tool of monetary policy.

Think for a moment about how the discount rate would work. Imagine that the central bank raises the discount rate. It charges a higher discount rate to individual banks. When the central bank does that, it's going to encourage banks to keep money on hand, because they know that, if they run over and they do need to borrow from the central bank, they need to pay a high interest rate. So, banks will be encouraged to leave an extra margin—not just the reserve requirement—but some extra margin, to make sure they don't bump into that reserve requirement. That extra margin means that banks would loan out a little bit less than they otherwise would. A higher discount rate from the central bank discourages banks from loaning a little bit, and will reduce the amount of money that's out there in the economy.

Conversely, what happens if the central bank reduces the discount rate? Well, if it reduces the discount rate, then banks are going to be less concerned that they don't have enough on reserve at the central bank. If they're less concerned that they don't have enough, then banks are going to be more willing to lend right up to the maximum possible, because they know that if they need to borrow money from the central bank, it's not a big deal. It's not going to be a high rate of interest that they need to pay. These are extremely short-term loans; often, they're literally overnight; so a low rate of interest overnight isn't going to be a big deal.

Although this is a perfectly good theoretical tool of monetary policy, in practice, the Federal Reserve, most of the time, lends relatively little money at the discount rate. Before a bank borrows from the Federal Reserve to fill out its needed reserves, the bank is expected to first try and borrow from other available sources, like other banks. So, this discount rate, which is the rate charged from the central bank to individual member banks, doesn't have as much of an effect as you might think, because not very much is borrowed at that rate. Instead, the key interest rate is probably the rate at which banks charge each other for these overnight loans.

Ultimately, the discount rate doesn't get moved up and down a whole lot; it does in some cases, but it's not a very commonly used tool of monetary policy.

The third tool is really the main tool of monetary policy. The third tool is referred to as open market operations. Open market operations occur when a central bank buys or sells bonds with the goal of decreasing or increasing the money supply.

Think about how this works. Banks are holding assets. They've got these deposits that people have given them, and they need to invest those deposits one way or another. Some of the deposits banks, in effect, loan out to people, and they get interest rates in that way. But most banks also hold a certain amount of money in bonds, usually in government bonds, and they receive some interest just from holding those bonds.

The Federal Reserve can buy and sell bonds with banks. Let's say that the Federal Reserve goes to banks and buys bonds; we're talking about bonds issued by the U.S. government. So, the Federal Reserve goes to the banks; the Federal Reserve gives the banks money; the banks give bonds to the Federal Reserve. In that situation, the banks now have more money to lend, while the Federal Reserve is holding the bonds.

When the Fed buys bonds from the banks, the banks end up with more money to lend out. Remember, bonds are not money. They're not part of M1, or M2, or M3. A bank that is holding bonds, which has invested depositors' money in treasury bonds, can't lend out the bonds. That money is, in effect, tied up. So, when the Federal Reserve buys the bonds, it loosens up that money; it provides money to the bank, and then the bank can lend out more than it otherwise would.

What's the intuition on the other side? What if the Federal Reserve takes some of the treasury bonds that it's built up over time, and it sells those bonds to banks? Then, the banks have more bonds and the Federal Reserve has more money. The banks have handed over money in the sense of M1, or M2, or M3 to the Federal Reserve and now, the assets of the bank are tied up in these bonds, which they can't lend out. When that happens, then the bank is going to have less money to lend out. The quantity of loans in the economy will be smaller, and the aggregate demand will be diminished as well.

Open market operations are the most primary, direct, and commonly used tool of monetary policy. The real reason for that is that the reserve requirement and the discount rate require thinking about how banks will react to a change in rules, and how banks will react and think about what they're going to do if this interest rate goes up, or this reserve requirement goes up. That's a bit of a sketchy thing to try and think about. One can never be entirely sure. But with an open market operation, you can order a specific quantity of bonds to be bought or sold. You can see the result, and if you want to do more, you can do more. So it's fairly direct and predictable; it's a lever that really seems to work.

The open market decisions about buying and selling bonds are made by something called the Federal Open Market Committee, the FOMC. The Federal Open Market Committee is actually made up of 12 members rather than just the seven on the Board of Governors. It includes the seven people on the Board of Governors, but it also includes five representatives from bank districts all around the country; and that group rotates over time. Decisions about open market operations are not just made by these presidential appointees, although they do have a majority of the group of 12 on the Federal Open Market Committee. There is also input from people who are actually involved in banking all around the country.

Banks create money through this web of interconnected loans. One bank makes a loan; it's deposited in another bank; it provides the basis for an additional loan, and so on. Essentially, these tools of monetary policy all work because they make banks either more or less eager to lend; or, to put it a little differently, more or less able to lend.

To nail down this point, consider how monetary policy directly influences lending, aggregate demand, and interest rates. If you want money supply to be larger, what can you do? Well, you could either have a lower reserve requirement or a lower discount rate—both of which mean banks are willing to lend out more—or you can have an open market operation of buying bonds from the banks, so the banks would have more money and fewer bonds.

All these steps to expand the money supply can be referred to as expansionary policy—a term used for fiscal policy—or looser monetary policy. They all tend to reduce interest rates, and they all encourage more lending and more overall demand in the economy. In terms of our aggregate supply-and-demand model, they increase the amount of aggregate demand that's out there in the economy.

On the flip side, what steps would be necessary to reduce the growth in the money supply, or at least to restrain the rate of growth in the money supply that might otherwise have happened? What would be involved with a contractionary, or a tight, monetary policy? Well, it would be a higher discount rate, to discourage banks from lending; it would be open market operations of selling bonds, so banks have more bonds and less money; or it could be a higher reserve requirement. All of these would tend to change the money supply in such a way that you would have tighter money supply; you would have higher interest rates; and there would be less lending and overall demand in the economy. In terms of our aggregate supply-and-demand model, all of these steps would reduce aggregate demand or limit the rise in aggregate demand.

When you hear news reports about the Federal Reserve, you typically hear something like the Fed has increased or decreased interest rates. But that isn't what is actually happening. The Fed doesn't have dictatorial powers where it just says, "We want interest rates to rise," or, "We want interest rates to fall." Instead, the Federal Reserve central bank affects the supply of funds that banks are willing to lend. With expansionary policy, more banks are willing to lend; with an increased supply of funds, interest rates fall. If the Fed uses contractionary monetary policy, banks lend less; with a decreased supply of loanable funds, interest rates rise.

More specifically, the Fed actually targets or aims at one specific interest rate, called the federal funds rate. The federal funds rate is the interest rate at which banks make short-term loans to other banks, which is the interest rate for those specific loans we were talking about before. As this interest rate goes up or down, the federal funds interest rate and other interest rates—like the rate on your car loan or your home loan—more or less move up and down with that rate.

While there are a number of other tasks that a central bank has in helping money and credit function smoothly in the economy, monetary policy and having interest rates rise or fall is the main task of the central bank, and the one that gets the most media attention. ∎

The preceding lecture was an excerpt drawn from The Great Course:

Economics, 3rd Edition
Course #550

We are all economists—when we work, buy, save, invest, pay taxes, and vote. It repays us *many* times over to be good economists. However, when the subject of economics comes up in conversation or on the news, we can find ourselves longing for a more sophisticated understanding of the fundamentals of economics.

Lecture Titles

Timothy Taylor

Timothy Taylor is Managing Editor of the *Journal of Economic Perspectives*, a quarterly academic journal produced at Macalester College and published by the American Economic Association. He received his Bachelor of Arts degree from Haverford College and a Master's degree in Economics from Stanford University.

At Stanford, he was winner of the award for excellent teaching in a large class given by the Associated Students of Stanford University. At Minnesota he was named a Distinguished Lecturer by the Department of Economics and voted Teacher of the Year.

If you would like to order this course, please contact us at:

Phone: 1-800-TEACH-12
Web: www.TEACH12.com
For more information on our pricing policy, see page 245.

Frequently Asked Questions

How did The Teaching Company begin?

The Teaching Company was founded in 1990 by Thomas M. Rollins, former Chief Counsel of the United States Senate Committee on Labor and Human Resources. Years earlier, as a Harvard Law School student, Rollins had an unforgettable experience that opened his eyes to the extraordinary power of a great lecturer captured on tape.

Rollins was facing an important exam in the Federal Rules of Evidence, but was not well prepared. He managed to obtain videotapes of 10 one-hour lectures by a noted authority on the subject, Professor Irving Younger. "I dreaded what seemed certain to be boring," Rollins says. "I thought that few subjects could be as dull as the Federal Rules of Evidence. But I had no other way out."

Rollins planted himself in front of the TV and played all 10 hours nearly nonstop. The lectures, he says, "were outrageously insightful, funny, and thorough." Watching Professor Younger's lectures was one of Rollins's best experiences as a student. Rollins made an "A" in the course. And he never forgot the unique power of recorded lectures by a great teacher.

After many years of government service, Rollins founded The Teaching Company to ignite people's passion for lifelong learning by offering great courses taught by great professors.

What does The Teaching Company do?

The Teaching Company records the finest lecturing university professors in the world to create a curriculum in the arts and sciences available to people who love to learn. More than 2,000 hours of topics in literature, philosophy, history, fine arts, religion, and the sciences are currently for sale.

Since 1990, great teachers from the Ivy League, Stanford, Georgetown, and other leading colleges and universities have crafted more than 200 courses for lifelong learners. We provide the adventure of learning without the homework, pressure, or exams.

What are The Great Courses®?

The Great Courses are intellectual investigations into the most fascinating ideas in the world, and, as such, we believe that to do these investigations justice requires an in-depth approach. That's why our courses are between six and 42 hours long and come to you in a series of 30- or 45-minute lectures on CD, DVD, audiotape, printed transcripts, and MP3 and MPEG-4 formats downloadable directly from our website.

Each six-hour course segment comes with its own Course Guidebook containing a syllabus, outlines of each lecture, glossary, bibliography of suggested readings, and—when appropriate—maps, diagrams, illustrations, and a timeline.

How do you choose the professors?

America has nearly 500,000 college professors. We have identified the top 1 percent of professors based on their teaching awards, published evaluations of them, newspaper writeups of the best teachers on campus, and other sources.

Each year, our professional recruiters travel the country—from Harvard to Stanford, UCLA to UNC—and listen to hundreds from the top 1 percent. Of these, we select about 1 in 20 to give an audition lecture for The Teaching Company. Each audition is reviewed by hundreds of our customers. The professors who get high scores from our customers are invited to craft new courses. More than 15,000 of our customers have voted on audition lectures to select our faculty.

How do you make the courses?

We work closely with our customers and professors to create The Great Courses. Here's how:

- Customers choose the professors. Only one in 5,000 professors meets the standards set by our customers, who vote on all professors we retain.
- Customers choose the courses. We interview thousands of customers to find out what titles they want and how they want us to make our courses.
- The professors carefully prepare each course. Months of prep-

aration ensure that a course will satisfy our customers. Long before a word is spoken on our sound stage, every professor outlines and prepares each lecture and writes the extensive Course Guidebook. Our own producers help to slate each image that will be included in the video version of the course.

- We control the quality by recording courses in-house. Professors come to our studio in Chantilly, Virginia (near Washington, DC) to deliver their lectures.
- The video of each lecture is recorded on broadcast-quality equipment and media.
- The audio for each lecture is recorded on CD-quality equipment and media.
- We then devote weeks to include all appropriate images and text in the videos and to professionally master the sound for the audio and video versions of our courses.

What media formats are available for the courses?

We offer courses in the following formats:
- Digital Video Disc (DVD)
- Audio Compact Disc (CD)
- Audiotape
- Transcript Book
- Audio download files in MP3 or MPEG-4

Digital media—DVDs, CDs, and our download files—provide the highest quality for video and audio.

Transcript Books are attractive, soft-bound books of 170–250 pages. They contain all the information that's in the Course Guidebooks you receive with every course, and lightly edited transcripts of all the lectures.

Should I buy audio or video?

The choice between audio and video depends on how you want to use the course and on its content.

The audio version is very flexible, allowing you to listen to The Great Courses almost anywhere and at any time you like: while commuting, jogging, gardening, even swimming.

The video version contains all the images that a professor would find useful in teaching. Some visual elements (e.g., charts, graphs, illustrations, physical experiments) enhance the professor's presentation. If a course requires visual elements to illustrate the material, we issue the course only in video. In most cases, our professors are able to explain the visual contents of a course to the "audio audience," and we issue the course in both audio and video.

Each detailed course description in our catalogs and on our website includes a section at the end to help you choose the right format.

When and why do courses go on sale?

Every course we make goes on sale at least once a year. This revolving sales approach allows us to provide you with great value and great service.

Producing large quantities of only the sale courses keeps our manufacturing and inventory costs down, and we pass the savings on to you. This approach also enables us to fill your order immediately: 99 percent of all orders placed by 2:00 pm eastern time ship that same day.

To find out which courses are on sale, please check our catalogs, newsletters, or website. The catalogs and newsletters clearly identify the courses currently on sale. On the website, visit the "On Sale" section, or visit the "Your Account" section and try our Sale Notifier, which will inform you when specific courses of interest to you go on sale.

Are the courses guaranteed?

Yes. If a course is ever less than completely satisfying, you may exchange it for another or we will refund your money promptly. Or, if a tape or disc ever breaks, warps, or gets damaged, we'll replace it, as long as the course is in print, free.

Most publishers do not guarantee you will be satisfied with their books or recordings. But we do. We guarantee your satisfaction for a lifetime because we want you to be our customer for a lifetime of learning.

This guarantee, which we have honored every day since we

opened our doors, not only protects your investment in learning, it compels us to produce great courses and nothing less; otherwise, we'd go out of business.

How can I contact The Teaching Company?
You can reach us by:

E-mail: custserv@teachco.com
Phone: 1-800-TEACH-12 (1-800-832-2412)
  Our office hours are 9 am to 12 midnight eastern time, Monday through Friday; and 9 am to 5 pm eastern time, Saturday. After hours, an automated voicemail system is available.
Fax: 703-378-3819
Mail: The Teaching Company
        4151 Lafayette Center Drive, Suite 100
        Chantilly, VA 20151-1232

If you have further questions, please contact our Customer Service Team at custserv@teachco.com, or visit us online at www.TEACH12.com.

Image Credits:

Cover: © Bruce Burkhardt/CORBIS; xii: Prints and Photographs Division, Library of Congress; p. 3: Prints and Photographs Division, Library of Congress; p. 5: Prints and Photographs Division, Library of Congress; p. 9: © Bettmann/CORBIS; p. 10: © 2007 JupiterImages Corporation; p. 11: Prints and Photographs Division, Library of Congress; p. 13: © Masterfile; p. 17: Prints and Photographs Division, Library of Congress; p.18: Prints and Photographs Division, Library of Congress; p. 30: © 2007 JupiterImages Corporation; p. 33: Courtesy NASA and the NSSDC; p. 34: Courtesy NASA and the NSSDC; p. 37: Courtesy Alex Filippenko; p. 41: © 2007 JupiterImages Corporation; p. 46: Prints and Photographs Division, Library of Congress; p. 55: © 2007 JupiterImages Corporation; p. 58: The Teaching Company Collection; p. 61: Prints and Photographs Division, Library of Congress; p. 63: Prints and Photographs Division, Library of Congress; p. 69: Prints and Photographs Division, Library of Congress; p. 76: © 2007 JupiterImages Corporation; p. 81: Prints and Photographs Division, Library of Congress; p. 90: © 2007 JupiterImages Corporation; p. 92: © 2007 JupiterImages Corporation; p. 95: © 2007 JupiterImages Corporation; p. 97: Prints and Photographs Division, Library of Congress; p. 98: Prints and Photographs Division, Library of Congress; p. 101: Prints and Photographs Division, Library of Congress; p. 105: Prints and Photographs Division, Library of Congress; p. 106: © Bettmann/CORBIS; p. 108: Prints and Photographs Division, Library of Congress; p. 110: Prints and Photographs Division, Library of Congress; p. 111· Prints and Photographs Division, Library of Congress; p. 112: Prints and Photographs Division, Library of Congress; p. 114: © 2007 JupiterImages Corporation; p. 121: Prints and Photographs Division, Library of Congress; p. 126: © Royalty-Free/Corbis; p. 129: The Teaching Company Collection; p. 130: © 2007 JupiterImages Corporation; p. 133: The Teaching Company Collection; p. 138: The Complete Encyclopedia of Illustration; p. 141: © 2007 JupiterImages Corporation; p. 143: © Corel Stock Photo Library; p. 146: The Teaching Company Collection; p. 149: The Teaching Company Collection; p. 150: The Teaching Company Collection, p. 154: © Corel Stock Photo Library; p. 157: © Digital Stock Corporation; p. 158: Prints and Photographs Division, Library of Congress; p. 161: The Teaching Company Collection, © 2003 ROBESUS, INC. robesus@robesus.com, p. 162: Photograph from the U.S. Coast Guard Collection in the U.S. National Archives; p. 165: The Teaching Company Collection; p. 167: © 2007 JupiterImages Corporation; p. 168: Prints and Photographs Division, Library of Congress; p. 171: Prints and Photographs Division, Library of Congress; p. 175: Prints and Photographs Division, Library of Congress; p. 183: © 2007 JupiterImages Corporation; p. 184: © Wood River Gallery; p. 190: © 2007 JupiterImages Corporation; p. 192: © Images.com/Corbis; p. 195: Dore Bible Illustrations, Courtesy of Dover Pictorial Archive Series; p. 207: © 2007 JupiterImages Corporation; p. 208: © Charles & Josette Lenars/CORBIS; p. 209: © 2007 JupiterImages Corporation; p. 210: The Teaching Company Collection; p. 213: Prints and Photographs Division, Library of Congress; p. 218: © 2007 JupiterImages Corporation; p. 220: © 2007 JupiterImages Corporation; p. 223: The Teaching Company Collection; p. 226: © Royalty-Free/Corbis; p. 229: © Masterfile; p. 232: © 2007 JupiterImages Corporation; p. 234: © 2007 JupiterImages Corporation.

More Praise for The Great Courses®

"Consistently high quality lectures on a wide variety of topics, always informative, never disappointing. Your [courses] have changed my commuting time from drudgery to pleasure."

—Richard Dorsey, Newport Beach, CA

"These courses have opened up subjects I didn't have time to take in college. The professors have a passion for their subject and easily convey their enthusiasm for the material."

—Kristie Fitzgerald, Draper, UT

"Real life answers to real life questions."

—Steve Grossmann, Dallas, TX

"I travel by car often. Your courses have added a new dimension of enjoyment to my business trips. Thank you!"

—Larry Kuss, Albuquerque, NM

"Your courses offer a unique approach to life long learning. Excellent approach to making technical subjects fun and understandable."

- –R. Meiser, McAlisterville, PA

"I used to regret not having attended college. No more! Thanks for your outstanding products and service."

—Dave Polson, Omaha, NE

"I really enjoy your courses. I view them while walking on my treadmill. You've made my retirement and exercise regime much more enjoyable."

—Allen Weingast, Cortlandt Manor, NY

"For those of us with busy lives and full schedules, it's a wonderful opportunity to make use of commute time to improve our minds and enrich our lives."

—Linda Bauer, Urbana, IL

"I am recently retired and had planned to take courses at a local community college—then I found The Teaching Company. I could not be more pleased—Thank you."

—George Bauer, Castro Valley, CA

"I was so impressed I've already bought three more courses and recommended that a catalog be sent to a friend."

—Lewis G. Billard, Dartmouth, NS

"These audio courses are perfect for the car, clear, well recorded and well packaged. A fantastic opportunity to make better use of your time."

—Rick Bradley, West Lafayette, IN

"As an engineer I was taught well but poorly educated. Your courses are helping me to fill my educational lapses."

—Robinson Buck, Wethersfield, CT

"You have given me hours of relaxing contemplation far from the ordinary cares of the day."

—Lawrence D'Antonio, Westchester, PA

"Great material, excellent professors, it doesn't get any better than this for lifelong learners."

—Kate Felix, Littleton, CO

"You are the university of the world."

—Njaal Helle, Pleasant View, TN

"I am a Harvard graduate and the courses are comparable!"

—Laurie Hillsberg, Charlestown, WV

"Traffic jams increase my IQ."

—Charles Jeanner, Los Angeles, CA

"The course was like sitting back in the college classroom listening to an excellent teacher."

—Helen Jones, Dayton, OH

"I was concerned that shipping seemed so expensive—until the package arrived and I saw how much material there was. I was somewhat overawed at the concept of 84 lessons. It didn't sink in until I saw it. This was my first order, but certainly not the last."

— Lilly Jones, Phoenix, NY

"I love these courses! I listen to them while driving and no longer mind traffic jams. I intend to eventually listen to all your courses."

—Janet Kennedy, Timonium, MD

"I have a master's degree and have been an ardent reader all my life. With your great courses I can now do other things—painting, sewing, etc. —while enjoying literature and acquiring knowledge."

—Muriel Kolb, Highlands, NC

"It's probably safe to say that the customers don't want to graduate from this. There's a stunning array of courses to pick from. And The Teaching Company keeps coming up with new courses that are impressive as ever."

—James Lehr, Norfolk, VA

"TTC's courses were an answer to my prayers. I wanted to expand my intellectual horizons but had no time to attend classes. TTC's courses turned out to be better than attending classes!"

—Betsy Lyman, Boyertown, PA

"A brilliant idea. With the cost of continuing education and higher education going up and up, these courses are both a delightful resource and a bargain. I ADORE being able to learn at my own convenience from such engaging professors."

—Andrea Matthews, Needham, MA

"These courses provide an excellent way to explore new areas of learning and to resume former passions."

—Stanley McCracken, St. Anne, IL

"These lectures are equal to if not often superior to those I had at Princeton for a tiny fraction of the cost and can be listened to and relistened at my convenience."

—Brian Mitchell, Boca Raton, FL

"As a retired professional person (CPA) I could not imagine a better opportunity for learning and expanding my horizons!"

—Nancy Myers, Austin, TX

"I'm delighted to have these courses that are taught by such excellent professors available to me. My commute time to work is now worthwhile!"

—Mary Ross, Cupertino, CA

"An extraordinary experience for a retired university professor. I'm now studying courses outside my major and minors with delight."

—Jack Scott, Cresson, TX

"My only complaint is that these courses are so good that I have become something of a learning addict! Keep up the great work!!"

—Larry Scott, Houston, TX

"On the list of things I can't live without your courses are right up there with my morning coffee. In fact, my favorite thing to do is to listen to a course while drinking my morning coffee! Your courses have enriched my life immeasurably."

—Ann Squire, Katonah, NY

"Your return policy has encouraged us to try topics we otherwise might not have attempted. Some of the courses on unfamiliar topics have been a great success, others a disappointment. In any case, we have freely recommended your courses to friends and coworkers."

— Cynthia St. John, Limestone, TN

"I am listening to four courses—it's just like being back in college! And all are not new info for me, but refresher courses that I need now that I've been out of school for 20 years."

—Mary Van Voorhees, Greenbrae, CA

"No more going to community college and paying large sums for adult courses with inferior teaching."

—Fred Widom, Fountain Hills, AZ

"I had been thinking about buying a course for years before I finally did it. Good thing I didn't wait forever—it is wonderful! A whole new world opened up to me."

—Connie Zelinsky, Placerville, CA

"As an educator and administrator (Vice-Principal) I rely on these courses for my enrichment and the professional development of my staff."

—Jack McDonald, Anaheim, CA

"I've enjoyed my courses so much that I'm tempted to tackle subjects that would normally intimidate me."

—Mary Rowe, Cambridge, MA

"Teaching Company courses have brought me pure pleasure. I have taken many and enjoyed them all."

—Jeanne Tiernan, Douglas, MA

"How wonderful to download lectures to my i-Pod. I can listen in the car or anywhere."

—Marylou Wilkinson, New Canaan, CT

"One is never bored or lonesome traveling into the wonderful past with The Teaching Company."

—Kenneth Weygant, Burlington, IA

"In a busy life, I find the listening material to be a very effective way to satisfy my curiosity."

—Mehmet Yuce, Yorktown Heights, NY

"The Teaching Company gives me the tools to effectively improve my knowledge on a very tight schedule."

—Eric Ball, Helena, MT

"These classes are fabulous, I'm on #5 now, and plan to keep going, getting caught up on topics I've always wanted to know better. Thank you so much!"

—Bill Chambers, Palm Desert, CA

"At 54 years old I have been re-energized. These courses take me out of my daily thought patterns, and re-open my eyes and mind."

—Steven Cross, Redmond, OR

"The Teaching Company has improved my life immeasurably! In life's uncertainties, there is one certainty: My daily Great Courses lecture will be uplifting!"

—Simeon Herbert, Garland, TX

"These courses are absolutely outstanding. They are engaging and entertaining. This kind of learning is tremendous fun!"

—Kim Working, Lebanon, TN

"It's better than being in a classroom. When I do not understand, or get distracted, I can rewind it until it is totally clear."

—Marga Friedman, Great Neck, NY

"I am very satisfied with all the courses I have purchased. I like to learn at my own pace and The Teaching Company makes that possible."

—Richard Goepfert, Seattle, WA

NOTES

NOTES

NOTES

NOTES

NOTES